T0344842

FOLLOWING THE TREND

FOLLOWING THE TREND

Diversified Managed Futures Trading

Second Edition

Andreas F. Clenow

WILEY

Library of Congress Cataloging-in-Publication Data is Available:

ISBN 9781119908982 (Hardback)
ISBN 9781119908999 (ePDF)
ISBN 9781119909002 (epub)

Cover Design: Wiley
Cover Image: © aydinmutlu/Getty Images

Set in 12/14 pt Perpetua Std by Straive, Chennai, India

SKY10039714_120822

CONTENTS

v

Jerry Parker

My trend-following journey started over 40 years ago when I was in my twenties. I read everything I could find on trend following, trading, markets, futures, and stocks. I was instantly hooked and I knew I needed to exit the accounting field and find my way into the exciting life of a trader. I was open-minded about futures, commodities, shorting, leverage, and especially trend following. I thought trend following was the greatest thing I'd ever heard about. I believed in it from cover to cover as soon as I heard the phrase "take small losses and let profits run." My question was: would the infrequent big winning trades pay for the frequent losses? I didn't know but I wanted to find out.

Books like *Following the Trend* were hard to find back in those days but I was on a hunt and I would not be denied a place in the trend-following world. When I got my big opportunity to work for Richard Dennis, I was ready. Well, at least I thought I was ready. I had a lot to learn and they were the best teachers, real geniuses.

I learned that the best trend-following rules are not complex and they are not overly optimized. The best trend-following systems have only a few rules. I have been tempted over the years to make my system more complex but that has only resulted in fewer profits and me having to revert back to the basic rules of trend following that make sure you never miss a big trade and that you continually and, in all situations, limit the losses to a small percentage of your AUM. "Keep it simple" really does work better than complexity. Of course, I got better at system development and discipline as I became more experienced but frequently I thought, "I wish I didn't know

now what I didn't know then." This book will teach you the basics and make you loath to give up on the basics!

There is no way around the pain and anxiety of trading and having to sit still during drawdowns in order to profit from the markets. A disciplined approach to following rules is a requirement to maximize trading opportunities. Following the trends with a rules-based strategy with almost no discretion was and still is appealing to me. The struggle of watching profits turn into losses and big profits turn into small profits will always be a part of trading. Practice and teach yourself how to fall in love with your systematic approach. We were taught that we should "do the right thing" and "do the hard thing." Easy and comfortable approaches to trading don't usually work well. Trading is rewarding intellectually and financially, so it is only fitting that it should be difficult and counter-intuitive for most of us normal people.

The best traders that I have known play for the big trends, let profits run, take small losses, and trade many markets, both long and short. Diversification is one of the not-so-secret secrets of success. I started out trading 20 markets, I now trade over 200 markets. Successful systematic traders must have dogged consistency and discipline. The best traders do every trade, regardless of the recent losses and drawdowns. It takes practice and a commitment to your system. My only regret in trading has been when I haven't followed my system the way I should have. Enjoy this book as I did and revisit it over the coming years to be reminded of how basic and powerful trend following is. The trend is truly your friend!

Jerry Parker
CEO, Chesapeake Capital

This book is an excellent training manual for anyone interested in learning how to make money as a trend follower.

I know a bit about trend following because I was part of the famous Turtle experiment in the 1980s when Richard Dennis, the Prince of the Pits, showed the world that trading could be taught and that people with the right sort of training and perspective could make consistent returns that far exceeded normal investments. Ultimately, that ordinary people could learn to trade like the most successful hedge funds. I started as a 19-year-old kid and by the time I was 24 in 1987, I took home $8 million, which was my cut of the $31.5 million I earned for Richard Dennis as a trend follower.

I even wrote a book about it, *Way of the Turtle*. It became a bestseller because many traders wanted to know the secrets of our success and to hear about the story first-hand which had been kept secret because of confidentiality agreements and our loyalty to Richard Dennis, a great man and a trading legend.

I'd thought about writing a follow-on book a few times in the intervening years; something meatier and with more detail. My book was part-story and part-trading manual and I thought about writing a book that was all trading manual.

In *Following the Trend*, Andreas F. Clenow has written a trend-following trading manual I would be proud to put my own name on. I'm very picky too, so I don't say this lightly.

Very few trading books are worthy of an endorsement of any sort. Too many are filled with tips and tricks that don't stand the test of the markets, let alone the test of time. Too many are written by those who are trying to sell you something like a course, or their seminars. Too many want your money more than they want to create an excellent book.

That's why I don't often speak at conferences and you won't see me endorsing many books. There is too much self-serving propaganda in the trading industry that makes its money by fleecing the unsuspecting newcomers; too many lies designed to rope in the neophytes with promises of easy profits and quick money that will never pan out.

Following the Trend is different.

It is solid, clearly written, covers all the basics, and it doesn't promise you anything that you can't actually get as a trend follower.

If you want to be a trend follower, first, read *Reminiscences of a Stock Operator* (2010) to learn from Jesse Livermore. Then, buy Jack Schwager's *Market Wizards* books to learn about the great traders who have been trend followers, like Richard Dennis, my trading mentor, Ed Seykota, Bill Dunn, John W. Henry, and Richard Donchian. They will get you excited about the possibilities but leave you wondering how; how can you too learn to be a trend follower?

Then, when you are ready to move from desire to reality. When you are ready to do it yourself. To make your own mark.

Read *Following the Trend*.

Curtis Faith
Savannah, Georgia

This book is in essence about a single trading strategy based on a concept that has been publicly known for at least two decades. It is a strategy that has worked remarkably well for over 30 years with a large number of hedge funds employing it. This strategy has attracted much attention over the past few years and in particular after the dramatically positive returns it generated in 2008, but it seems nevertheless to be constantly misunderstood, misinterpreted, and misused. Even worse, various flawed and overly complicated iterations of it are all too often sold for large amounts of money by people who have never even traded them in a professional environment. The strategy I am alluding to goes by many names, but it is in essence the same strategy that most trend-following futures managers (or CTAs/Commodity Trading Advisors, if you prefer) have been trading for many years.

This book differs in many aspects from the more traditional way in which the trading literature tends to approach the subject of trend-following strategies. My primary reason for writing this book is to fill a gap in that literature and to make publicly available analyses and information that are already known by successful diversified trend followers, but understood by few not already in this very specialised part of the business. It is my belief that most books, and therefore most people aspiring to get into this business, are focusing on the wrong things, such as entry and exit rules, and missing the important aspects. This is likely related to the fact that many authors don't actually design or trade these strategies for a living.

There have been many famous star traders in this particular sector of the industry and some of them have been raised to almost mythical status and are seen as kinds of deities in the business. These people have my highest respect for their success and pioneer work in our field, but this book is not about hero worship and it does not dwell on strategies that worked in the 1970s but might be financial suicide to run in the same shape today. The market has changed and the hedge-fund industry even more so, and I intend to focus on what I see as viable strategies in the current financial marketplace.

This is not a textbook where every possible strategy and indicator is explored in depth with comparisons of the pros and cons of exponential moving average to simple moving average, to adaptive moving average, and so on. I don't describe every trading indicator I can think of or invent new ones and name them after myself. You don't need a whole bag of technical indicators to construct a solid trend-following strategy and it certainly does not add anything to the field if I change a few details of some formula and call the new one by my own name, although I have to admit that 'The Clenow Oscillator' does have a certain ring to it. Indicators are not important and focusing on these details is likely to be the easiest way to miss the whole plot and get stuck in nonsense curve fitting and over-optimisations. I intend to do the absolute opposite and use only the most basic methods and indicators to show how you can construct strategies good enough to use in professional hedge funds without having unnecessary complexity. The buy and sell rules are the least important part of a strategy and focusing on them would serve only to distract from where the real value comes.

Also, this is not a get-rich-quick book. If you are looking for a quick and easy way to get rich, you'll need to look elsewhere. One of my main points in this book is that it is not terribly difficult to create a trading strategy that can rival many large futures hedge funds but that absolutely does not mean that this is an easy business. Creating a trading strategy is only one step of many and I even provide trading rules in this book that perform very well over time and have return profiles that are marketable to seasoned institutional investors. That is only part of the work, though, and if you don't do your homework properly, you will most likely end up either not getting any investments in the first place or blowing up your own and your investors' money at the first sign of market trouble.

To be able to use the knowledge I pass on here, you need to put in some really hard work. Don't take anyone's word when it comes to trading strategies, not even mine. You need to invest in a good market data infrastructure, including effective simulation software and study a proper programming language, if you don't already know one. Then you can start replicating the strategies I describe here and make up your own mind about their usefulness, and, I hope, find ways to improve them and adapt to your own desired level of risk and return. Using someone else's method out of the box is rarely a good idea and you need to make the strategies your own in order to really know and trust them.

Even after you reach that stage, you have most of the work ahead of you. Trading these strategies on a daily basis is a lot tougher than most people expect, not least from a psychological point of view. Add the task of finding investors, launching a fund or managed accounts set-up, running the business side, reporting, mid-office, and so on, and you soon realise that this is not a get-rich-quick scheme. It is certainly a highly rewarding business to be in if you are good at what you do, but that does not mean it is either easy or quick.

So despite the stated fact that this book is essentially about a single strategy, I will demonstrate that this one strategy is sufficient to replicate the top trend-following hedge funds of the world, when you fully understand it.

■ Why Write a Book?

Practically no managed futures funds will reveal their trading rules and they tend to treat their proprietary strategy as if they were blueprints for nuclear weapons. They do so for good reason but not necessarily for the reason most people would assume. The most important rationale for the whole secrecy business is likely tied to marketing, and the perception of a fund manager possessing the secret formula to make gold out of stone will certainly help to sell the fund as a unique opportunity. The fact of the matter is that although most professional trend followers have their proprietary tweaks, the core strategies used don't differ very much in this business. That might sound like an odd statement, since I have obviously not been privy to the source code of all the managed futures funds out there, and because they sometimes show quite different return profiles, it would seem as if they are doing very different things. However, by using very simple methods, one can replicate very closely the returns of many CTA funds and by tweaking the time horizons, risk factor, and investment universe, one can replicate most of them.

This is not to say that these funds are not good or that they don't have their own valuable proprietary algorithms. The point is merely that the specific tweaks used by each shop are only a small factor and that the bulk of the returns come from fairly simple models. Early on in this book I will present two basic strategies and show how even these highly simple models are able to explain a large part of CTA returns, and I then go on to refine these two strategies into one strategy that compares well with the big established futures funds. I present all the details of how this is done, enabling the reader to replicate the same strategies. These strategies are tradable with quite attractive return profiles just as they are, and I show in subsequent chapters how to improve upon them further. I will introduce more advanced concepts as well, such as how to exploit the unique futures effect of term structure and how to go about constructing counter-trend strategies.

And why would I go and tell you all of this? Wouldn't the spread of this knowledge cause all trend-following strategies to cease functioning, free money would be given to the unwashed masses instead of the secret guild of hedge-fund managers, and make the earth suddenly stop revolving and fling us all out into space? Well, there are many reasons quantitative traders give to justify their secrecy and keep the mystique up and a few of them are even valid, but in the case of trend-following futures, I don't see too much of a downside in letting others in on the game. The trend-following game is currently dominated by a group of massive funds with assets in the order of US$10–50 billion, which they leverage many times over to play futures all over the world. These fund managers know everything I've written in this book and plenty more. The idea that me writing this book may cause so many people to go into the trend-following futures business that their trades would somehow overshadow the big players and destroy the investment opportunities is a nice one for my ego, but not a very probable one. What I describe here is already done on a massive scale and if a few of my readers decide to go into this field, good for them, and I wish them the best of luck.

What we are talking about here are simply methods to locate medium- to long-term trends typically caused by real economic developments and to systematically make money from them over time. Having more people doing the same will hardly change the real economic behaviour of humankind that is ultimately behind the price action. One could of course argue that a significant increase in assets in this game could make the exact entries and exits more of a problem, causing big moves when the crowd enters or exits at the same time. That is a concern for sure, but not a major one. Overcoming these kinds of problems resides in the small details of the strategies and will have little impact over the long run.

There are other types of quantitative strategies that neither I nor anyone else trading them would write books about. These are usually very short-term strategies or strategies with low capacity that would suffer or cease to be profitable if more capital comes into the same game. Medium- to long-term trend following, however, has massive liquidity and is very scalable, so it is not subject to these concerns.

Then there is another reason for me to write about these strategies. I am not a believer in the black-box approach, in which you ask your clients for blind trust without giving any meaningful information about how you will achieve your returns. Even if you know everything that this book aims to teach, it is still hard work to run a trend-following futures business and most people will not go out and start their own hedge fund simply because they now understand how the mechanics work. Some probably will and if you end up being one of them, please drop me an email to let me know how it all works out. Either way, I would like to think that I can add value with my own investment vehicles and that this book will not in any way hurt my business.

■ Ten Years On: A Second Edition

Well, here we are, ten years after this book, my first, was originally published and it has been quite a ride. I have to admit that ten years ago, I hadn't expected many people to be interested in a book on trend following by some odd European that they had probably never heard of. The overnight success of *Following the Trend* came as a complete surprise and it has been an amazing decade since then. Still to this day, the most common question I get, though usually phrased a little more politely, is whether I make a lot of money from writing books. No, certainly not, but that question is missing the point. Writing books is not only intellectually challenging and fun, it has opened doors I never thought I'd walk through. Yes, it has led to significant business deals over the years, which is a nice bonus, but what I value the most is the contact with all kinds of people I have met because of my books.

The books made me a frequent keynote speaker at various conferences around the world, and I very much enjoy the interaction and conversations I have had with so many people at these conferences. And there is the matter of other speakers whom I have met through such conferences, many of whom have become good friends. Back in the 1990s, when I was dreaming of getting into serious finance, I must have read each one of Jack Schwager's *Market Wizards* books at least a dozen times, and when I suddenly find myself on the other side of the planet, on a stage in front of hundreds of people, signing books next to one of the market wizards, well, then I know that my decision to write this book was the right call.

CHAPTER 1

Cross-Asset Trend Following with Futures

There is a group of hedge funds and professional asset managers who have shown a remarkable performance for over 30 years, consistently outperforming conventional strategies in both bull and bear markets, and during the 2008 credit crunch crisis showing truly spectacular returns. These traders are highly secretive about what they do and how they do it. They often employ large quant teams staffed with top-level PhDs from the best schools in the world, adding to the mystique surrounding their seemingly amazing long-term track records. Yet, as this book shows, it is possible to replicate their returns by using fairly simple systematic trading models, revealing that not only are they essentially doing the same thing, but also that it is not terribly complex and within the reach of most of us to replicate.

This group of funds and traders goes by several names and they are often referred to as CTAs (for Commodity Trading Advisors), trend followers or managed futures traders. It matters little which term you prefer because there really are no standardised rules or definitions involved. What they all have in common is that their primary trading strategy is to capture lasting price moves in either direction in global markets across many asset classes, attempting to ride positions as long as possible when they start moving. In practice, most futures managers do the same thing they have been doing since the 1970s: trend following. Conceptually the core idea is very simple.

Use computer software to identify trends in a large set of different futures markets and attempt to enter into trends and follow them for as long as they last. By following a large number of markets covering all asset classes, both long and short, you can make money in both bull and bear markets and be sure to capture any lasting trend in the financial markets, regardless of asset class.

This book shows all the details about what this group does in reality and how the members do it.

The truth is that almost all of these funds are just following trends and there are not a whole lot of ways that this can be done. They all have their own proprietary tweaks, bells and whistles, but in the end the difference achieved by these is marginal in the grand scheme of things. This book sheds some light on what the large institutional trend-following futures traders do and how the results are created. The strategies as such are relatively simple and not terribly difficult to replicate in theory, but that in no way means that it is easy to replicate them in reality and to follow through. The difficulty of managed futures trading is largely misunderstood and those trying to replicate what we do usually spend too much time looking at the wrong things and not even realising the actual difficulties until it is too late. Strategies are easy. Sticking with them in reality is a whole different ball game. That may sound clichéd but come back to that statement after you finish reading this book and see if you still believe it is just a cliché.

There are many names given to the strategies and the business that this book is about and, although they are often used interchangeably, in practice, they can sometimes mean slightly different things and cause all kinds of confusion. The most commonly used term by industry professionals is simply CTA (Commodity Trading Advisor) and though I admit that I tend to use this term myself, it is in fact a misnomer in this case. CTA is a US regulatory term defined by the National Futures Association (NFA) and it has little to do with most so-called CTA funds or CTA managers today. This label is a legacy from the days when those running these types of strategies were US-based individuals or small companies regulated onshore by the NFA, which is not necessarily the case today. If you live in the UK and have your advisory company in London, set up an asset management company in the British Virgin Islands and a hedge fund in the Caymans (which is in fact a more common set-up than one would think), you are in no way affected by the NFA and therefore not a CTA from their point of view, even if you manage futures in large scale.

■ Diversified Trend Following in a Nutshell

The very concept of trend following means that you will never buy at the bottom and you will never sell at the top. This is not about buying low and selling high, but rather about buying high and selling higher or shorting low and covering lower. These strategies will always arrive late to the party and overstay their welcome, but they always enjoy the fun in between. All trend-following strategies are the same in concept and the underlying core idea is that the financial markets tend to move in trends, up, down or sideways, for extended periods of time. Perhaps not all the time and perhaps not even most of the time, but the critical assumption is that there will always be periods where markets continue to move in the same direction for long enough periods of time to pay for the losing trades and have money left over. It is in these periods and only in these periods that trend-following strategies will make money. When the market is moving sideways, which is the case more often than one might think, these strategies are just not profitable.

Figure 1.1 shows the type of trades we are looking for, which all boils down to waiting until the market has made a significant move in one direction, putting on a bet that the price will continue in the same direction and holding that position until the trend has seized. Note the two phases in Figure 1.1 separated by a vertical line. Up until April there was no money to be made in following the trends of the NZ Dollar, simply because there were no trends around. Many trend followers would have attempted entries both

FIGURE 1.1 Phases of trend following.

on the long and short side and lost money, but the emerging trend from April onwards should have paid for it and then some.

If you look at a single market at any given time, there is a very high likelihood that no trend exists at the moment. That not only means that there are no profits for the trend-following strategies, but can also mean that loss after loss are realised as the strategy enters position after position only to see prices fall back into the old range. Trend-following trading on a single instrument is not terribly difficult but quite often is a futile exercise, not to mention a very expensive one. Any single instrument or even asset class can have very long periods where this approach simply does not work and to keep losing over and over again, watching the portfolio value shrinking each time can be a horrible experience as well as financially disastrous. Those who trade only a single or a few markets also have a higher tendency of taking too large bets to make sure the bottom line of the portfolio will get a significant impact of each trade and that is also an excellent way to go bankrupt.

With a diversified futures strategy you have a large basket of instruments to trade, covering all major asset classes, making each single bet by itself almost insignificant to the overall performance. Most trend-following futures strategies do in fact lose on over half of all trades entered and sometimes as much as 70%, but the trick is to gain much more on the good ones than you lose on the bad and to do enough trades for the law of big numbers to start kicking in.

For a truly diversified futures manager it really does not matter if we trade the S&P 500 Index, rough rice, bonds, gold, or even live hogs. They are all just futures which can be treated in exactly the same way. Using historical data for long enough time periods we can analyse the behaviour of each market and have our strategy adapt to the volatility and characteristics of each market, making sure we build a robust and truly diversified portfolio.

■ The Traditional Investment Approach

The most widely held asset class, in particular among the general public, is equities, that is, shares of corporations trading on stock exchanges. The academic community, along with most large banks and financial institutions, have long told the public that buying and holding equities over long periods of time is a safe and prudent method of investing and this has created a huge market for equity mutual funds. These funds are generally seen as responsible long-term investments that always go up in the long run, and there is a good chance that even a large part of your pension plan is invested in equity mutual funds for that very reason. The ubiquitous advice from banks is that you should hold a combination of equity mutual funds and bond mutual funds and that the younger you are, the larger the weight of the equity funds should be. The reason for the last part is that, although equities do tend to go up in the long run, they are more volatile than bonds and you should take higher financial risks when you are younger since you have time to make your losses back. Furthermore, the advice is generally that you should prefer equity mutual funds over buying single stocks to make sure that you get sufficient diversification and you participate in the overall market instead of taking bets on individual companies which may run into unexpected trouble down the road.

This all sounds very reasonable and makes for a good sales pitch, at least if the core assumption of equities always appreciating over time holds up in reality. The idea of diversifying by holding many stocks instead of just a few companies also sounds very reasonable, given that the assumption holds up that the correlation between stocks is low enough to provide the desired diversification benefits of lower risk at equal or higher returns. Of course, if either of these assumptions turns out to be disappointing in reality, the whole strategy risks falling down like the proverbial house of cards.

In reality, equities as an asset class has a very high internal correlation compared to most other types of instruments. The prices of stocks tend to move together up and down on the same days and while there are large differences in overall returns between a good stock and a bad one, over longer time horizons the timing of their positive and negative days are often highly related, even in normal markets. If you hold a large basket of stocks in many different countries and sectors, you still just hold stocks and the extent of your diversification is very limited. The larger problem with the diversification starts creeping up in times of market distress or when there is a single fundamental theme that drives the market as a whole. This could be a longer-term event such as a dot com bubble and crash, a banking sector meltdown and so on, or it can be a shorter-term shock event like an earthquake or a surprise war. When the market gets single-minded, the correlations between stocks quickly approach one as everyone panic sells at the same time and then re-buys on the same euphoria when the problems are perceived to be lessened. In these markets it matters little what stocks you hold and the diversification of your portfolio will turn out to be a very expensive illusion.

Then again, if stocks always go up in the long run, the correlations should be of lesser importance since you would always make the money back again if you just sit on the stocks and wait a little bit longer. This is absolutely true and if you are a very patient person, you are very likely to make money from the stock markets by just buying and holding. From 1976 to 2011, the MSCI World Index rose by 1,300%, so in 35 years you would have made over ten times your initial investment. Of course, if you translate that into annual compound return, you will see that this means a yield of just around 8% per year. If you had been so unlucky as to invest in 1999 instead, you would still hold a loss 13 years later of over 20%. Had you invested in 2007, your loss would be even greater. Although equities do tend to move up in the long run, most of us cannot afford to lose a large part of our capital and wait for a half a lifetime to get our money back. If you are lucky and invest in a good year or even a good decade, the buy-and-hold strategy may work out but it can also turn out to be a really bumpy ride for quite a low return in the end. Going back to the 1,000% or so made on an investment from 1976 to 2011, the largest drawdown during this period was 55%. Looking at the buy-and-hold strategy from a long-term return to risk perspective, that means that in order to get your 8% or so return per year, you must accept a risk of losing more than half of your capital, which would translate to close to seven years of average return.

You may say that the 55% loss represents only one extreme event, the 2008 credit meltdown, and that such scenarios are unlikely to repeat, but this is not at all the case. Let's just look at the fairly recent history of these so-called once-in-a-lifetime events. In 1974, the Dow Jones Industrial average hit a drawdown of 40%, from which it took over six years to recover. In 1978, the same index fell 27% in a little over a year. The same thing happened again in 1982 when the losses amounted to 25% in about a year. From the peak in August 1987 to the bottom in October, the index lost over 40%. Despite the bull market of the 1990s, there were several 15–20% loss periods and when the markets turned down in 2000, the index had lost about 40% before hitting the bottom. What you need to ask yourself is just how high an expected compound return you need to compensate for the high risks of the stock markets, and whether you are happy with single-digit returns for that level of volatility.

If you do choose to participate in the stock markets through an equity mutual fund, you have one more factor to consider, and that is whether or not the mutual fund can match or beat the index it is supposed to be tracking. A mutual-fund manager, as opposed to a hedge-fund manager, is tasked with trying to beat a specific index and, in the case of an equity fund, that index would be something like the S&P 500, the FTSE 100, the MSCI

World or similar. It can be a broad country index, an international index, a sector index or any other kind of equity index, but the task is to follow the designated index and attempt to beat it. Most mutual-fund managers have very little leeway in their investment approach and they are not allowed to deviate much from their index. Methods to attempt to beat the index could involve slight over- or under-weights in stocks that the manager believes will perform better or worse than the index, or to hold a little more cash during perceived bad markets. The really big difference between a mutual-fund manager and a hedge-fund manager or absolute-return trader is that the mutual-fund manager's job is to follow the index, whether it goes up or down. That person's job is not to make money for the client but rather to attempt to make sure that the client gets the return of the index and, hopefully, slightly more. If the S&P 500 index declines by 30% in a year, and a mutual fund using that index as a benchmark loses only 25% of the clients' money, that is a big achievement and the fund manager has done a very good job.

There are of course fees to be paid, including a management fee and sometimes a performance fee for the fund as well as administration fees, custody fees, commissions and so on, which is the reason why very few mutual funds manage to beat their index or even match it. According to Standard & Poor's Indices Versus Active Funds Scorecard (SPIVA) 2011 report, the percentage of US domestic equity funds that outperformed the benchmark in 2011 was less than 16%. Worst that year were the large-cap growth funds where over 95% failed to beat their benchmark. Looking over a period of five years, from 2006 to 2011, 62% of all US domestic funds failed to beat their benchmarks. The worst in that five-year period was the mid-cap growth funds where less than 10% reached their targets. The picture that the S&P reports paint is devastating for the mutual-fund business. If active mutual funds have consistently proved to underperform their benchmarks year after year, there is little reason to think that this is about to change any time soon.

There are times when it's a good idea to participate in the general equity markets by buying and holding for extended periods of time, but then you need to have a strategy for when to get out of the markets when the big declines come along, because they will come along. It makes sense to have a portion of your money in equities one way or another as long as you step out of that market during the extremely volatile and troublesome years, but personally I'm not entirely convinced about the wisdom of putting the bulk of your hard-earned cash into this asset class and just holding onto it in up-and-down markets, hoping for the best. For participating in these markets, you may also want to consider investing in passive exchange-traded funds (ETFs) as an alternative to classic mutual funds, because the index-tracking ETFs hold the exact stocks of the index at all times and have substantially lower fees, making them track and match the index with a very high degree of precision. They are also very easy and cheap to buy and sell as they are directly traded on an exchange with up-to-the-second pricing.

■ The Case for Diversified Managed Futures

There are many viable investment strategies that tend to outperform buy-and-hold equities on a volatility adjusted basis and I employ several of them. One of the top strategies is trend-following managed futures for its consistent long-term track record of providing a very good return-to-risk ratio during both bull and bear years. A solid managed futures strategy has a reasonably high expected yearly return, an acceptable drawdown in relation to the yearly return and a lack of significant correlation to world equity markets, and preferably slightly negative correlation.

The list of successful traders and hedge funds operating in the trend-following managed futures markets is quite long and many of them have been around for decades, some even from the 1970s. The very fact that so many trend traders have managed not only to stay in business for this long period, but also to make consistently impressive returns, should in itself prove that these strategies work.

Table 1.1 shows a brief comparison between the performances of some futures managers to that of the world equity markets. As mentioned, MSCI World has shown a long-term yield of 8% with a maximum drawdown (DD) of 55%, which would mean that more than seven normal years of performance were given up in that decline. This could be compared with funds like EMC, which over the same period had a return of 17% and only gave up 27% at the most, or the equivalent of one and a half years only. Transtrend gave up even less of its return and even Dunn, which, after a stellar track record, suffered a setback some years ago, only lost four years of performance and still holds a much higher compound rate of return than the equity index.

Looking at the funds' correlation to MSCI World you should notice that none of them have any significant correlation at all. This means that with such a strategy, you really don't have to worry about whether the world

TABLE 1.1	Performance comparison				
Name	Annualised compound return (%)	Max DD (%)	Correlation to MSCI World	Annualised volatility	Starting date
MSCI World TR	8.1	−54.6		15.1	31 January 1988
Chesapeake Classic	10.1	−31.6	0.17	18.9	1 February 1988
Dunn World Monetary and Agriculture	12.9	−57.9	−0.09	32.1	1 November 1984
Eckhardt Evolution	10.9	−27.1	0.02	18.1	1 August 1991
EMC Classic	17.4	−45.4	−0.11	42.7	1 January 1985
Estlander Alpha	7.9	−29.7	0.04	13.6	1 October 1991
Fort Global Diversified	10.0	−17.5	−0.07	15.8	1 March 2002
ISAM Systematic Trend	11.2	−37.8	−0.20	18.2	1 June 2001
Mulvaney Global Markets	12.5	−45.1	−0.12	33.1	1 May 1999
Tactical Institutional	16.3	−41.5	−0.05	23.3	1 April 1993
Transtrend Enhanced	11.3	−15.7	0.01	13.7	1 January 1995

equity markets are going up or down since it makes little difference to your returns. It does not mean that all years are positive for diversified futures strategies, only that the timing of the positive and negative returns is, over time, unrelated to those of the equity market. The observant reader might be asking if that does not make these strategies a very good complement to an equity portfolio, and the answer is that it absolutely does, but we are getting ahead of ourselves here.

■ Criticism of Trend-Following Strategies

Although certain criticisms of trend-following trading have some validity, there are other commonly recurring arguments that may be a little less thought through. One somewhat valid criticism is that there is a survival bias in the numbers reported by the industry. The argument is that the funds that are part of the relevant indices and comparisons are only there because they did well and the funds that did not do well are either out of business or too small to be part of the indices, and that this effect makes the indices have a positive bias. This is of course a factor, much the same way as a stock can be knocked out of the S&P 500 Index after it had a bad performance and its market capitalisation shrunk. Survival bias is a fact of life with all indices and it makes them all look a little better than reality would dictate. This is not a problem specific to the asset class. Anyhow, the arguments made in this book regarding the performance of diversified futures strategies are not dependent on the performance of indices; the comparisons asset managers included consist of a broad range of big players, some of which had some really difficult periods in their track records. There are some excellent aspects of these strategies and there are some serious pitfalls and potential problems that you need to be aware of. I deal with all of these in this book and have no intention of painting a rosier picture of the real situation than my experience reflects. Doing so would be both counterproductive and also, quite frankly, unnecessary.

Another common argument is that the high leverage makes the strategy too risky. This is mostly based on a lack of understanding of the two concepts of leverage and risk, which are not necessarily related. Defining leverage is a tricky thing when you are dealing with cross-asset futures strategies and simply adding up notional contract values and dividing with the capital base simply does not cut it. As I demonstrate and explain further on, having a million pounds' worth of exposure to gold and having a million pounds' worth of exposure to the Euribor are a world apart in terms of actual risk. While gold often moves several per cent in a day, a normal move in the Euribor would be a couple of basis points. Certainly, these futures strategies may have quite high notional contract exposures but don't go confusing that with risk. To be sure, these strategies can be risky, but buying and holding a portfolio of stocks are not necessarily less risky.

Most trend-following futures strategies will need to sell short quite often, and often as much as you buy long. Critics would highlight that when you are short you have an unlimited potential risk, which again is a misunderstanding of how markets work. Just as with equities, you risk losing what you put on the table but not more than that. While the pay-out diagram for a futures contract in theory has an unlimited loss, unless you have an unlimited amount of margin capital in your account, this is simply not the case in reality. In my experience, it is harder to trade on the short side than the long side, but that does not necessarily make it riskier, in particular when done in the context of a large diversified portfolio. Rather, on the contrary, the ability to go short tends to provide a higher skew of the return distributions and thereby increase the attractiveness as a hedging strategy.

Managed futures funds sometimes have large and long-lasting drawdowns. This is an absolutely valid criticism and something you need to be very aware of before setting out on this path. People like to hear percentage numbers, such as a common drawdown is 20%, for example, but this is not really helpful since you can tweak the risk factor up and down as you please by adjusting position sizes, as I explain in detail in later chapters. The question should rather be whether the long-term return numbers compensate for the worst drawdown scenarios and in this case it is hard to argue with the numbers. Drawdowns are painful when they occur but to say that they are worse than for the classic buy-and-hold equity alternative would be untrue. At the bottom of the equity bear market of 2008, based on MSCI World, you would have lost 55% from the peak and gone back to the levels of the mid-1990s. Losing almost 15 years of accumulated gains is practically unheard of for diversified futures strategies, yet the buy-and-hold strategy is considered by many the safer alternative.

Of course, just because a strategy worked for the past 30–40 years does not necessarily mean it will work in the next decade or two. We are not dealing with mathematical certainties here and we are not trying to predict the future. What we are doing is trying to tilt the probabilities slightly in our favour and then repeat the same thing over and over a large number of times. There will be years that are very bad for trend followers and there will be very good years. Over time the strategy is highly likely to produce strong absolute returns and to outperform traditional investment methods, but we are dealing in probabilities and not in certainties. There are no guarantees in this business, regardless of which strategy you choose. I don't expect any major problems that would end the profitable reign of trend-following futures trading, but it would be arrogant not to admit that the dinosaurs probably did not expect a huge stone to fall from the sky and end their party either. Neither event is very likely but both are quite possible.

■ Managed Futures as a Business

This book primarily deals with how to trade trend-following futures strategies as a money manager, trading other people's money, and it would be fair to wonder why one would want to share the profits with others. Some would take the view that once you have a good strategy with dependable long-term results, you should keep it to yourself and only trade your own money. There are instances where this may be true, in particular with strategies that are not scalable and have to be traded in low volume. For a truly scalable strategy, however, there is no real downside to sharing the spoils and quite a bit to be gained.

For starters, you need a large capital base to trade trend-following futures with sufficient diversification and reasonably low volatility, and even if you master the trading side, you may not have the couple of million pounds required to achieve a high level of diversification with acceptable risk. Pooling your money with that of other people would then make perfect sense. Given that you can charge other people for managing their money along with your own makes the prospect even more appealing, because it gives you an income while you do the same work you might have done yourself anyhow, and apart from your own gains, you participate in your clients' trading gains as well.

If you go the hedge-fund route and accept external money to be pooled with your own and traded like a single account, the overall workload increase is quite minor on a daily basis but your earning potential dramatically goes up. If you choose to manage individual accounts you may get a little higher workload on the admin side but a quicker and cheaper start-up phase and the economic upside is essentially the same. For starters you will have a reasonably stable income from the management fee which allows you to focus on long-term results. This strategy requires patience and if you feel economic pressure to achieve profitable trading each month, this will not work out. There can be long periods of sideways or negative trading and you need to be able to stick it out in those periods. Your incentive should always be towards long-term strong positive returns while keeping drawdowns at acceptable levels. As you get a percentage of the profits created on behalf of external investors, the earning potential in good years vastly exceeds what you could achieve with your own money alone.

If you have US$100,000 and make a 20% return one year, you just made US$20,000, which is great for sure. But if you also have US$1 million of external investor money in the pot and charge a management fee of 1.5% and a performance fee of 15%, you just made another US$30,000 in performance fee as well as over US$15,000 in management fee. By doing the same trades on a larger portfolio you make US$65,000 instead of US$20,000, and the beauty of managed futures trend following is that it is very scalable and you can keep piling up very large sums of external money and still trade basically the same way with very little additional work.

Managing external money means that you have a fiduciary responsibility not only to stick strictly to the strategy you have been given the mandate to trade, but also to create relevant reports and analyses and keep proper paperwork. This may seem like a chore but the added required diligence should be a good thing and ensure that you act in a professional manner at all times.

The negative part with managing other people's money is that you have a little less freedom, because you need to stick to the plans and principles that you have sold to your investors. You likely need to take lower risk than you would have done with your own account as well. Some traders who just manage their own money may be fine with the prospect of losing 60–70% of the capital base in return for potential triple-digit annual returns, but this is a very tough sell for a professional money manager. Investors, and in particular institutional investors with deep pockets, tend to prefer lower returns with lower risks.

The business of managing futures can be a highly profitable one if done carefully and with proper planning. There are a large number of famous traders who have achieved remarkable results in this field since the 1970s and the number of public funds in this space keeps increasing.

From a business point of view, the deal is quite straightforward compared to most other types of enterprises. A little simplified, it could be described in these steps:

1. Find clients to invest money with you.
2. Trade futures on their behalf.
3. Charge clients a yearly fixed fee for managing their money, usually 1–2%.
4. Charge clients a yearly performance fee if you make money for them, usually 10–20% of the profits.

The nicest part of this business model is that it is no more difficult to manage US$20 million than to manage US$10 million; your cost base would be more or less the same but your revenues would double. This business model is very scalable and until you reach a very large asset base, you can use the same strategies in the same manner and just adjust your position sizes. Once you reach US$500 million to US$1 billion, you will for sure get a whole new set of problems when it comes to asset allocation and liquidity, but that is rather a pleasant problem to have.

When first starting out, most of us discover that the biggest problem we have is finding clients to invest in a brand new manager with a brand new product. Unless your rich uncle Bob just retired and has got a few millions he does not mind investing with you, it may be an uphill battle to get that first seed money to get started. Before you start approaching potential clients you need to have a solid product to sell them, that is, your investment strategy along with your abilities to execute it, and be able to show them that you know what you are talking about. Designing an investment strategy is where this book comes in and I hope you will have a good platform to build upon once you reach the end.

There are two main paths for building a futures-trading business, as opposed to just trading your own money:

- *Managed accounts:* This is the traditional approach, where clients have accounts in their own names and give a power of attorney to the trader to be able to execute trades directly on their behalf. This is quite a simple approach in terms of set-up and legal structures and it provides the client with a high level of flexibility and security. Each account is different, and so the client may have special wishes in terms of risk and such which the trader is usually able to accommodate.

  If this is not a desired feature and you wish to simplify trading, you can also get onto a managed-accounts platform for a bank or prime broker where you essentially trade one account and have trades automatically *pro rata* split on the individual client accounts. Since the money is in the client's own account, the individual has the added flexibility of being able to view the account status at any time or to pull the plug on the trading without any notices or otherwise intervene. The client does not need to worry about dealing with a possible new Madoff, because there are no middle men and the bank reports the account status directly to the client. For the money manager, the managed-account solution can mean a little more administrative work at times than if a hedge-fund type structure is employed.

- *Hedge fund:* With this approach, there is one big account for all clients. Well, in practice, there may be several accounts at several banks, but the point is that all money from all clients is pooled together in one pile and traded together. This greatly simplifies the business side when it comes to handling client reporting and paperwork, but it requires a more complex legal structure, sometimes with a combination of onshore and offshore companies.

Regardless of which of these two main paths you decide to take, you need to do some proper homework on the pros and cons of either solution. More and more professional investors have a preference for managed accounts because they reduce legal risks, but for most managed-account setups you need larger amounts from each client than you would need for a hedge-fund set-up. The situation also varies a lot depending on where you and your potential clients are domiciled. Look into the applicable legal situation and be sure to check what, if any, regulations apply. You may need licences from the local regulators and breaching such requirements could quickly end your trading career.

■ Differences between Running a Trading Business and Personal Trading

Marketability of Your Strategy

When you trade your own account, and sometimes even manage accounts for trusted people, you can trade on pretty much anything you think makes sense without having to convince anyone of how good your ideas are. If you are truly a very strong trader and you have a stellar track record, you may be able to do the same thing for a hedge fund or professional managed accounts, but the days of the black box funds are mostly in the past. Simply telling prospective clients to just trust you and only hinting at how your strategies work no longer make for a good sales pitch. If you are dependent on raising assets for your new fund, as most of us are, you need a good story to be able to paint a clear picture of what your fund does and why it can make a big difference. This does not mean that you need to disclose all your mathematics and hand over source code for your programs, but the principal idea of what your strategy is about, what kind of market phenomenon you are trying to exploit and how you intend to do so, need to be clear and explicable. You also need to be able to explain how your risk and return profile will look, what kind of return you are targeting, and at what kind of volatility level. Even if you have a good story for these aspects, you still need to be able to explain why your product is unique and why the prospective client should not just go and buy another similar fund or hand money to a different futures manager with a successful track record of many years.

You need to work on presentation and marketing. If you have solid simulations for your strategies, use the charts and data in your material. Make professional-looking fact sheets that describe your philosophy and strategy, showing exactly why your product is so well positioned for this particular market and why your strategy is stronger than the established competitors.

Don't underestimate the difficulty and the amount of work needed to raise the initial seed money for your business. This can be a colossal task that can make or break your whole project. It often comes down to connections and friends in the market who can help you by putting up some initial cash and if you lack such connections, you may find yourself having tough time. Even if you have a great strategy, a proven track record with individual accounts and a strong personal reputation in the markets, you are still very vulnerable in this phase and you may be forced to make deals against your better judgement, such as paying a yearly fee for referred funds, in order to secure enough seed capital to make a fund launch possible.

Volatility Profile

Volatility is the currency used to buy performance. If customers don't get what they pay for, they will leave very quickly. There simply is no loyalty in this business and that is probably a good thing in a strictly Darwinian sense. An old adage states that there is no such thing as a third bad year for a hedge fund; after the second bad year all the investors are gone and the fund is out of business.

In your strategy simulations as well as in your live trading, you need to pay attention not only to the overall return numbers but also to the drawdowns and volatility. Try to simulate realistically what your maximum drawdown would have been trading with the same strategy for the past 30 years, and then assume that something much worse will happen after your fund or trading product is launched. Drawdown is defined as your current loss from the highest historical reading of the fund or strategy. If you gain 20% in the first three months of the year, and then back down to +10% on the year in the next three months, you are in an 8.3% drawdown despite being up 10% year to date.

You need to be aware what magnitudes of drawdowns are normal for your strategy and how long it normally takes to recover, and of course what the longest recovery time was in the simulations. Even if your drawdown was not big, it is hard to retain clients if it takes years to reach a new peak. Remember that investors may come in at any time during the year, normally at the start of any month. Even if the investor who bought in at a lower price might be okay with a bit of a drawdown, the one who bought at the top may be a little grumpier.

Managed-accounts clients are generally stickier, as the industry term goes, than hedge-fund clients. This refers to the notion that the managed-account clients tend to stay longer with a manager and it takes more for them to close the relationship than for a hedge-fund client. This is largely due to the fact that the manager has much more personal interaction with a managed-account client than with a hedge-fund client, who is often completely anonymous to the manager. On the flipside, it is generally more difficult to find managed-accounts clients in the first place and they require more admin and relationship management.

A common concept in measuring risk-to-return profile is the Sharpe ratio. This ratio measures return above risk-free interest rate, divided by the standard deviation of the returns. For systematic strategies, anything above 0.5 is normally considered acceptable, and the higher the better, of course. A fair case can be made against the use of Sharpe ratio for these kinds of strategies, however, because it penalises both upside and downside volatility where only one of them is negative to an investor. The Sharpe ratio is very well known, easily explainable to clients and comparable across funds and so it does have some merits, but a good complement to use is the Sortino ratio. This is a very similar concept but punishes volatility only on the downside, or below a required rate of return.

When analysing your strategies' potential drawdowns and recovery times, you also need to consider the crasser factor of your own profitability. Although you should target to be able to at least break even on the management fee alone, all hedge-fund and futures account managers are, sometimes painfully, aware of the fact that the real money comes from performance fees. If you are in a drawdown for two years, you don't get paid any performance fees for two years and that could mean a very large difference in your own bottom line. After all, you are still running a business.

■ Subscriptions and Redemptions

Client money inflow and outflow can create a headache for many money managers. You need to have a clear plan for how to handle this aspect and what to do when money comes in or goes out. This is a larger problem than it might sound and can have a significant effect on the return. When you get money coming in, do you simply add to all positions at the same ratio, increase selectively, open new positions for that money or leave it in cash? If you are still a fairly small fund and have a large diversified portfolio of futures, you might find yourself having three to four contracts of some futures and if you get subscriptions increasing your assets under management by 15%, you just cannot increase your positions proportionally. The same naturally goes for an equivalent redemption.

If you get 15% new money coming in and you decide it's too little to increase position sizes, you effectively dilute the returns for everyone who has already invested. The correct thing to do is to adjust every single position *pro rata* according to the subscriptions and redemptions coming in, but for a smaller portfolio you will need manual intervention. If you only hold a few contracts of some assets, that is likely to mean that you already have a rounding error in your position size and you could use the subscriptions and redemptions to attempt to balance these rounding errors out. If you have new subscriptions, you could selectively increase the positions where you are slightly underweight due to previous rounding errors and vice versa. Unless you have a large enough capital base, some discretionary decisions will be needed in these cases.

One nice thing about futures strategies compared to other strategies based more on cash instruments, such as equity funds, is that you will always have enough cash on the accounts to pay for normal redemptions. You probably don't need to liquidate anything to meet the payments for clients who want to exit or decrease their stake, as long as the amounts are not too large a part of the total capital base.

■ Psychological Difference

When you review your simulation data and look at a 15% drawdown, it might not sound so bad but the first time you lose a million pounds, things will feel quite different. The added stress of watching the net asset value of your fund ticking in front of you in real time will further assault your mental health. It takes a tremendous amount of discipline to sit tight and follow a predetermined path of action when a bad day comes along and you see a wildly ticking red number in front of you, losing tens of thousands by the second. Making rash decisions in this situation is rarely a good idea and you need to have a plan in advance for how to react to any given situation. If your simulation tells you that 5% down days are possible but far out on the tail, you cannot pull the plug on the strategy and step to the side if it suddenly occurs in front of your eyes, no matter how painful it might be.

This type of advice is easy to give but very hard to follow. It is obvious common sense but most people need to go through some really tough market periods and probably do this several times before this starts becoming less difficult. The temptation to override your strategy when it does badly will always be there and you need to have a rule in advance about whether you are allowed to override, and, if so, under what conditions and in what manner. Never make the decision on the stressful bad day; just follow your predetermined plan.

To attempt to maintain your sanity, it might help to try to distance yourself from the monetary numbers. Try not to view the fund's assets as real money but merely a way of keeping score in the game, like Monopoly money. If you start thinking about what the million you just lost could have bought in the real world, you lose your perspective and risk further losses or missing out on the rebound. Even worse, never calculate what the recent loss means in terms of your own management fee or performance fee and what you would have done with that money. After all, it's just Monopoly money.

An unwritten rule says that hedge-fund managers should have a large part of their net worth in their own fund. There are, however, two sides of that coin. The common argument is that having your own money in the fund ensures that your financial interests are aligned with your investors, so that if they lose, you lose as well, and vice versa. This is of course true, but on the other hand, as manager, you make most of your money on the performance fee of the fund and so the interest should already be aligned. There is then the added psychological stress of having your own money in the fund. It is certainly a lot harder to look at the fund as Monopoly money if you have a large part of your own money in it. Many investors will see that as a good thing, forgetting that if managers can distance themselves from the asset values and take a more rational perspective on the strategy, the performance might in fact be better. Emotions and investment decisions make a very bad mix.

CHAPTER 2

Futures Data

■ Futures as an Asset Class

Futures Exchanges

There are quite a few futures exchanges around the world, although a few large exchanges in the US are the most important for the typical diversified futures manager. Most exchanges have excellent web pages with tons of useful information about the products they offer and they are worth having a read through. You can always look up the exact specifications for a contract or any other detail you might be interested in.

Futures and Currency Exposure

If you are an international investor or trader and mostly used to cash instruments such as stocks, the concept of currency exposure when it comes to futures will be quite different from what you are used to. With cash instruments the currency exposure is always very clear and straightforward but that is not necessarily the case with futures. If you are a Swiss-based investor buying US$100,000 worth of IBM in New York, you also need to buy the dollars to pay for it, at least if for a moment we disregard Lombard financing and such. That means that after the transaction you have US$100,000 exposure to the stock price of IBM and at the same time US$100,000 worth of exposure to the US dollar (USD) against the Swissie (CHF). This exposure can have a major impact on the return of your investment and is a major factor in any quantitative analysis of the trade. Consider the following example:

- You are a Swiss-based investor buying 1,000 shares of IBM in May 2007 at exactly US$100 each.

- The exchange rate is about 1.21, so you have to exchange 121,000 CHF to pay for the purchase.

- Three and a half years later the price of IBM is up to 122 and you would like to sell and take home your 22% gain.

- The exchange rate now is about 1.01.

- When you sell your IBM stocks for US$122,000 and then exchange it back to Swissie, you only have 123,000 Swissie left, leaving barely enough to pay for commissions.

This is an age-old problem with cash equities strategies where one needs a strategy for whether to hedge all currency risks, run an overlay currency trading on top of the strategy or simply accept all currency exposure. With futures, the situation is quite different.

When you open a futures position, no money actually changes hands except from your commission fees. What you opened is just a commitment to buy or sell something at a future time. As mentioned, an overwhelming majority of all futures contracts are of course closed out by taking an offsetting position before it is time to buy or sell, but that is beside the point here. The fact that no money changes hands on initiation of the position means that you have much less foreign exchange risk than you do with cash instruments. Consider a similar example to the IBM trade above:

- You are a UK-based investor buying 10 contracts of the big Nasdaq futures at the price of US$2,000. The exchange rate at the time of purchase is 1.56, but that is in fact almost irrelevant.

- You close the position by selling offsetting contracts at the price of US$1,834 just a few weeks later.

- Now your loss is US$166,000, which you calculate by taking the price difference of 166 points, multiplying by the point value (which in the case of the Nasdaq contract is 100) and finally multiplying by the number of contracts held, to end up at US$166,000.

- The exchange rate at the time of closing the position is 1.44 and so your loss in your own currency ends up at more or less £115,300, and the exchange rate at the time of opening the position has no actual bearing on this number.

As seen here, the only exchange rate that has any bearing on the final settlement of the position is that of the closing day, or rather when you bring the resulting profit or loss back to your own base currency, but don't let that lead you to believe that exchange-rate fluctuations have no bearing on your futures profits and losses. You certainly have to have an exposure to currencies with futures, just not on the notional amount as you do with cash instruments. Your exposure is instead on the profit and loss (P&L), and so only your current profits or losses are subject to currency risk. You therefore have a very dynamic currency exposure and the extent of it varies day by day and even hour by hour as your positions move. This is a much smaller factor than what you have to deal with in cash-instrument strategies, but a much more difficult one to hedge. You may also need to keep some cash in various currencies with your broker just to make sure you don't get charged fees unnecessarily for overdrawing accounts when you make losses.

The important point is to understand that you always have a currency risk on your futures P&L and it requires additional care to manage.

■ Futures Data

Dealing with Limited Life Span

When trading commences for a new contract there is usually quite a long time left to the expiry date and very little trading activity to be seen. Few people are interested in trading wheat with a delivery several years from now and as such the contract will remain relatively illiquid until it gets closer to expiry. At any given time, there will be one contract in each market, corn, orange juice, gold and so on, which is the most liquid and the contract that almost everyone is trading at the moment. This can sometimes be the contract that is closest to the expiry date, but this is far from certain and there are no firm rules for when the liquidity switches to another contract or even which contract it switches to. For some markets this is very predictable and very straightforward, such as for equity index futures and currency futures, where the most liquid contract with a high degree of certainty is simply the one that has the least time left to expiry and the switch happens on the expiry date itself or just one or two days before it. In some commodity markets both the timing of the switchover and the selection of the next active contract are completely unpredictable.

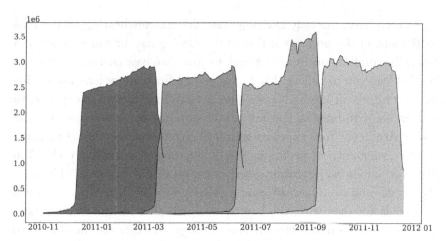

FIGURE 2.1 Open interest moving from month to month.

For someone focused just on a single market, it is possible to stay close enough to that market to be aware right away when the attention of the traders switches from one contract to another, but as a systematic trader covering a large number of markets you need to find a way to automatically detect such changes. From the perspective of the typical trader, the most liquid contract is the only one that really matters. Although there are CTA managers exploiting pricing differences between different delivery months in the same market, the most common strategies focus solely on the most heavily traded delivery month.

Figure 2.1 shows the open interest for the S&P 500 futures for three delivery months in 2011. This particular market offers only contracts for March, June, September and December so when the March moves to expiry the trading will normally move to the June contract and so on. The June contract expires on June 16 and shortly before that the open interest starts moving down for that contract while moving up in the next. At the same time, Figure 2.2 shows that the volume spikes up sharply in both the June and the September contract around this time as well. Remember that the open interest will tell you how many contracts are outstanding, that is how many are still uncovered in that particular delivery month. If you buy one S&P contract, you will add one to this number, and when you sell it you will decrease this number, and the same is true for the reversed trade, of course.

The reason why the volume goes up while the open interest rolls to the next delivery is that everyone is busy rolling their position, switching out of the June contract and into the September and thereby generating a lot of trade tickets. Since this is a non-deliverable financial future, you could in

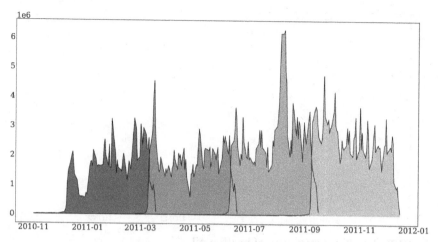

FIGURE 2.2   Volume spiking at rollover time.

theory stay with it all the way until it expires, but as you can see in these figures, very few people ever do that. If your desire is to maintain your position in the underlying asset, in this case, the S&P Index, you will want to have control over your rollover and buy one month and sell the other at the same time, so that you don't have any open price risk between closing one contract and opening the other or vice versa.

What you need is a clear method for when to switch from one contract to another and a notification of when you need to do the rollover. Common methods are to use the volume, the open interest or both in combination and then roll when a new contract has higher open interest and/or volume. Some prefer to require a couple of consecutive days or higher values before rolling, whereas some roll on the first day one contract exceeds another. In the end, this does not make a huge difference as long as you make sure you stay with a highly liquid contract and are aware of how and when to roll.

Term Structure

The term structure, or yield curve, of a futures market refers to the shape of the curve you get if you plot the price of each successive delivery month in a graph, such as in the heating oil example in Figure 2.3 and Table 2.1. The price of an asset to be delivered in one month is generally quite different from the price of the same asset to be delivered in six months and the overview graph of how these prices change for different delivery dates is called the term structure.

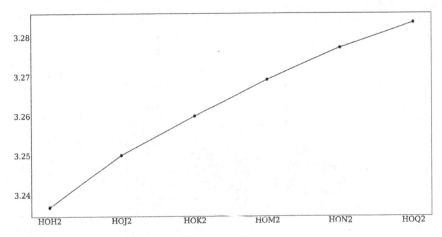

FIGURE 2.3 Term structure of heating oil.

Ticker	Name	Last
TABLE 2.1	Term structure table	
HOH2	Heating Oil March 2012	3.2367
HOJ2	Heating Oil April 2012	3.2499
HOK2	Heating Oil May 2012	3.2598
HOM2	Heating Oil June 2012	3.2690
HON2	Heating Oil July 2012	3.2771
HOQ2	Heating Oil August 2012	3.2835

In this example, the price level of heating oil for each successive month is going up, which is the normal case. A term structure chart that slopes upwards such as this one is said to be in *contango*. In some instances the term structure can take on a downward slope and such a situation is called *backwardation*. These two words are the legacy of a system of deferring payments for stocks on the London Stock Exchange in the mid-nineteenth century, which may explain the rather esoteric terminology.

To understand why the prices are usually higher further in the future, you need to think of the cost of hedging the position. The fair price of any position is the cost of hedging it, so if you can hedge something, you can also price it. If someone sells open 100 gold contracts with delivery one year from now, the way to hedge this would be to buy 10,000 ounces (283 kilograms) worth of physical gold in the spot market now and store it until the time of delivery. Storage of gold is not entirely free unless you really want to keep it in your basement and you would be locking up cash during this year, which you could have received interest on or otherwise used. You would of course need to be compensated for this or the position is not worth taking.

For financial futures, such as equity index futures and bond futures, the interest rate is the main driver of the term structure shape because there is no physical storage required for hedging; you just need to deliver the cash upfront. Therefore, you see less of a steep curve for financial futures than for deliverable ones. On the other hand, there are commodities with severe storage cost where this is the overwhelming factor in the term structure shape. Natural gas, for instance, is very expensive to store and it therefore tends to show very steep contango.

Backwardation, or downwards-sloping term structure, is less common but not an anomaly. Backwardation can be caused by seasonality, interest rate conditions or unusual storage cost situations and is not uncommon for softs and perishable commodities.

Basis Gaps

The current price of two contracts with the same underlying but different delivery months will always be different and this is reflected in the term structure. The April gold contract will be traded at a different price than the December gold contract for the same year, and the same logic goes for any other market as well. Usually the price of the December contract will be higher than the April contract of the same year, in which case we have a contango situation, and this has nothing to do with the expectations of gold price changes. It may be intuitive to think that the higher price of the December contract reflects traders' view that the gold spot price should move up, but this is not at all the case. Instead the hedging cost, or carry cost if you will, is the core factor in play. The difference in base price between two contracts becomes acutely important when the currently traded contract comes to the end of its life and you need to roll to the next.

Figure 2.4 shows the May and July 2012 rough rice price where the July contract is the lighter, broken line. Note that the July is consistently more expensive than the May. This is the normal case but there are times when the relationship can reverse as well and the longer contract can be cheaper than the shorter.

The reason for this price discrepancy should now be clear: it's primarily related to hedging or carry costs. The problem that this creates for us is that when creating a continuous time series for long-term simulations, we

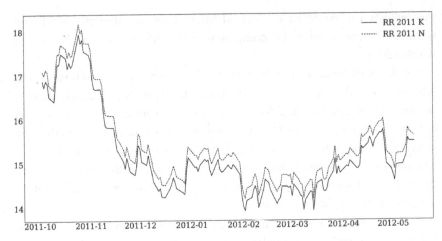

FIGURE 2.4 Rough rice basis gap.

cannot simply put one contract's price series after another. Doing so would introduce artificial gaps in the data where there really are no gaps in the actual market. What is required to do proper back-testing simulations is a continuous time series that reflects the actual market behaviour, which does not necessarily mean that it reflects the actual prices at the time. Consider the time series in Figure 2.5, which is a completely unadjusted time series where contract after contract have just been put back to back. The closest contract has always been selected and held until expiry, when the next

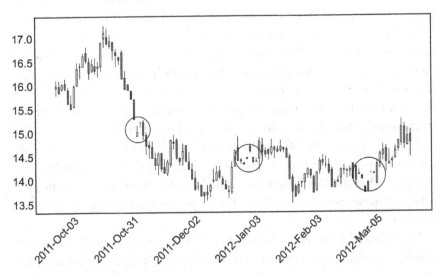

FIGURE 2.5 Unadjusted time series for rough rice.

contract has taken over. This is the default way of looking at continuous futures time series in many market data applications and if you, for instance, chart the c1 codes in Reuters, this is what you get. In this example, it is easy to see right away when the contract rollovers occurred, even without the circles that I put in. The seemingly erratic behaviour of the price during these periods does not at all reflect the actual market conditions at the time and basing your simulations on such data will produce nonsense results.

Now compare this with the more normal-looking price curve in Figure 2.6. Notice how it is no longer possible to see where the contract rollovers occurred and the artificial gaps have been removed. If you look even closer, you will notice that while the final price is the same in the end, there are significant price differences between the two series on the left-hand side of the x-axis. Whereas the unadjusted peak reading in October was about 17.3, the adjusted chart shows a peak of over 30. The difference can occur in either direction, depending on whether there is a positive or negative basis gap at the time of the roll.

The reason for this price discrepancy in the past prices is that I use back-adjusted price charts here. For a back-adjusted chart, the current price is always correct at the right-hand side of the series, but all previous contracts will have a mismatch. When the roll occurs, the back-adjusted series will adjust all series back in time and remove the artificial gap. This means that the whole time series back in time will have to be shifted up or down to match the new series.

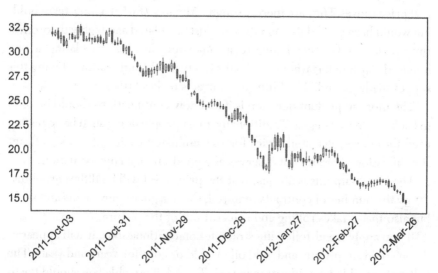

FIGURE 2.6 Properly adjusted time series for rough rice.

There are several possible ways to achieve this adjustment and most good market data applications offer a choice in this regard, but it does not make a huge difference for the bigger picture which exact method you choose. My preferred method is to identify the liquid contract based on open interest and to link the contracts together so that the old contract's close matches the new contract's close on the rollover date, keeping any actual gaps on that day and back-adjusting the entire time series all the way from the start of the data. So if you look at the adjusted time series to see the exact price of corn in June of 1985, it will be very different from what the actual price was at the time since there have been countless adjustments done with all the rollovers that have occurred since. However, the real trends of the price series over time have been properly preserved and the most recent price in the series represents the actual price in the market.

Other methods of adjusting prices can involve using ratios of two contracts, forward adjusting, and different methods of using volume and open interest to find the most liquid issue. These are details which are not too important for the long-term strategy but worth experimenting with if you want to look at the finer details. For a comprehensive look at rollover methods, see Jack Schwager's (1995) book, *Schwager on Futures: Technical Analysis*.

The Change in How Continuations Are Used

The obvious problem with these calculated continuations is that they are not real. They are not tradable instruments, and they do not represent actual, real price moves. They are merely rough estimates of what a long-term holding would have looked like and they are just calculated and highly theoretical time series. If you need long-term analytics, such as calculating a one hundred-day moving average, you absolutely need continuations. Doing this sort of maths on individual futures contracts makes little sense.

The more important question is if and how continuations should be used in back-testing strategies. Traditionally, most people doing such back-testing used these pre-calculated series for the simulated trading. It's a significant simplification of reality but it serves as a good-enough approximation.

The issue with this is not just that the price level will be different, obfuscating the number of contracts required, the margin requirements and such, but also that it takes rolling and roll cost out of the picture.

If you apply trend-following strategies on continuations, it will appear as if you could simply buy and hold oil or gold or corn for years and years. The rolling is an added complication in real life, and, if possible you should try to include this in the backtest logic.

The good news is that there's been remarkable development in this space since the first edition of this book came out in 2013. Back then, there really wasn't any choice but to use continuations, not if you were a retail trader or even a smaller-scale professional. There wasn't any readily available software solution for backtesting on individual futures contracts and even if you wanted to build your own, computing power and memory were clearly limiting factors back then.

Even if you had the ability to construct your own back-tester, you still needed hardware capable of dealing with tens of thousands of individual contracts and their time series, and that just wasn't commonplace until fairly recently.

For all the research in this book, I have used individual contracts in order to get as close to reality as possible. The software that I used is something which I wish had been readily available ten years ago, a software which is able to base analytics and trading logic on on-the-fly calculated continuations and execute trades based on real contracts. On-the-fly in this case means that the back-test would calculate the continuation each day, the way it would have looked on that day, rather than using a pre-calculated single series for the entire time. It would be a close approximation of real-life trading.

■ Futures Sectors

Agricultural Commodities

Purists may take issue with my definition of agricultural commodities, because I include softs, grains, fibres, meats, and so on in this sector, but I prefer a practical and pragmatic sector definition to a textbook definition. There is nothing wrong with subdividing this sector into all those components, but it does not add value in this context.

The agricultural sector might start feeling slightly comical for traders who are used to dealing with stocks, currencies, and bonds. In the agricultural space there are quite a few different futures markets where everything from coffee and cotton to lean hogs and livestock can be traded, making it a veritable supermarket. This is, in a way, an excellent sector because the internal correlation between these different markets is not particularly high. Although it never hurts knowing a little bit about what you trade, you can essentially treat each market as just pure numbers, without having to care about what the market driver for, say, wheat demand really is.

Most agricultural futures are traded in Chicago or New York, but you also find some interesting markets in Tokyo, London, and even Winnipeg. The variety of available instruments in this sector is a dream for the diversified futures manager, such as coffee, cocoa, cotton, orange juice, sugar, corn, wheat, lumber, rubber, oats, rice, soybeans, soybean meal, soybean oil, live cattle, and lean hogs. They are all affected by inflation to some degree as well as by the US dollar, but these tend to be of lesser importance over the long run and the individual markets show their own clear trends. It is certainly no coincidence that the business of diversified futures started within the commodity sector, and traders even still retain their name from those days: commodity trading advisors (CTAs).

The volatility of the different markets in this sector can vary significantly. The contracts in this sector are highly driven by fundamental developments specific to the commodity in question, such as adverse weather in an important production region, crop results, and inventory reports. When significant news comes out, there may be substantial moves not only on the day in question, but also for a prolonged period of time. This can be very nice when the move is in your favour, but make sure you are able to take the pain when the moves go against you. Seasonality is also a factor to consider in some of these commodities where cyclical demand or supply can affect the price patterns.

The exchanges often have so-called limit rules on these markets, meaning that there is a maximum amount the price is allowed to move in a single day. When the price has moved the maximum amount and buyers and sellers agree that the fair price lies beyond, the trading comes to a halt and is said to be in limit lock. The following day the price can move the same amount again, or less if the participants have calmed down by then.

In this sector all futures are in theory deliverable, which means that if you hold a contract, long or short, past the critical date you may be forced to take or make delivery of the underlying asset. For all deliverable futures contracts, such as gold, live cattle, corn, and so on, you need to close out your position long before the actual expiry date. The market conventions and terminology vary between markets, but usually you need to be out before the so-called first notice day. After that day, you could be called upon to make good on your commitment, which means either deliver or take delivery of the underlying. I don't know about you, but nothing ruins my day like a truckload of live cows parked outside my office.

For most traders this is only an amusing theoretical scenario with no actual risk, because most brokers will not allow these contracts to go to delivery and therefore shut them down for you in case you had forgotten and could not be reached, but this is not something you want to happen either. Make sure you are always aware of when you should close or roll a position or there will be negative consequences.

The units used for agricultural commodities are usually a mass unit such as pounds or a volume unit such as bushels, but with various exceptions such as feet for lumber (see Table 2.2 for all the details).

In the agricultural commodities sector the small player has a clear advantage in that there are a large number of less liquid instruments available with low correlation to other assets. They are liquid enough for trading accounts of a few tens of million dollars, perhaps even over a hundred million, but the big players in the field simply cannot get any useful profits out of them because of their size. It simply is not possible to trade huge amounts of Japanese rubber or European potatoes and this keeps the huge CTA funds away. If you manage reasonably small accounts, this is the sector where you can go nuts and add all kinds of obscure markets to help improve your risk-adjusted returns. The relatively low internal correlation in this sector means that you can get significant diversification benefits from adding more markets.

TABLE 2.2   **Agricultural commodity futures**

Name	Point value	Unit	Currency	Exchange
Azuki red beans	2,400	Kg	JPY	TGE
Coffee	37,500	Lbs	USc	CSCE
Corn	5,000	Bsh	USc	CBOT
Cotton	50,000	Lbs	USc	NYCE
Lean hogs	40,000	Lbs	USc	CME
Live cattle	40,000	Lbs	USc	CME
Lumber	110,000	Feet	USD	CME
Oats	5,000	Bsh	USc	CBOT
Orange juice	15,000	Lbs	USc	NYCE
Canola	20	Tons	CAD	WCE
Rough rice	2,000	Cwt	USc	CBOT
Rubber	10,000	Kg	JPY	TOCOM
Soybean meal	100	Tons	USD	CBOT
Soybeans	5,000	Bsh	USc	CBOT
Sugar	112,000	Lbs	USc	CSCE
Wheat	5,000	Bsh	USc	CBOT

Non-Agricultural Commodities

This is again a pragmatic sector definition, which you are unlikely to find in the more purist literature on the subject. I have mixed energies and metals into one sector because they fit more together with each other than they do with the agricultural commodities (see Table 2.3).

The energy group is a bit limited in terms of instruments, but offers some interesting opportunities. The dominating theme in this sector is oil and its different products, where light sweet crude oil forms the core. This is essentially the product they pump out of the ground in various regions of the world with horrible climates and extremist leaders, such as Saudi Arabia, Texas, and Alaska. The main products from crude oil are heating oil, gasoil, and gasoline, all tradable and highly liquid in the futures market. These four markets usually have a fairly high correlation to each other, but at times the driving factors behind them work independently and their trends can decouple for extended periods. They are all very prone to long-term trends and well suited for a diversified futures trend-following method.

There is another highly interesting instrument within the energy sector as well, which is usually not very correlated to the oil theme, and that is the Henry Hub (HH) natural gas. This is a bit of a special animal and rather unique in its behaviour. Natural gas is mainly used for power generation and is pumped out of the ground, chiefly in Russia and the US. The unique property of this particular commodity is its persistently sharp contango, which means that the prices of contracts deliverable further in the future are more expensive than contracts that expire sooner, and that the term structure chart thereby is sloping upwards. Most commodities display somewhat of a

TABLE 2.3	Non-agricultural commodity futures			
Name	**Point value**	**Unit**	**Currency**	**Exchange**
Gasoil	100	Tonne	USD	NYMEX
Crude oil	1,000	Barrels	USD	NYMEX
Heating oil	42,000	Gallons	USD	NYMEX
Natural gas (HH)	10,000	mmBTU	USD	NYMEX
Gasoline	42,000	Gallons	USD	NYMEX
Gold	100	Troy Ounces	USD	COMEX
Copper	25,000	Pounds	USc	COMEX
Palladium	100	Troy Ounces	USD	NYMEX
Platinum	50	Troy Ounces	USD	NYMEX
Silver	5,000	Troy Ounces	USc	COMEX

contango due to the cost of hedging the position, as explained earlier (the main reasons being cost of storage and opportunity cost of capital, although for some markets seasonality is a large part of the explanation as well).

For natural gas, the contango is very large and for good reason. This particular commodity has a very low density, which makes storage extremely expensive. The method of hedging a short futures contract of natural gas would be in theory to buy it today, store it in huge domes or silos that are often located underground, and then deliver it against the contract upon expiry (or of course to just let it stay in the ground and take it up later on instead). As a futures trader, of course, you are not concerned with dealing with the actual physical commodity, but the hedging method is still theoretically valid for pricing and you need to understand why the term structure chart looks the way it does, and how it can work in your favour. The cost-of-carry hedging model applies mainly to commodities that can be stored and, for assets such as oil, this is the core driver of the term structure shape. For natural gas, with its highly complicated and nigh impossible storage situation, the curve is also in large part driven by the seasonal demand patterns for the underlying asset (Figure 2.7).

At the time of writing, the price difference in the May contract and the September 2012 contract is nearly 5%. The actual price by expiry is often quite stable while the futures contracts are traded much higher, depending on how far out they are. This means that the points on the term structure curve tend to slowly move down while they are moving left, which is where the profit opportunity lies; commodities with a sharp persistent contango trend strongly downwards and the money is on the short side of the game as long as the shape persists.

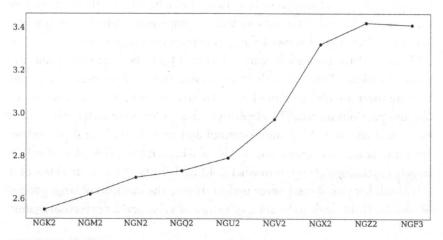

FIGURE 2.7 Term structure of natural gas.

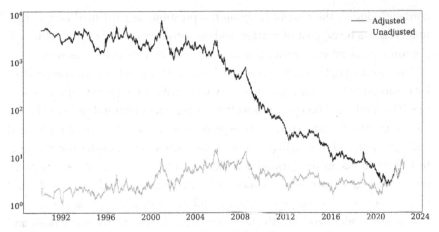

FIGURE 2.8 Adjusted versus unadjusted data for natural gas.

Sharp contango situations, as well as backwardation, can offer great opportunities but also require that you really take care of the problem of obtaining corrected time series. The trend in something like natural gas will look highly different if you simply paste one futures contract after the next as opposed to adjusting properly for basis gaps when they are spliced together. Figure 2.8 illustrates the problem, where the lighter line lacks any adjustment and simply displays the actual prices of each contract followed by the next contract upon expiry, while the second one uses a back-adjustment method as described earlier. So did the actual price move up or down? It depends on your point of view, but for a futures trader it absolutely collapsed and there was a ton of money being made on staying short. The spot price did not change anywhere near as much and actually went up over time, but if you traded the futures that is completely irrelevant because the contango effect overshadowed the spot price moves over time.

Then we have the metals where you find both the base metals and the more shiny kind. There are only four precious metals of interest for a trader because there are no liquid markets in ruthenium, osmium, and other more obscure precious metals. The elephant in this sector is naturally gold, which has a dual use as a shiny status symbol and as a psychological protection against inflation and various end-of-the-world scenarios. The value of gold is largely psychological and somewhat political because the industrial use of it is limited, but one should never underestimate the madness of large groups of people. Gold tends to be seen as a store of value and a protection against inflation, deflation, wars, riots, and zombie attacks. It does have these properties in some sense, but only because a lot of people have agreed on this logic. If the state of the world turns ugly in a serious way and the chanting crowds with the pitchforks are approaching your house, you are probably better off with canned food and a shotgun than with gold bars. Still, gold shows excellent long-term trending patterns and certainly should be included in a diversified futures strategy.

Often seen as the little brother of gold, silver has a fairly high correlation to gold, but it has its own merits as well. This metal has more industrial use and in many respects different drivers of performance. Apart from these two well-known precious metals, there is also platinum and palladium, which both at times can show truly excellent trending patterns. These two metals are less liquid than gold and silver but for a small- to medium-sized managed futures fund, they are absolutely liquid enough.

The most common futures market in base metals is copper, traded in Chicago. Most other base metals are primarily traded in London on the London Metal Exchange (LME), and are not in fact futures but forward contracts. In that exchange you can find the less exciting sounding metals such as zinc, aluminium, lead, and so on. They can be traded on the same principles as their futures brethren and the differences between the futures and forwards markets are not that significant.

Currencies

If you are not used to trading currencies, you may need some time to get used to the concept. A Euro-based investor who buys a contract of the German MDAX future is doing something very straightforward: buying a basket of stocks traded in her own currency. If the same investor buys gold futures, she is buying gold against the US dollar, which is still fairly straightforward, but when the same person buys the Mexican peso contract, she is long peso against dollar and is taking a bet on two completely different currencies. Trading currencies makes it more important to understand that in every single position, regardless of asset class or sector, you are always long something and short something. If you buy IBM shares, you are long IBM and short dollar, and so on. Yes, you might already have the cash dollars to pay with, but the acquisition of those dollars belongs to a different position with its own long and short leg.

In the same way, when you enter a currency future you are long one currency and short the other. There are many available currency futures and quite a few of them are very liquid. The spreads are very tight and often better than on the forwards. The currency markets are the most liquid in the world and the spot market can swallow just about any volume. This is highly useful for very large CTA funds that tend to trade a large portion of their funds in currencies when they get so big that it is getting difficult and expensive to move positions in many other markets. If you study the asset allocation of the extremely large trend followers with assets in the billions, you will find that they have the bulk of their money in the currency markets.

Many currency futures are crosses against the USD and if only one currency is named, it is implied that it is against the USD (see Table 2.4). Therefore, the CHF future is a bet on the exchange rate between the CHF and the USD. There are also a growing number of non-USD crosses, such as the Euro/Yen future and so on. This sector offers some interesting diversification possibilities if you use these types of crosses. Always be aware of the danger of stacking up USD risk and be sure to monitor the risk you are taking here. If you are long the euro future, long the CHF future, the yen future, the British pound future and the Aussie future, you are really just short dollar and when the dollar recovers, you get hit on all positions at once. Taking these positions may still at times be a good idea, just as long as you are aware of the risk and model it properly so you know what to expect when things turn against you.

TABLE 2.4	Currency futures			
Name	Point value	Unit	Currency	Exchange
AUD/USD	100,000	AUD	USD	CME
GBP/USD	62,500	GBP	USD	CME
EUR/USD	125,000	EUR	USD	CME
CAD/USD	100,000	CAD	USD	CME
JPY/USD	1,250	Million JPY	USc	CME
NZD/USD	100,000	NZD	USD	CME
NOK/USD	200,000	NOK	USD	CME
ZAR/USD	500,000	RND	USD	CME
SEK/USD	200,000	SEK	USD	CME
CHF/USD	125,000	CHF	USD	CME
EUR/CHF	125,000	EUR	CHF	CME
EUR/GBP	125,000	EUR	GBP	CME
EUR/JPY	125,000	CHF	JPY	CME

Equities

This is the largest futures sector in terms of amount of available instruments and the easiest for most people to relate to. Buying a basket of stocks in a well-defined market is a very straightforward concept and understanding the potential risk and reward of such a trade is fairly intuitive. The percentage moves of the underlying indices are published daily on news websites, TV screens, and in newspapers. We are only dealing in equity index futures in this book and not with single stock futures and the reason for this is not just simplification, as one might think, but rather that I find single stock futures of much less interest and they are just not terribly helpful in diversified futures strategies.

Just as single cash equities have high internal correlation, so of course do equity futures. It can be very tempting to include a large number of equity futures in your strategy because there are so many to pick from, but I would advise against allocating too high a risk to this sector, as it can easily put you in a corner portfolio with the illusion of diversification when you are in fact just putting on massive bets on equity beta. Nevertheless, equity futures do have a place in a diversified futures strategy and representative contracts from several different geographical markets should be included. As Table 2.5 shows, I include the large US futures such as the S&P 500 and the Nasdaq 100 as well as European representatives such as the Euro Stoxx 50, the FTSE 100, the GDAX and CAC40, and a few Asians such as Hang Seng and Nikkei 225.

TABLE 2.5	Equity futures				
Name	Point value	Unit	Currency	Exchange
CAC 40	10	Index points	EUR	Euronext
DAX	25	Index points	EUR	EUREX
Euro Stoxx	10	Index points	EUR	Euronext
FTSE 100	10	Index points	GBP	Euronext
Hang Seng	50	Index points	HKD	HKEX
Hang Seng China Enterprises	50	Index points	HKD	HKEX
IBEX 35	10	Index points	EUR	MEFF
MSCI Taiwan	100	Index points	USD	SGX
Nasdaq 100	100	Index points	USD	CME
Nikkei 225	5	Index points	USD	CME
S&P 500	250	Index points	USD	CME
S&P 60	200	Index points	CAD	ME
SPI 200	25	Index points	USD	ASX

In Asia you also have some interesting Chinese exposure opportunities by including the Hang Seng China Enterprises and the MSCI Taiwan.

One thing to keep in mind here is that most diversified futures strategies go both long and short and that the short side of equities usually has a very different profile from the long side. When equities are in a bull market, they can move slowly upwards in an orderly fashion for long periods of time, compounding gains week after week and be highly profitable. On the downside, equity moves tend to be swifter and more violent. Sharp drop-downs followed by v-shaped reversals create a very dangerous trading environment. Many strong diversified futures programmes struggle on the equity sector and it is not uncommon even for good systems to lose money consistently over time on that game. Even so, I would not recommend that you cut out short equity futures from your trading universe. You are likely to end up without significant profits in the long run, perhaps even in a loss, but in the shorter run it provides a very valuable diversification and can smooth out returns. When the bad years for the equity markets come along, the short side of your equity trades can make very good money and help you recover from what otherwise might be a very bad year for you.

The unit used for equity index futures is simply points on the relevant index, which makes this a very simple calculation in terms of profit and loss. For example, if you buy five contracts at 100 and sell them at 110 and the point value for this particular contract is 10, your gain is $((110 - 100) \times 5 \times 10 \times 1) = 500$ of the currency in question.

Rates

In this sector I include practically everything on the yield curve, from the far left to the far right. The behaviour of instruments very far apart on this scale can seem like very dissimilar instruments in that the level of volatility will be extremely different and that has to be taken into account for position sizing. The far left of the yield curve always has a much lower volatility than the far right since these instruments have much lower duration and therefore a much lower interest rate risk, but going into the finer points of fixed income mathematics is far outside the scope of this book. You don't need to have read all Fabozzi's books on the subject to be able to trade bond futures but it does not hurt to get a little basic knowledge. The key point to understand is that volatility decreases drastically on the far left side and it goes up the farther on the right you move.

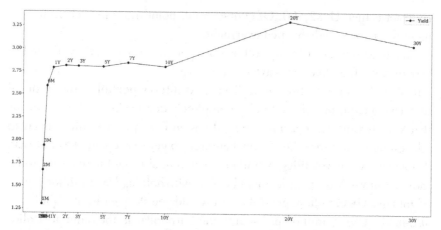

FIGURE 2.9 US benchmark yield curve.

Take a look at Figure 2.9. Starting on the left end we have the short-term interest rate futures, often based on loans of 30 or 90 days. These futures, often shorted down to just STIRs, are bets on changes in interest rates on the left side of the curve. The major difference between this sector and the bond futures is the aforementioned massive difference in potential price moves on the left and the right side of the curve. If the 30-year US Bond moves 1% in a day, that is a slightly larger than normal move, but nothing to write home about; a 1% move in a STIR future, on the other hand, would take a cataclysmic world event. The quick conclusion from this should be that one needs to take massive leverage in STIRs to get any form of profit or loss that actually matters, as scary as that might sound.

Also be careful to get the underlying contract value and the point value right since this works a little differently than for other sectors. Let's take the Eurodollar as an example, which is based on the three months US Dollar LIBOR – although don't confuse this with the currency rate Euro/Dollar which is something completely different. The term Eurodollar was coined long before the European currency was conceived and refers to the interest rate of time deposits in USD outside the United States. The notional underlying of this contract is US$1 million and quoted as 100 minus the annual three months LIBOR rate. To get to the point value, you therefore need to first divide the notional by 100, just like you would with bond futures, but you also need to divide again by four because the contract is for the quarterly rate and not the annual, despite being quoted as such. So if the Eurodollar contract moves from 98 to 99, the profit or loss impact on one contract is then US$2,500. Of course, a full point move in such an instrument does not exactly happen overnight.

Short-term interest futures often scare people away because you need to take on what feels like a massive position to get any sort of real profit or loss out of it. As you will find, in a diversified futures portfolio, the notional underlying exposure of the fund is completely dominated by this sector for that very reason. Comparing with gold as an example, you often need to take on up to 50 times the notional amount to get to the same level of risk, if normalised for volatility, or rather for potential price fluctuations, to be more accurate. Most people might be okay with holding US$1 million worth of gold in a US$5 million portfolio, but would you sleep easily at night if you also held a US$50 million position in the Eurodollar in the same portfolio? Nevertheless, this is essentially a fallacy to avoid and you should be concerned with actual risk and not with notional amounts.

From about year 2 on the curve we have the bond futures where there is an actual underlying bond to be delivered at expiry. Bond futures are quoted in per cent of par, just as a normal bond. That means of course that as yields move up, bond futures move down and vice versa. Each bond futures contract has certain specifications, such as maturity, coupon, issuer and so on, and in theory there are often several different actual bonds that could be delivered against the contract upon expiry. In reality, however, only one bond will be cheapest to deliver and that is the one that will change hands between those who choose to keep their contracts open to the end. As a trader, you don't want to keep your contracts open until expiry though, as you would then have to deal with the actual bonds. The most liquid and therefore most interesting bond futures are those on bonds issued by the respective governments of the USA, Germany, the UK, Australia, Canada, and Japan, although other countries' debt may also be of interest to you should you want to expand in this sector.

A bond future is tied to a certain, although often approximate, maturity. For the US, for instance, the contracts of interest are the 2-year note, the 5-year note, the 10-year note, and the 30-year t-bond. In Germany, the terminology is less straightforward, where the longest-term contract is called the Buxl and represents a German government debt with a remaining term of 24–35 years. There is also the Bund with a duration of 8.5–10.5 years, the Bobl with 4.5–5.5 years and the Schatz with 1.75–2.25 years (see Table 2.6).

The price moves in the bond futures depend on the interest rate changes, which in turn are a factor of many things from inflation to investors' propensity to take risk and the perceived solvency of the issuer.

TABLE 2.6	Rates futures			
Name	Point value	Unit	Currency	Exchange
AU 10Y	1,000	Bond price	AUD	ASX
AU 3Y	1,000	Bond price	AUD	ASX
AU 90 Day	2,500	Price	AUD	ASX
Bobl	1,000	Bond price	EUR	Euronext
Bund	1,000	Bond price	EUR	Euronext
CD 10Y	1,000	Bond price	CAD	ME
CD 90 Day	2,500	Price	CAD	ME
Euribor	2,500	1 million EUR	EUR	Euronext
Euroswiss	2,500	1 million CHF	CHF	Euronext
JP 10Y	1,000	Bond price	JPY	TSE
Long gilt	1,000	Bond price	GBP	Euronext
Schatz	1,000	Bond price	EUR	Euronext
Short sterling	1,250	£500,000	GBP	Euronext
US 10Y	1,000	Bond price	USD	CME
US 2Y	2,000	Bond price	USD	CME
US 5Y	1,000	Bond price	USD	CME

The contract value of bond futures is normally 100,000 of the currency in question, although as the pricing is in percentage terms, this need to be divided by 100 to arrive at the most common point value for bond futures of 1,000. As a futures trader, the point value is always more important for you to know than the actual contract value. They may often be the same but when they differ, focus on the point value.

Bond futures as a group have a fairly low level of volatility; however, the longer durations always have a greater volatility than the shorter ones. The longer ones have a higher sensitivity to changes in interest rates and the prices will move much quicker. They are still slower than most other sectors, but there is a very large difference in volatility between a 10-year note and a 2-year note.

CHAPTER 3

Constructing Diversified Futures Trading Strategies

45

In this chapter and the next two, I demonstrate how extremely simple strategies can be used to achieve results very close to what the big managed futures managers display. Some large futures funds treat their proprietary strategies as if they are photos of the Roswell alien landing and like to talk about how they have vast staffs of PhDs and massive research budgets, and, in most cases, this is true. The question you should ask, however, is just how big a difference this really makes. Once you reach the size of having a few hundred million under management, hiring a staff of researchers to improve details is a good idea, but in fact a single person can replicate the bulk of the returns with some decent software and a bit of hard work.

I describe two very basic trend-following strategies using the most common approaches to capturing trends. I then make some slight adjustments to these strategies and combine them into a single, and more realistic, strategy. I will analyse the resulting strategy in detail and compare it with the results of the big-name futures funds.

Through this exercise I intend to show that you don't need complicated mathematics to construct a working trend-following portfolio strategy and that the exact buy-and-sell rules are largely irrelevant. The concept is important but the common focus on entry and exit rules is misguided.

■ They Are All Doing the Same Thing

I make the somewhat bold claim in this book that all the trend-following futures managers out there are more or less doing the same thing and that this is not a very complicated thing to replicate. I have to admit that part of the reason I make this claim is that the controversy of the statement itself should catch your eye and if you are still reading this book, I have probably succeeded so far, but I am serious in my statement and I intend to prove it. Of course, many funds have their own clever little tweaks which may make a substantial performance difference over time and my statement is in no way intended to belittle the successful futures managers in this field, rather the contrary. There is a clear difference between understanding how to construct a successful strategy and having the ability, drive, and willpower to make it happen in reality. That is the tough part that can never be properly taught. The entrepreneurs who started the funds I mention in this book have achieved incredible success and should receive their proper credit for it.

The first chart I show (Figure 3.1) is not so much for comparison purposes but to provide an overview of the performance profile for this type of fund. Figure 3.1 shows you a number of funds in this field and how they have performed since their inception and because they all have different dates of

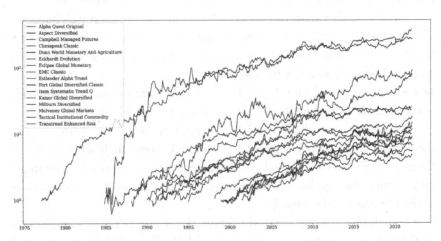

FIGURE 3.1 Trend-followers' performance.

inception the starting point will be different for them. Millburn is the one with the longest official track record and I include both old legendary funds and newer and less well-known funds. These funds have different volatility profiles and different investment universes, but if you look closely, you can see that they quite often show peaks and troughs at the same time. We can also see that a few of the funds with very strong long-term track records had really bad starts but picked themselves up and moved on, something that is extremely hard to do in reality.

To better put the numbers into context, consider Table 3.1 with some basic performance data. The compound annualised return of these funds is quite high, with most over or around double digits over extended periods of time. In the light of the fairly modest drawdowns, they far outpace traditional investment approaches. Of course, what truly makes them stand out is the low correlation to the equity markets.

Since 1977 when the oldest manager in our example list, Millburn, was founded, the MSCI World Index has yielded a compound annual return of 8%. To further put these numbers into perspective, the world stock market had an annualised standard deviation of 15% and a maximum drawdown (DD) of 55%, making it a highly inferior investment vehicle any way you look at it.

TABLE 3.1 Trend-followers' performance

	Annualised compound return (%)	Max DD (%)	Correlation to MSCI World	Starting date
MSCI World TR	8.12	−54.57		1988-01-01
Millburn Diversified	13.25	−25.65	0.02	1977-02-01
Dunn World Monetary and Agriculture	12.85	−57.88	−0.09	1984-11-01
Chesapeake Classic	10.06	−31.58	0.17	1988-02-01
Campbell Managed Futures	8.27	−31.77	−0.04	1990-01-01
Eckhardt Evolution	10.85	−27.11	0.02	1991-08-01
Estlander Alpha Trend	7.86	−29.71	0.04	1991-10-01
Tactical Institutional Commodity	16.34	−41.53	−0.05	1993-04-01
Transtrend Enhanced Risk	11.25	−15.67	0.01	1995-01-01
Mulvaney Global Markets	12.49	−45.08	−0.12	1999-05-01
Alpha Quest Original	9.85	−29.39	−0.08	1999-05-01

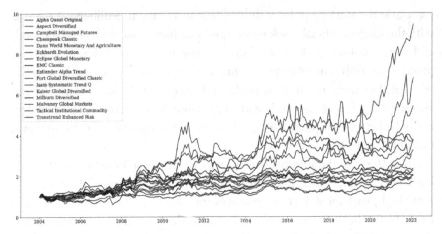

FIGURE 3.2 Performance comparison of futures funds since 2004: unadjusted.

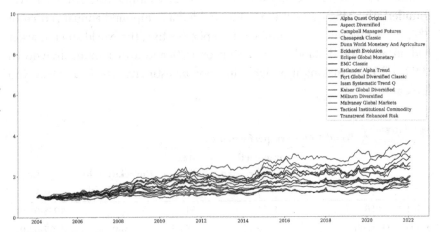

FIGURE 3.3 Performance comparison of futures funds since 2004: normalised for volatility.

Obviously these strategies have very different risk profiles because their annualised return numbers and risk numbers come out quite far apart, and so you may be wondering where I am going with this argument about them all doing almost the same thing. Have a look at Figures 3.2 and 3.3, which should help prove my point. Figure 3.2 shows the performance of a representative group of futures funds rebased to 1 in 2004. The data is the pure track record of each manager and as you can see they don't look too similar at first glance except that almost all were profitable in this period. The similarities are not that large until you start digging into the details. Don't worry about identifying which line is for which fund; that's not important to the point I am making. It is the same set of funds shown in Table 3.1 and the important point here is to observe the similarities.

Figure 3.3 shows the exact same funds and, more importantly, the exact same y-axis scale. The only difference is that the return of each fund has been adjusted based on the standard deviation of its returns. In essence, I have merely normalised the returns for volatility to compare them on an equal footing. Naturally you can still see some difference between the funds, but the notion that they are all working with the same base concepts should be very clear from this figure. Some perform better than others but they all react at the same time to the same events. The main differences between these funds are what investment universe they use, more specifically how their sector allocation looks, what time frame they primarily operate on, and what risk level they are using.

It is my intention in this book to dig into the gritty details of what these funds actually are and how they are creating these superior results. As you will see, the underlying methods need not be overly complex and it is completely possible for any determined individual to get into this business and compete with the big players.

■ Cracking Open the Magic Trend-Following Black Box

The Investment Universe

To achieve long-term success with a diversified futures strategy, you must cover multiple markets and multiple instruments per market. Running a trend-following strategy like these ones on a single market or a single asset class is at best plain silly and at worst suicidal. If you take these strategies and then go and trade only the Nasdaq 100 with it, don't come blaming me when that margin call comes along. And when I say you need multiple markets, I don't just mean that you need both the S&P 500 and the NDX. If you don't include a large variety of futures markets in different asset classes, you should not do this in the first place. Sometimes there are several years in a row when a single market or even a whole asset class just keeps losing and losing, and then some years later that turns out to be the big winner. The whole point here is that you trade everything, even if you keep losing on some markets. As long as the winners pay for the losers, it is worth having these markets in for diversification. You never know when the market regime will switch and the losing market becomes the winner. I cannot stress enough the importance of multiple markets. Using a single strategy on a single instrument is for those people with either extreme skill or for those who simply have a death wish.

There is often a trade-off between number of markets and complexity of the strategy. More markets can increase diversification and create more trading opportunities but adding too many will complicate your strategy and your operational side. The exact number you settle on should be a result of your own simulations and matching your risk acceptance. I will use a fairly well balanced and broad universe here, one with a tilt towards agriculture (Table 3.2).

TABLE 3.2 **The investment universe**

Agricultural	Non-Agricultural	Currencies	Equities	Rates
Cotton	Gasoil	AUD/USD	CAC 40	Bunt
Corn	Light sweet crude oil	GBP/USD	DAX	Schatz
Lumber	Heating oil	EUR/USD	FTSE 100	Long Gilt
Live cattle	Brent Crude	JPY/USD	HS China Enterprises	Canadian Bankers' Acceptance
Lean hogs	Natural gas (HH)	NZD/USD	Hang Seng	US 2-year note
Oats	Gasoline	CHF/USD	Nasdaq 100	US 10-year note
Rough rice	Gold	CAD/USD	Nikkei 225	Eurodollar
Soybeans	Copper	MXN/USD	S&P 500	Euroswiss
Sugar 11	Palladium	Dollar Index	Euro Stoxx 50	Euribor
Wheat Chicago	Platinum		Russell 2000	Short sterling
Soybean Oil	Silver		S&P 400	Euro-BTP Long-Term
Cocoa			S&P/TSX 60	Euro-Bobl
Milk Class III			Dow Jones	5-Year U.S. T-Note
Feeder Cattle			Volatility Index	U.S. T-Bond
Coffee Arabica				10-Year Govt. of Canada Bond
Coffee Robusta				30 Day Federal Funds
Wheat Kansas				
Sugar White				
Orange Juice				
Canola				
Soybean Meal				

Why these particular markets? They are all highly liquid and easily traded, and that's the most important part. The typical trend-following futures fund would use around 100 different contracts and some make artificial markets by trading spreads between, for instance, gold and silver.

I use daily data only, not just to simplify but also because you can successfully run these types of strategies without bothering with intraday data. Since this is futures data, you need to make sure that the data is properly adjusted, as I discuss in Chapter 2. Don't skip or underestimate the importance of this detail. If your futures data is not properly adjusted, you are simply wasting your time building strategies and will be wasting your money trading them later on.

Position Sizing

Without a decent position-sizing formula it really does not matter how good the trading rules are. The instruments included in our portfolio above show very different volatility profiles, not to say extremely different volatility profiles. The term volatility is admittedly used loosely here and what we are concerned with is the potential price fluctuations of different instruments based on their recent past.

Although the Euro Stoxx 50 index can easily move 1–2% in a day and sometimes even 4–5% in a very eventful day, a move of just 0.5% in a day would be practically unheard of for Eurodollar. So if we were simply to put the same notional dollar amount in each trade, the portfolio would immediately be dominated by the volatile instruments and not much impact at all would come from the less volatile. This is not what we want to do, so instead we need to find ways to take the volatility of each instrument into account when deciding how many contracts to buy or sell in each market. There are several variations on how to do this: some prefer to base it on average true range, others on standard deviation and some may prefer to make their own formulas. In essence, the methodologies used by most CTAs are more or less the same, the principle being that you take larger sizes of less volatile instruments with the aim of having each position theoretically capable of making the same bottom line profit or loss impact on the overall strategy.

For our strategies in this book I use a method based on so-called average true range, which has been widely known for a long time and used for at least four decades. It aims to measure how big a normal daily move is for each instrument and then use that as a basis for position sizes. The true range refers to the price span in which the instrument was traded for one day based on the high, low, and close values. The formula for the true range for day t is:

$$TR_t = \max\left(H, C_{t-1}\right) - \min\left(L, C_{t-1}\right)$$

The lowest price of today's low and yesterday's close is subtracted from the highest of today's high and yesterday's close, and we arrive at the range in which we have been trading for today. To get to the average true range (ATR), you just need to take an average of these numbers. I use an exponential moving average to arrive at the normal trading range for each instrument over time. You may see other smoothing methods for the ATR in other books, but it usually matters very little which one you use.

The point with using the ATR as volatility estimation is that it provides not only a comparable number that we can use it to standardise position sizes, but also as an estimation of how large a move we can expect on any given normal day. We can use this information to set a target impact of the position on the portfolio as a whole. This target impact number will in turn act as a kind of leverage factor which could be scaled up or down to shift the risk level of the strategy up or down.

For our initial strategies we use a risk factor of 20 basis points, so the theoretical average daily impact on the portfolio for each position should be 0.2%. Imagine the current portfolio as a whole is worth US$1 million. Since we want each position to have a theoretical impact of 20 basis points, that translates to US$2,000. We get a buy signal in gold and the ATR of this instrument happens to be exactly US$10 at that time, and because we know that the Comex Gold contract has a point value of 100, each contract we buy has a theoretical impact of US$1,000. So we buy two of them.

The reason I keep using the phrase 'theoretical impact' is that you must always be aware that volatility is not stationary and can change dramatically over the course of a position's lifetime. This position-sizing method does not depend on a stationary volatility, it just uses the ATR at the time of position entry as a reasonable estimation of potential price moves. The position size is kept constant through the life of the position and not increased or reduced over time. The last part is something you may or may not want to tweak in your final strategy.

The formula employed here is:

$$Contracts = \frac{0.022 * Equity}{\left(ATR_{100} * PointValue\right)}$$

Equity is the full value of the account being traded, or the amount of the account allocated to the strategy in question, and I discuss the ATR above (if you are not aware of what point value is, read up on it in Chapter 2). The denominator of this equation is the normal daily move in the instrument, should volatility remain on the same level. Note that if you are dealing with futures denominated in different currencies, this number must be converted to the same currency as the account equity; also remember that the point value is not always the same as the underlying amount of the contract. We can, of course, only buy whole contracts and not fractions of a contract, so the number is rounded down to make sure we err on the conservative side.

The magic value here is the figure 0.002, or 0.2%, which I refer to as our risk factor. This is a more or less arbitrary number and changing it can scale the risk of your strategy up or down very quickly. I suggest you experiment with the outcomes of simulations and find a risk factor that you are comfortable with. A lower number gives you lower returns and lower risk, while a higher number gives you higher risk and higher returns.

I use the ATR method for position sizing because it is the simplest to explain and does the job well enough. There are several similar approaches possible, all striving to adjust the size of the position to the expected price moves of the instrument so that you get a common risk basis. Another popular method is to use standard deviation instead of ATR. Note that if you use this approach, you need to calculate the standard deviation of the daily returns and not on the prices themselves.

Although I have always shied away from it myself, I know of futures hedge funds with excellent results that use only margin to equity as their position sizing and risk measurement. This is a different approach than using historical volatility estimations but aims to accomplish the same thing. The exchanges set the margins of each futures market based primarily on their view on volatility to minimise the risk of defaults by market participants. By trusting that the margins accurately reflect the risk of the instrument, you could use this as a basis, for example, always taking 0.5% margin to equity risk of each position, where equity represents your full account value. This method has always made me wary of the somewhat subjective part in the exchanges' decisions for setting the margin and the history of sudden and unexpected changes in margin requirements in some markets. It is also tricky to simulate results back in time because it can be hard to get hold of accurate historical data for margin requirements. Still, there are large funds using this concept with very strong results and so I won't write it off.

Slippage and Commission

For all backtested strategies in this book, I have applied realistic fees and slippage. Commissions for futures trading has gone down quite a bit over the years but it remains a factor which has to be taken into account. In this book, I have assumed a commission of 1 dollar per contract, plus an exchange fee of 1.5 dollars. On top of that, I have also assumed that we always get poor executions, because life tends to have a mean sense of humour. I have applied a volume-based slippage algorithm, which attempts to provide realistic executions based on actual volumes traded in the market. These estimates are never perfect, but you should always try to err on the side of caution and rather overestimate your costs. It's much nicer to get positive surprises in reality.

Strategy Personality

There is an old industry adage that the way to make money from the markets is to buy low and sell high. This is certainly not how trend-following futures traders operate and you need to get comfortable with a very different way of working. As a trend follower, you will be buying high and selling higher as well as selling low and buying back lower. You will often take positions that seem crazy, such as buying an instrument that already went up 20% in a month and just had a massive spike up, showing extreme overbought readings. When everyone else thinks something has gone so far that it just has to stop and reverse, that is often when you enter.

Trend-following strategies look easy and highly profitable when you look at long-term return charts, but you need to study the shorter term down to daily variations and trades to be able to judge whether you can really follow the strategy in real life. It's a matter of your own personality and whether you could and want to trade in the style that the strategy dictates, and the matter of how your clients will see the results. Many of these strategies have drawdowns of up to 30% and can sometimes take a year or more to recover. If you launch your trading product just before a larger drawdown occurs and you are sitting there half a year later trying to explain to a client why he still has a substantial loss on his investment, you might wish you had chosen a different strategy or a different risk level. But certainly, the more volatile strategies are also the most profitable in the long run and it's all a matter of how much you and your clients can stomach.

In Chapter 4, I describe two trend-following methodologies that are deliberately picked because of their simplicity and widespread usage. These strategies form a good starting point for getting familiar with the principles of trend-following futures trading and although they are profitable over time, I don't recommend using them in their original form. Don't worry though; I am not going to play the usual trick of describing simple models that cannot be used in real life. As the book progresses, we will improve upon these strategies and arrive at methods that are perfectly usable in a real-life hedge fund.

Anatomy of a Trend-Following Strategy

The aim of trend-following strategies is to enter into a trend that is already under way and then stick with the trend until it makes a move against you and is likely to turn. That means that you are targeting the middle of a trend, deliberately forsaking the beginning and the end. The underlying principle involved here is that markets tend to move in extended trends. For the most part, any given instrument lacks a real trend to exploit and trend followers either stay out or keep losing over and over by trying to enter into potential new trends that don't materialise. Any single instrument might stay in such a non-trending mode for a very long time, perhaps even years. It is therefore crucial that the serious trend-following trader systematically trades many different instruments in many different sectors. If your intention is to run these types of strategies on a single instrument or perhaps just a few of them, you might as well go and buy a lottery ticket.

Often books on this subject spend too much time talking about entry rules while often neglecting the really important aspects of a strategy. In reality, the buy-and-sell rules are far subordinate in importance to position sizing and diversification. Non-professionals tend to spend an excess of time and energy on the buy-and-sell rules and neglect the infinitely more important aspects of diversification and risk. For a trend-following strategy, it is quite possible to have flawed entry and exit rules in combination with good diversification and risk rules and still be profitable, but the other way around is a recipe for disaster.

Looking at classic futures trending systems, some of which have published or otherwise disclosed, there are two main methods commonly used by these traders. The first method is to buy positive breakouts and to short negative breakouts, which means you need to find a good way to define a breakout (see Figure 3.4).

The second main method is to use some classic trending indicator, such as a moving average, and enter on various cross-over rules (see Figure 3.5). The simplest example would be to plot a moving average over a price chart and buy whenever the price crosses above it and short whenever the price crosses below.

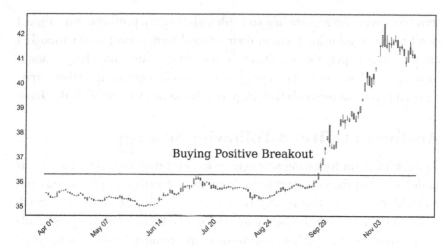

FIGURE 3.4 Buying positive breakout in rough rice.

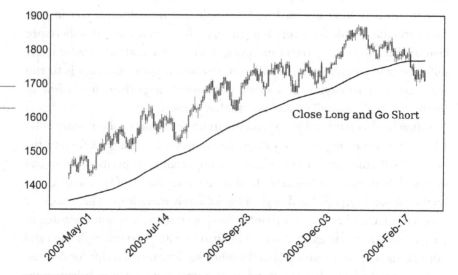

FIGURE 3.5 Reversing position on moving average cross in the Nasdaq.

As stated, entry rules are the least important part of a trading strategy and accordingly you should spend the least amount of time on them. That does not mean they are irrelevant and should be skipped over, but the other components are very much more important to your actual trading results over time.

Often a filter rule accompanies the trending rules, making sure that buys only occur when the market is in a bullish phase and vice versa for shorts. Many trend followers would want to avoid accidentally going against a strong trend just because there was a short-term counter-move, and a good filter rule can help you with that. An easy method is to use two layers of trend measurement of different time horizons, such as a 200-day moving average for a long-term trend filter and a shorter moving average for trend-entry signals. Requiring both indicators to agree ensures that you only enter into trades in the direction of the longer-term predominant trend. For the initial strategies presented in this section of the book, I don't employ a trend filter. The point of doing so is just to keep the models as simple as possible for the first demonstration, and then I will add more features to them later to see how the results are impacted.

CHAPTER 4

Two Basic Trend-Following Strategies

Instead of lingering too long on the theoretical aspects of constructing trading strategies, in this chapter I use examples that you can replicate and test yourself, so that you can make up your own mind about what works and what does not. I start by introducing two very basic trend-following methods, which have been used at least since the 1970s and perhaps even earlier. These particular methods have been chosen for their simplicity and widespread use, in order to make a point. I intend to demonstrate that these very simple and well-known strategies, even without any complex modifications, can achieve results comparable with many of the professional trend-following funds out there. I describe the details of these strategies along with a common position-sizing formula they both use as well as the diversification plan; then we can see how well these strategies perform over time and how they measure up against the competition in the hedge-fund world.

The first strategy we investigate is a real classic and very easy to model and trade. The basis of the strategy is the moving average, that is, the average price for the past *X* number of days. In this variant of the strategy, two moving averages are used with a different number of days used for the look-back period, so that we have one fast-moving average and one slow-moving average.

Observant readers of the first edition of this book may notice that I have changed quite a few things around this time. The rules have been changed in various ways, in practically all parts of this book. There are two reasons for that.

First, what I try to do with this book is to demonstrate concepts. For concepts to work, they cannot be overly dependent on exact parameters. This book is about showing how simple and robust rules can explain a large part of the multibillion dollar trend-following industry, and how you can build your own models to rival the professionals. It's not about parameter optimisation.

Second, I think it would be quite lazy of me to write a second edition after ten years, and just use the same rules as before. After all, the publisher is paying me for this.

So, for that reason, our first model will use exponential moving averages of 50 and 100 days (see Figure 4.1). Why these numbers? you ask. Why not these numbers? I say. They are reasonably arbitrary and I do encourage you to test all kinds of combinations and find out for yourself how little they really matter.

Exponential moving averages use a weighting scheme where more reason points carry higher weight than those a long time ago. In the last edition, I used a simple moving average, and that is the main reason for going exponential this time.

This strategy trades both on the long and short side of all instruments and it will always be in the market, which means that, for each futures contract we include in the strategy universe, we always have a position, long or

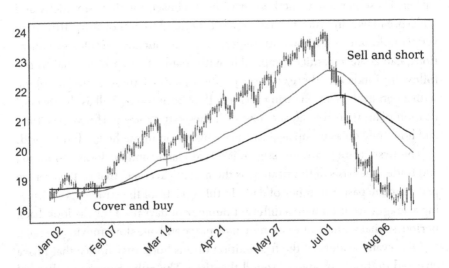

FIGURE 4.1 Standard moving average cross-over strategy.

short. As soon as we get a stop from the long strategy, we immediately open a short position and vice versa. No trend filter or similar is employed at this stage, so we simply follow the moving average cross-signals as they come along. The strategy is being run on daily data and always trades the day after a signal. The last part is a safeguard to prevent so-called data snooping, a common mistake of modelling strategies that trade on data that may not be available in reality at the time of the trade. If a signal is generated on a Tuesday, the strategy simulation assumes that we buy on Wednesday morning and that we get a generally bad entry price with the slippage and commission assumptions mentioned in Chapter 3.

The logic of the strategy is very simple. If the faster-moving average is above the slower-moving average. that means that the trend of the instrument is up. Since the trend is up, we buy with the assumption that if the price moves against us we will get stopped out fairly soon with a small loss, whereas if the price continues up, we have a theoretically unlimited upside.

Our second strategy attempts to enter into new trends and stay with them as long as possible. This model too has been shaken up a little since the last book. Using the same code and same logic would have been easy, but also lazy and of less value to readers of both editions. In comparison with the first edition, I will make this simple breakout demonstration a bit more long-term, by simply doubling both the breakout window and the stop window.

The rules are again very simple: if today's close is higher or equal to the highest close in the past 100 days, we buy tomorrow; if the close is below or equal to the lowest close for the past 100 days, we sell open tomorrow and go short. A similar logic is used to get out of positions, where a long trade is sold when the close reaches the lowest point in 50 days and a short trade is covered when the price makes a 50-day high (see Figure 4.2). Analytics are done on daily closing prices and trades are always taken one day after the signal.

As opposed to the moving average cross-strategy, the breakout strategy does not have to be in the market the whole time. After a position is stopped out, it can be out for some time before the next signal comes along.

■ Strategy Performance

It is important to view the performance of any strategy in the proper context. Simply looking at the compounded annual return number does not tell you much about whether the strategy is viable or not, or even whether

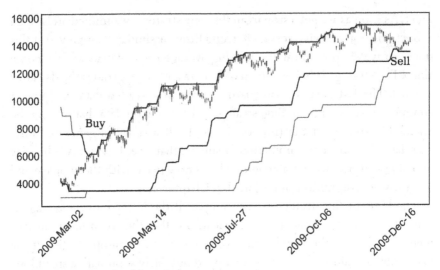

FIGURE 4.2 Standard breakout strategy.

it is better or worse than another strategy. To figure out which strategy is preferable over another, you need to look at various risk measurements but also study the equity curve of the strategy in detail to see whether it is something you can realistically live with or not. Some highly profitable strategies have very scary periods and if you cannot stomach them, you should find a different strategy that fits you and your investors.

The equity curve in Figure 4.3 tells us that both strategies seem to be profitable over longer time spans, but it is easy to fall into the trap of making premature assumptions. A simple visual inspection of such a long-term

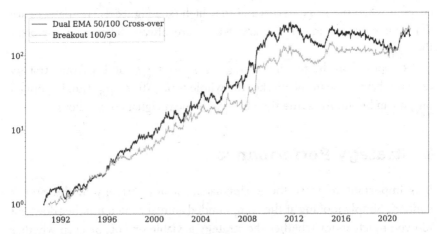

FIGURE 4.3 Moving average and breakout strategies.

equity curve would not make it easy to judge whether the moving average strategy is in reality a better strategy than the breakout, for instance. In this time span you would have made more money with the latter, but seeing which one would be better from a volatility adjusted point of view is not easy. Note that the y-axis uses a logarithmic scale to make the chart more readable. With the large percentage moves over time that we see here, a linear chart would just look plain silly, to use the technical term for it, and for that reason practically all charts in this book employ the same scale.

What should be really interesting in Figure 4.3 is seeing how remarkably close the two are to each other. Even a quick visual inspection can tell us that these two strategies are more or less the same. They move up and down at the same time and even though one of them fared slightly better during a couple of tough periods, they really trade the same thing.

To put the long-term performance of the basic strategies into context, I include four comparison items, or benchmarks, if you will. The first is simply MSCI World, which is a common benchmark for world equity performance because it covers over a thousand stocks in many regions, and the second is Barclay BTOP 50, an index that seeks to replicate the overall composition of the managed-futures industry (see Figure 4.4). I also include (in Figure 4.5) the Millburn Diversified Futures Program and the Dunn World Monetary and Agricultural Program. Millburn is one of the pioneers in the business and it has been running a highly successful business since the 1970s, making it an excellent benchmark for performance. As with Millburn, Dunn is a very successful long-term performer and one of the legends of the business. These two funds are chosen to represent the industry because they

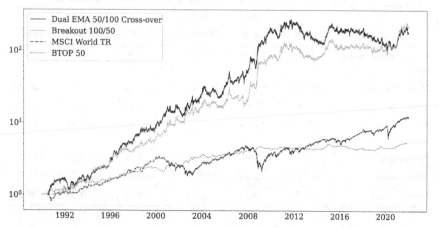

FIGURE 4.4 Base strategies compared to benchmarks.

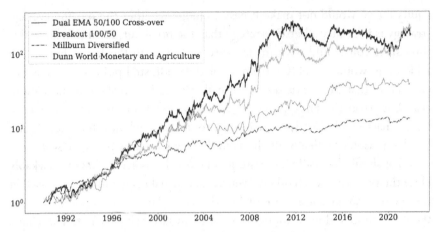

FIGURE 4.5 Base strategies compared to CTA funds.

both have long official track records available and show very respectable performance.

We can see from these figures and the summarised data in Table 4.1 that the most basic strategies, which have been published over and over again for decades, outperform traditional investments in a big way. Start by considering the long-term performance of equities. During the period covered by the simulation, world equities had an annualised performance of less than 9%, which is still above what you would expect to see from the equity markets over longer periods. This number is very much inflated by the prolonged bull market which we have been seeing since 2009, and which is

TABLE 4.1 Simple strategies compared to benchmarks and competition

	Breakout	MA Cross	MSCI World TR	BTOP50	Millburn	Dunn
Compounded annual return	17.90	18.18	8.88	4.95	7.02	13.12
Worst drawdown	−47.19	−64.67	−56.23	−17.30	−22.94	−57.88
Annualised volatility	25.74	28.65	15.46	8.17	13.77	30.75
Percentage profitable months	53.74	57.18	62.64	45.98	57.47	55.17
Best month	48.70	37.94	12.21	10.00	14.59	29.55
Worst month	−19.29	−21.04	−19.79	−7.00	−11.51	−23.52
Sharpe (zero)	0.77	0.73	0.63	0.63	0.56	0.55

still in effect as of writing this in early 2022. Over considerably longer periods, covering a multitude of market regimes, the stock markets tend to return closer to 5%.

There is a perception among the public that equities always go up and that one always has to be invested in this asset class. For some periods in history this has been true, but it can also be a dangerous illusion. Consider as an example if you had invested US$100 in the global stock markets in 1999. Ten years later, you would still have a loss on your investment. Similarly, if you had invested your hundred dollars in 2007, half of it would be gone in a little over a year, and ten years later you would have a total profit of about 8%.

This in no way implies that you shouldn't hold a general exposure to the stock markets. For the vast majority of investors, it makes perfect sense to keep a portion of your portfolio in stocks or equity-based funds. But that, in turn, does not imply that you should keep the lion's share of your assets in this often fickle asset class. Alternative investments, such as futures, can make for an excellent portfolio diversification, providing for stronger long-term results.

What we see here from the futures models aren't all clear skies either. Attentive readers of the first edition of this book should notice how the performance of these two simplistic model iterations have been struggling in the years after that book came out. The purpose of these two initial models were to show how even rules so simple that they can be drawn on a napkin can provide sufficient results to prove the viability of the concept. As such, they still stand up, despite some clear issues.

Both of these strategies showed concerning drawdowns, larger than what had been seen in the previous edition. The fact that they underperformed equities in a strong bull market isn't surprising or worrying in itself. When the stock markets are on fire, they will outperform everything. The true value in futures models is in providing uncorrelated results, not to beat stocks in a bull market.

The most concerning thing that we see is not the depth of the drawdown, but the length. The past ten years have indeed been more difficult for purist trend followers than the decade before that. That does not mean that it was unprofitable or that trend following somehow stopped working. It was just a bit more difficult to generate returns, and many industry players started diversifying across strategies to seek additional sources of return. What is really interesting of course, is that even after a tough decade, during which the stock markets rallied, the trend-following futures models still hold up really well and show strong long-term outperformance.

The astute reader might at this point ask about the dividends you would have received on the stocks if you had bought and held the index constituents for this time, and whether this would not make the equity index perform better in real life. The answer is simple: no. The MSCI World data I present here is the total return series, and so the dividend effect is already included.

So let's look at the second index, Barclay's BTOP 50. This shows a solid long-term performance, which speaks in favour of these types of strategies of course. It compounded at about 5%, despite the clear underperformance of the futures markets in the past years. The worst drawdown suffered was a little over 17%, which seems quite reasonable, given the annual return number. Keep in mind, of course, that this is an index consisting of the performance of many diversified futures traders and so the volatility is naturally lower than most of the individual constituents. Compare the return profile of the BTOP and the MSCI indices in Figure 4.4 and you can see that the managed-futures index provides a much smoother return, which remains stable through good and bad years for the stock market. It is not prone to the large declines as the equity index is.

To compare against the big guys in the business, I include two managed-futures houses that have been around for quite some time and are highly respected in the business. Millburn has had a compounded annualised return since inception of around 14% since 1977, which would beat pretty much any benchmark you throw at it. Dunn has been around since 1984 and compounded around 13% since then. There are many top-notch trend-following managers out there, and we'll look closer at them later on, but for now these two will have to represent the competition in our initial comparisons. For full disclosure, I don't get paid, directly or indirectly, by any fund or similar to say nice things in this book, but in case you manage a hedge fund and would like me to mention it in my next book you should know that I'm partial to gold bars and Audemars Piguet watches.

So, how did our two test strategies fare against the indices and the big competitors? The moving average strategy compounded at 18% with a worst drawdown of 64% and the breakout strategy yielded 24.5% annualised while having a max drawdown of 60%.

Those are some pretty hefty drawdowns and that shows the dangers of running such naïve strategies. Clearly a drawdown of 60% can be the death of any portfolio and measures must be taken to avoid such events. What is interesting though is that despite this, the long-term performance of these models is still attractive, and given how they tend to outperform during slow or negative equity markets, there is every reason to believe that they will do well going forward.

Obviously our two strategies are more volatile than the benchmarks and show larger numbers for both return and risk. In the current shape they may seem a bit overly volatile but as long as the profits are strong in relation to the risk taken, there is no need for concern. The volatility level itself is not a problem, because it can be dialled back and forth very easily by modifying our position-sizing factor and thereby simultaneously decreasing risk and return at the same time. How this works is explored in detail in Chapter 5. Therefore, the ratio between the two is of much more importance than the absolute return and drawdown numbers.

A common way to compare strategies of different volatility is the Sharpe ratio. It is often seen as a universal way to rank strategies where you simply choose the one with the highest ratio. Before I explain why this is a bad idea, let me briefly explain what the Sharpe ratio is. The formula as such is quite simple: take the annualised historic return, deduct the so-called risk-free return, and then divide the result by the standard deviation of the strategy's return.

The real problem with this ratio is in how it reacts to volatility. Since we have volatility, in the shape of standard deviation of the returns in the denominator, the formula is of the distinct opinion that volatility is always bad and should be severely punished. The core idea is not wrong and it is certainly better to have smooth returns than volatile returns, but the way in which the standard Sharpe ratio is calculated makes no real sense for evaluating different styles of trading. The standard deviation formula is based on a theoretical mean return and whenever actual returns are far away from this, the deviation rises and causes a negative impact on your Sharpe ratio. Note that the standard deviation treats both positive and negative deviations equally, so if your strategy has a very strong run-up, such as occurred for most trend-following strategies during the second half of 2008, you may have excellent returns but your Sharpe ratio might not look so great.

Another reason why the Sharpe ratio is a bad idea for our kind of strategies is that we are essentially dealing with highly leveraged trading. Exactly how leveraged we are is a matter of debate when you deal in cross-asset strategies and many traditional measures of leverage may not make much sense in this context, but we are certainly leveraged. If you study the position-sizing formula presented earlier, you'll find that it has a key input

TABLE 4.2 **Simple strategies compared to benchmarks and competition, 2002 to 2021**

	Breakout	MA Cross	MSCI World TR	BTOP50	Millburn	Dunn
Compounded annual return	14.25	12.74	8.29	3.64	5.13	7.34
Worst drawdown	−47.19	−64.67	−56.23	−17.30	−22.94	−57.88
Annualised volatility	27.46	30.85	16.12	7.43	12.6	28.41
Percentage profitable months	52.92	54.17	62.08	45.98	57.47	55.17
Best month	48.70	37.94	12.21	7.00	12.13	29.55
Worst month	−19.29	−21.04	−19.79	−6.00	−11.51	−22.63
Sharpe (zero)	0.62	0.54	0.58	0.52	0.46	0.39

number that can be raised and lowered depending on how large a position you want and by extension how much risk you want on your strategy. By lowering this number, you get lower return numbers, lower drawdowns, and lower standard deviation, and vice versa if you raise the number. You are still, however, deducting the same risk-free rate from your returns, and so if you lower your number, you get a lower standard deviation but lose a much larger part of your return in the numerator of the Sharpe equation.

The data in Table 4.1 covers quite a long period, from the start of 1992, and we know of course based on the charts we saw earlier that a large amount of outperformance came from the first decade. This is both due to the strong trend-following performance of the 1990s, and part due to the bear market of 2000, where stocks fell and trend-following models didn't. In the first edition of this book, I limited the data period covered to 20 years, so let's have a look at the same data again, over the last 20 years (Table 4.2).

■ Correlations Between Strategies

What we are looking at here are monthly return correlations, that is, how closely the returns of one strategy are related to another. Be careful when you calculate your correlations and avoid the rookie errors that are still so common.

The most common mistake made by people not used to calculating correlations is to simply make a column in Excel with all the price series, NAV of a fund, price of a futures contract, and so on, and then use the same Correl() function, which will produce nonsense data. The problem is not the aforementioned Excel function, which is perfectly usable for this purpose, but that you need to have the right input data.

The most common way of calculating correlations is by doing it on log returns, but percentage return numbers will do as well. What you are looking for is the correlation between the changes, not in the absolute values. That's why you cannot use the prices themselves, or even dollar changes, but percentages or log returns.

To calculate the log returns, use the formula:

$$R_t = Ln\left(\frac{P_i}{P_{i-1}}\right)$$

where P_i is the price or value of your time series at point i in time, P_{i-1} would then be the price of the same time series one day earlier and the resulting R_i is your natural log return for data point i. If you are using Excel to do this, just put all your time series price data in a row and make a row next to it where you use the built-in Ln() function to calculate a new column with all the log returns. Then use the Correl() function on two sets of log returns and you are done.

Of course, if you're ready to step into a more modern world, you may want to ditch Excel and move straight to Python. This programming language is easy to learn, easy to code. and purpose-built for time series analysis just like what we are doing here.

The correlation coefficient itself will have a value between -1 and 1, which describes the nature of the relationship between the two series being compared. A value of 1 means that they are identical and move exactly the same, while -1 implies that they move exactly inversely to each ovther. Zero means that they are completely unrelated.

The correlation matrix in Table 4.3 demonstrates a few interesting points. First, even after the two naïve futures strategies decoupled somewhat after 2013, the overall long-term correlation between them remains fairly high. They were extremely close to each other before, and in the period from 1990 to 2012, they were almost identical.

More interesting is to see how both futures strategies and futures funds have a very low or negative correlation to the stock markets. This is what we are looking for, this is where the real value is. This means that they would

TABLE 4.3 Correlation comparison

	Dual EMA cross-over 100-50	Breakout 100-50	MSCI World TR	BTOP 50	Millburn Diversified	Dunn World Monetary and Agriculture
Dual EMA Cross-over 100-50	1.00	0.89	−0.12	0.57	0.44	0.54
Breakout 100-50	0.89	1.00	−0.17	0.62	0.52	0.58
MSCI World TR	−0.12	−0.17	1.00	−0.02	0.04	−0.08
BTOP 50	0.57	0.62	−0.02	1.00	0.80	0.80
Millburn Diversified	0.44	0.52	0.04	0.80	1.00	0.68
Dunn World Monetary and Agriculture	0.54	0.58	−0.08	0.80	0.68	1.00

work well as a complement to an equity portfolio, because they have positive return expectations and negative correlation to the market that would both improve return and reduce risk if held as part of a portfolio of stocks. In fact, all the diversified futures strategies here, including the Barclay index, have a slight negative correlation to world equities. The diversification effects of having vehicles in your portfolio that have a zero to slight negative correlation and still strong positive expectations can be huge.

The two futures funds correlate strongly to each other, which is to be expected and is a natural result of the nature of trend following.

■ Conclusions from the Basic Strategies

What we have established so far in this chapter is that even the simplest trend-following strategies can perform remarkably well over time. The point of this exercise was to demonstrate that the choice of trend-following method is not as important at people seem to think. It helps to have good buy and sell rules, but you can still achieve very good results using the most basic methods available to the public for decades. The secret sauce is not in the buy and sell rules.

■ Combining the Strategies

Trend Filter

The moving average strategy's biggest problem is that it is always in the market, even if there is really no trend at the moment. When there is a sideways movement in the market, this strategy tends to enter and exit time after time, losing on each turn. This is not only unprofitable, but also highly annoying, demoralising, and it makes little sense. Figure 4.6 shows this behaviour during a sideways phase of the mid-2000 in the S&P 500. Each time those two moving average lines cross each other, we reverse our position, and we keep losing money. What is missing here is some sort of trend filter to make sure that the strategy does not buy or sell when there is no trend available to profit from.

The breakout strategy does not have exactly the same problem, because it is not always in the market and only enters after a price breakout, but it does suffer from a similar symptom. Since the breakout will enter a long trade after seeing the highest price in a certain number of days and enter a short trade when a new low for the same number of days is made, it has a tendency to go against the main market trend at times. If there has been a very strong market trend for a while, it is not unusual to see a bit of a pullback. Such a pullback may for some strategies be a good place to take the profits and exit, but it is rarely a good point to enter a reverse position.

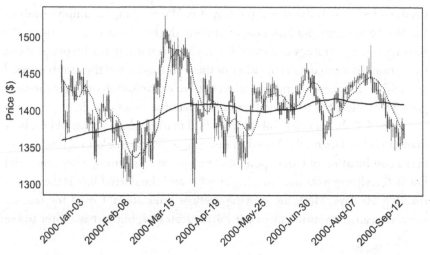

FIGURE 4.6 Moving average strategy overtrading without trend filter.

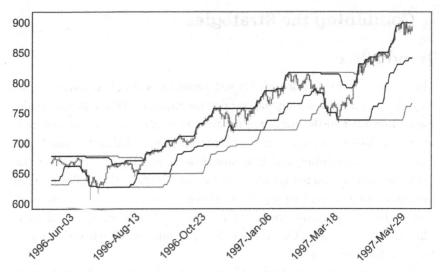

FIGURE 4.7 Breakout strategy without trend filter.

Figure 4.7 shows the breakout strategy in a strongly trending period of the S&P 500 at the height of the dot com bubble. Two things should be clear just from a quick glance: the strategy enters into shorts in a strong bull market, which does not make sense, and it over-trades, taking too many positions back and forth in a strong trending market.

The remedy for both these situations is to add a trend filter, which makes sure that we only trade in the direction of the main trend and that we don't get whipsawed by going in and out of positions every couple of days. The moving average strategy does in fact make for a pretty good trend filter by itself, so let's try to use it just the way it is. We're going to simply combine the two basic strategies into one, by trading the breakout strategy, using the moving average strategy as a trend filter. There is nothing really special about the parameters and details of either of these strategies and the numbers used are deliberately kept round and arbitrary. No optimisation or other shenanigans. The concept is what matters rather than the exact details.

Figure 4.8 shows crude oil during a bull market phase followed by a bear market phase. The method used to determine which market regime we are in is a combination of two exponential moving average lines, where the solid line is the slower 100-days moving average and the dotted line is the faster-reacting 50 days. Here the moving average lines are not used for trading signals because it was in one of our initial strategies, but just as a filter to see

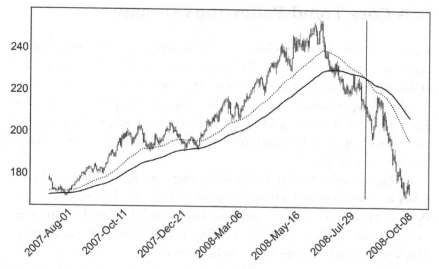

FIGURE 4.8 Using moving average as trend filter.

what market direction is dominating. If we set a criterion for our strategy that we are only allowed to buy when the overall market is in an uptrend and vice versa, we are likely to get two effects: the number of trades is reduced and there is a higher percentage of winners.

In Table 4.4, with data starting in 1992, we can see that the standard breakout strategy has significantly improved by using a simple trend filter. The annualised returns are up while the maximum drawdown is down and we got a few more positive months. Most importantly, the maximum drawdown has decreased significantly, and a much improved Sharpe ratio.

TABLE 4.4 Adding a trend filter

	Core model, combining the two	Breakout	MA Cross
Compounded annual return	15.81	14.25	12.74
Worst drawdown	−39.43	−47.19	−64.67
Annualised volatility	25.90	27.46	30.85
Percentage profitable months	57.08	52.92	54.17
Best month	37.04	48.70	37.94
Worst month	−18.37	−19.29	−21.04
Sharpe (zero)	0.70	0.62	0.54

■ A Core Trend-Following Strategy

Having combined the two basic trend-following strategies into one, we arrive at something that starts looking more reasonable. The rules we have at this point are still simplified compared to what actual futures traders use, but they do approximate the results close enough. The primary point that I am trying to make here, and really with this entire book, is that the bulk of the returns captured by trend-following futures trading can be explained with very simple rules.

Adding complexity may feel good, giving you the feeling that there is safety in complexity and it makes it harder to replicate. That is not necessarily true. Most of the complex parts for larger funds have to do with execution rules for various markets, volatility control, and risk management. Much of this is of less importance to hobby traders.

So let's take a look at what we have at this point. To recap, here are the rules that we are working with so far.

- Broad universe of futures markets traded, across all major sectors.

- Trading daily.

- Trend is considered bullish if EMA 50 is above EMA 100.

- Trend is considered bearish if EMA 50 is below EMA 100.

- Enter long on new 100-day high, if trend is bullish.

- Enter short on new 100-day low, if trend is bearish.

- Exit long if price falls to 50-day low, or trend turns bearish.

- Exit short if price rises to 50-day high, or if trend turns bullish.

- Position sizing uses 20-day ATR with a target of 15 basis points.

If we make a long-term graph of how this strategy stacks up against the two longest-running funds among our benchmarks, it looks quite striking (Figure 4.9). I would very much advise against drawing too many conclusions at this stage, though. Visual comparisons like this can be highly misleading, and it's remarkably easy to mislead people on purpose with such comparison charts.

A quick look at Figure 4.10 shows a massive outperformance. But again, this does not in itself imply that our core strategy is more attractive than these funds. As I will show you in a moment, it would be exceedingly simple

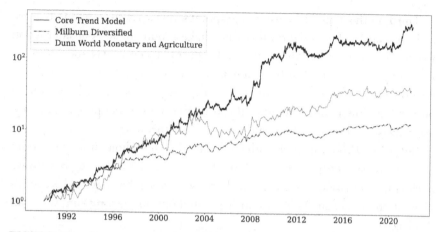

FIGURE 4.9 Core strategy compared to benchmark funds.

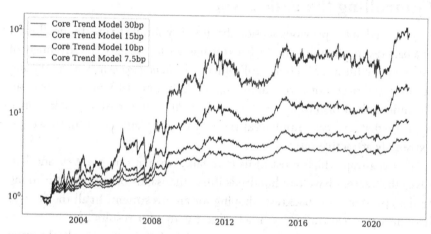

FIGURE 4.10 Toggling the risk level.

to manipulate our strategy results even further and provide an even greater outperformance. As Mark Twain famously said, there are three kinds of lies: lies, damned lies, and backtests.

Here are a few of the problems with comparing our theoretical strategy to that of the real-world results of these funds. First, our strategy is a backtest and thereby a theoretical return of strategy created after the fact. These rules are created to explain trend following as a phenomenon and to teach the principles behind it. They are a learning tool, and should be seen as such.

Second, these funds charge a management and performance fee for taking care of investors' money. Our strategy is not yet loaded with such fees, and therefore the comparison is not fair.

Third, in this type of long-term graph, it's very easy to overlook that we had a decade of almost flat performance. Take a moment and consider if you would really have stayed the course and kept trading every day, for ten years, without profits. That's 2,500 trading days of sideways performance. No matter how strongly you believe in your rules, ten years is a very long time to be in a drawdown. And, of course, if you are managing other people's money, your investors are unlikely to stay with you for that long.

But, sure, if you had stuck with these rules for this whole time, you would most likely have outperformed. In the long run, trend following has always performed remarkably well. Then there is always John Maynard Keynes's view on the long run. As he famously pointed out, in the long run, we're all dead anyhow.

Controlling the Risk Level

I mentioned in the previous section that it's very simple to create the illusion of a backtest profitability. In the backtesting world, we have the advantage of knowing the future. Much like Bill Murray in *Groundhog Day*, we can try and fail over and over, until we stumble upon a solution that works. We have all the time in the world to throw stuff on the wall until something sticks. Once we have that, we can simply dial the risk level up and down until we get extremely attractive returns.

This is a trap which most of us have fallen into at one point or another. Over the years, I have had hundreds if not thousands of enthusiastic young traders present their backtests, hoping for an investment. In all the years, I have never seen anyone present a backtest with poor results.

The focus of this book is not on the process of properly using backtesting tools for strategy development. For that, I would very much recommend the book *Systematic Trading* by Robert Carver. It's a subject which very much deserves its own book or two.

Depending on your background in trading, mostly if you come from the hobby trading side or the institutional side, you may think that the previous shown return of a bit under 16% per year is either very low or very high. Expectations on trading returns in general tend to vary substantially between the hobby segment and the industry crowd. The truth is that with backtests like this, you can make the return end up pretty much where you want it to, and that's why you should never trust a backtest that you haven't done yourself.

In this case, we have a basic trading model which appears to have positive expected returns over time. Knowing that, we can decide how high those returns should be, simply by changing the position-sizing mechanism. All we need to do is to take on larger positions and, hey, presto!, higher returns. Too bad that reality isn't as cooperative.

Remember how we use a position-sizing methodology based on Average True Range, with a target daily variation of 15 basis points? This is the key number to play with. For that reason, we're going to play with some variations.

I'm going to make one riskier version, and two less risky variants. Our base variant so far is using 15 basis points as the target daily variation, and I will show you versions based on 30 points, 10, and 7.5.

As you see in Table 4.5, we could crank the risk up to 30 points and get a return of nearly 26% per year. This is of course a very dangerous illusion and unlikely to be achieved in real life. Would you really want to put serious money at work on a strategy which would see losses of over 65% at some point? Always assume that real-life results will be worse than a backtest, so you might actually see losses of 75%, 80%, or more.

Here's a piece of simple maths to illustrate why a drawdown of 70% is a very bad idea. As simple as this example is, it is surprisingly often over-looked in the retail trading community. Imagine starting out the year with $100,000, and suffering a loss of 70%. You now have $30,000. If the next year returns +70%, you're not back to where you started. No, you'd still have a near 50% loss. $30,000 * 1.7 = $51,000.

TABLE 4.5 Controlling the risk level

	Core model 7.5bp	Core model 10bp	Core model 15bp	Core model 30bp
Compounded annual return	8.88	11.63	15.81	25.94
Worst drawdown	−22.23	−28.69	−39.43	−64.66
Annualised volatility	13.08	17.41	25.90	49.57
Percentage profitable months	58.30	58.80	57.10	57.50
Best month	17.30	23.50	37.00	69.30
Worst month	− 9.00	−12.20	−18.37	−35.90
Sharpe (zero)	0.72	0.72	0.72	0.71

So if you do end up having that horrific −70% drawdown, what would it take to return up to where you started? Answer: 234%. That's the trading gain you would need just to get back to where you started.

Setting the risk level is one of the most important decisions of your trading career. Set it too high, and you will very likely suffer crippling losses at some point and get knocked out of the game. Set it too low, and you might as well just buy the S&P 500 tracker and call it a day.

Cash Management and the Effect of Free Government Money

The readers old enough never to have used TikTok might remember the days when you were actually paid interest on your deposited money. Depending on which country you live in and when you read this, perhaps you can still get some of that cash.

The interest rate can be a very important factor in futures trading, much more so than most people may think. Keep in mind that when we are dealing in futures we don't need to pay cash for our positions the way that you normally would when buying stocks. All we need is to have enough cash on the books to cover the initial margin and enough to avoid risking margin calls in case the position goes against us. If the only position in the portfolio happens to be 10 contracts of wheat and the position was just opened at a price of 800 cents per bushel, we do in fact have a nominal exposure of US$400,000 worth of this particular grain, but that does not mean we need to have anywhere near as much money in our account. Exactly how much we need to hold in cash will vary based on the margin requirements on this commodity, which is set by the exchange where it is traded.

At the time of writing, the initial margin per wheat contract is about US$3,000, and so we would at least need to have US$30,000 to cover the 10 contracts just bought. The wheat contract has a maintenance margin of about US$2,250 at this time, which means that we need to make sure that there is at least that much cash per contract available in our account at all times, after any unrealised losses. If the price now drops to 780 cents, we have an unrealised loss on the position of US$1,000 per contract, given that the point value is US$5,000 and that the price quote is in cents. That means we just lost US$10,000 on the account on our 10 contracts and if we only have the minimum required US$30,000 on the account, we now get a margin call, because the cash on the account is not enough for the minimum US$2,250 per contract maintenance margin.

The margin call requires us to top up the account to US$30,000 or the position will be forcefully shut down. A margin call is not something that you want happening to you and proper cash management will prevent that from ruining your day. Don't ever put yourself in a situation where you may receive an unexpected margin call. Keep enough cash on the account to cover even quite large swings against you.

If you have a mandate or fund denominated in US dollars and you only trade on American exchanges, the cash situation is very straightforward. Of course, for most of us this is just not the case and you are likely to find yourself involved in five to ten currencies, depending on how many countries you want to trade in. You then face the added practical task of making sure each current account is properly funded as well as managing the currency exposure that this may entail.

But then again, no one is saying that you should keep all your cash lying around in some brokerage account. This is both a waste of money and an unnecessary risk. The risk here can be summarised in two words: Lehman Brothers. Although the failure of that unfortunate investment bank was the most spectacular, the same thing has happened to many others before and after. Many otherwise successful futures trading houses got burned in a big way on the MF Global implosion and there are no reasons to believe that these large blow-ups were the only ones masking horribly irresponsible companies behind smoke and mirrors. More spectacular failures of banks and brokerage houses are likely to come and it is not easy to predict who they will be.

If you hold stocks or bonds with a bank or broker when it suddenly goes bankrupt, it will be a messy and painful experience, but you and your investors will most likely get the stocks and bonds back in the end, because they are held directly under the account holder's name. When it comes to cash, however, the story is quite different. I am sure that if you have made it this far you are already quite aware of how fractional reserve banking works and why the money you think you have in your bank is not actually there. The details of this system and its merits and hazards are not a topic in this book, but the short and simplified story is that all cash coming into a bank goes into the same big old pile of money as everyone else's, to be lent out to people who go and buy things from people who put the money back into the bank to be lent out again.

Imagine that you find US$1,000 hidden in a mattress and you go to your local bank and deposit it in your savings account. The bank then keeps a fraction of that money in the bank, as required by law, and lends the rest out to someone. Now assume it lends out US$900 of your money to someone who goes to buy a used car. The person who sells the car deposits the money in his savings account at the same bank and all of a sudden there is US$1,900 in the bank, while the bank is just in the middle of lending out another US$1,710 to start the cycle again. If we for ease of calculation assume that the bank needs to hold a 10% reserve on deposits, your US$1,000 adds US$10,000 to the monetary system by the magic of banking.

In the end, everyone thinks that they have money in the bank but it's all the same money, and the illusion only works until everyone wants to get their money out at the same time. This of course never happens, unless the bank is about to go bankrupt or there is a perception that the bank might go bankrupt, in which case it becomes a self-fulfilling prophecy. What you need to understand about this is just that cash held with a bank is not secure and will be exposed to counter-party risk against said bank. If the bank goes belly-up, you will probably lose all your cash. Still, you do need some cash on the books and a reasonable amount of counter-party risk is the cost of doing business, but you should pick your broker well and not keep too much cash lying around for no reason.

A second reason not to keep all the money lying around in cash is that you receive little to no interest on it. Granted that as of writing this in 2022 the government yields are on a level where the interest income is almost insignificant, but at least you still get a little bit of free money while at the same time reducing risks. The core strategy described in this book normally operates at between 10–20% margin to equity ratio, so we have quite large amounts of money that will never be used. For a US$10 million fund running this strategy, you can easily keep US$6 million in government debt securities and probably even more.

Exactly how you keep this excess cash is something you need to think through and plan. I recommend sticking only to government debt with top-tier countries, preferably in your base currency, because it is not worth increasing risk to get a few extra basis points from lesser creditors. If you place the money only with the government that controls your fund's base currency, or in the case of the Euro, the most trusted of the member nations, your risk level is almost nonexistent. Regardless of the state of a nation's economy, a G7 nation will pay back debts in its own currency, because they own the printing presses. The exception is of course the Eurozone, but the strongest nations are still considered quite safe.

It is practical to pick a mix of varying durations to have different dates of expiry and keep rolling. Holding some in shorter-term papers and the bulk in 1–3-year securities is a common practice. Over time, the effect of proper cash management can be quite large, or at least it has been in the past.

I am sure by now that many readers have been wondering why I have barely mentioned the effects of interest income up until now. This is, after all, a huge factor for managed-futures returns and it can have an extremely large impact on overall results. Well, the reason is that this has been a major factor in the past but there is nothing to indicate that it will remain an important factor in the future, at least not anywhere near as important as it was in the 1980s and 1990s. The truth is that a significant part of the returns from many managed-futures strategies in the past 30 years has simply been free money from the government and this is a phenomenon we need to explore further.

Let's go back to our core strategy and look at the difference in returns if we keep all excess funds in cash versus allocating it sensibly to government securities. I make the simplified but reasonable assumption that on average we have 65% of the asset base in US debt instruments with an average duration of two years.

As both Figure 4.11 and Table 4.6 show, the effect of the interest on excess cash has gradually decreased and is currently (in 2022) very low. The impact of this factor is decreasing, because yields across the board have been decreasing for decades. There are two sides of that coin: on the one hand, we get less risk-free return on our excess cash, but at the same time the strategy has been long bond futures the whole time and making a killing on the same falling yields.

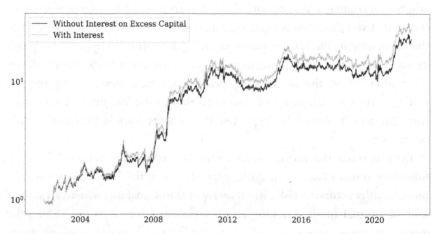

FIGURE 4.11 Effect of interest on excess capital.

TABLE 4.6	Effect of interest on free cash (%)		
Year	Without interest	Interest	With interest
2002	24.7	1.81	26.5
2003	22.5	1.19	23.7
2004	12.6	1.62	14.2
2005	6.9	2.37	9.3
2006	24.9	3.84	28.8
2007	3.1	2.74	5.9
2008	136.8	1.87	138.7
2009	25.7	0.68	26.4
2010	30.5	0.46	31.0
2011	2.7	0.30	3.0
2012	−20.1	0.16	−20.0
2013	2.2	0.19	2.4
2014	52.6	0.34	53.0
2015	−5.9	0.44	−5.5
2016	11.0	0.57	11.6
2017	3.7	0.88	4.6
2018	−6.2	1.53	−4.7
2019	−4.9	1.21	−3.7
2020	12.5	0.24	12.7
2021	51.3	0.25	51.6

The 1980s and 1990s were truly the golden years for a futures manager, where you could get 5% or more absolutely free, and still get a performance fee on it. Even though this extra side income is essentially free money from the government, the futures manager still gets paid for it. Always keep this in mind when analysing a futures manager's long-term track record. A significant factor in the diminishing returns we have been seeing for the managed-futures industry is of course related to the low interest rate environment and it should be expected that results looked better a decade or two ago.

Even without the impact of the interest income, the returns of trend-following futures have been quite attractive over the long run, showing a more healthy return to risk ratio than most traditional investment strategies such as mutual funds. Looking another decade back, into the 1980s, the interest income effect was much greater still. In such an environment, managing futures is very much easier than it is in the current climate. Just consider the seemingly odd situation of a futures manager who ended a year like 1985 flat, making or losing nothing on the trading, but gaining 7% on holding US government debt for the lion's share of the account. He would then be paid a performance fee on this 7%, despite a failed trading year. Don't expect this easy money environment to come back any time soon. Odds are that interests will stay low for some time and competition in our field will only increase.

Loading Fees

Getting the boost of interest on excess capital did wonders for our strategy and really helped to pump up the results. Now we're even further ahead of the benchmarks. But there are negative factors to consider as well. Most people who run diversified futures strategies do it on a professional basis. They primarily manage other people's money, just like the CTA hedge funds which we have been using as a comparison. As such, you charge fees. And those fees can be quite high over time. This can make quite a difference to the long-term net results.

The fee levels charged by futures managers vary somewhat, but the general structure tends to be the same. Managers charge two types of fees. First, a management fee, which is a flat percentage of assets under management. This is a base fee, charged no matter what the performance is and it is usually paid on a monthly or quarterly basis. The somewhat irreverent industry expression is that this is what you get paid for turning on the lights in the morning.

The second fee is called a performance fee, and this is where the real juice is. A futures manager gets paid a portion of the returns which they generate on behalf of their clients and this can be quite substantial. The performance fee is usually paid on a yearly basis and is based on a high-water mark principle. That means that we need to make a new high in the returns before we get paid.

For the remainder of the book, I will assume a management fee of 1.5%, paid on a quarterly basis, and a performance fee of 15%. Loading these fees will have a larger impact than what we saw from the interest rate effect, but in the opposite direction.

As we see in Figure 4.12, the effect over time is quite substantial. While that is bad news for the investors, it's good news for you, dear futures manager. The difference between these lines is your pay and the reason why you would want to read a book like this in the first place.

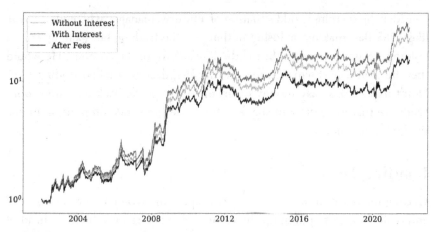

FIGURE 4.12 Effect of fees.

A word of advice for start-up futures managers. It's very easy to make the mistake of budgeting with a performance fee, and having unrealistic expectations of big bucks rolling in fast. If that happens, and it can, that's brilliant and more power to you. But you should always budget with zero performance. You, and your futures management business, must be able to survive on just the management fees. If not, you will be wiped out by a single bad year.

CHAPTER 5

In-Depth Analysis of Trend-Following Performance

This chapter uses the core strategy outlined in Chapter 4 to conduct an in-depth analysis into where the profit and loss in this type of strategy come from. I dig deeper into sector attribution and long versus short attribution and explain the consequences of the resulting analysis.

■ Strategy Behaviour

The strategy we now have in our hands seems to perform quite well over time, but before trading real money you need to be fully aware of how the strategy makes, and loses, money. To manage such a strategy you need to be very familiar with its characteristics before launching or else you will certainly get cold feet at the first sign of trouble and start overriding the rules. Too many strategy developers rely only on the overview statistics generated by their backtesting software to understand the strategy behaviour, and therefore I go in much deeper and show year by year how the sausage is really made. The statistics from your average backtesting software have their value too, at least some of them, but they only tell a very small part of the story. I start by giving you some general statistics on this strategy and then take a look at the real details.

The daily returns distribution is a good place to start. Figure 5.1 provides a quick overview of what you could expect your daily stress level to be like. This is a histogram showing the distribution of daily return numbers. What we can see here is that there is a strong concentration of returns around and slightly above the zero line.

You can also see that an overwhelming amount, over 90% of all days, see returns in the range of plus or minus 4%. There are very few outliers, but they are there, nonetheless. There are only a handful of double digit days, six positive return days in the double digits and only two negative. This is something that you would want to avoid, and when designing a live model you may want to take precautions to prevent or at least mitigate such days. It worked out in our favour here, but the stress level of having double digit days is no trifle.

Another way to get a better feel for how a strategy behaves in the long run is to look at the underwater plot, which is the drawdown over time. Figure 5.2 shows this information in black, behind the strategy curve itself. As you see there, we are underwater almost all the time, meaning that we almost always are in a drawdown. That's the nature of this kind of strategy, where we usually get a brief and sharp move up, followed by a pullback, and there's nothing worrying about that in itself. The thing to keep an eye on is the span between new highs, when that underwater plot goes back up to

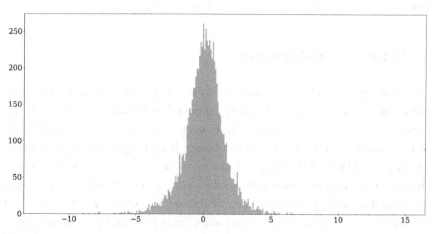

FIGURE 5.1 Daily returns distribution.

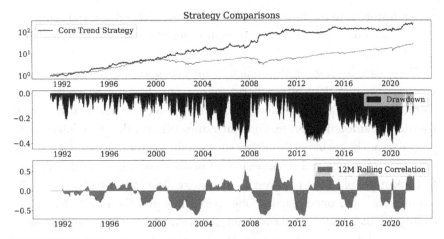

FIGURE 5.2 Core strategy underwater and plot.

zero. Clearly the time to recover during that last drawdown period is a bit too long and something to study closer. It's no longer than what we've seen in traditional markets like equities, but it's longer than we're used to in the trend following space.

The lower pane in Figure 5.2 shows the rolling 12 months correlation against the stock markets, in this case, represented by the S&P 500 Total Return Index. It would be easy to argue that this is the most important chart pane in Figure 5.2 and that this is where you find the real value in trend following.

What you see here is that the correlation in the long run is close to none, but that in the shorter term, it moves between +0.6 to −0.6. This means that we have a weak and variable correlation and if you are familiar with financial risk management and diversification principles, you will quickly understand how valuable this is. What is really interesting is how quickly the correlation drops into negative territory when the stock markets take a turn for the downside, and that will effectively work as a crisis hedge to your overall portfolio.

■ Strategy Long-Term Performance

If you look at the long-term graphs and data, it's easy to draw the conclusion that returns have stagnated permanently and that perhaps the strategy has stopped working. That's because we as humans tend to mentally extrapolate recent history into the future. Ironically, that's exactly what trend following is based on, but at the same time it tends to lead to poor investment allocation decisions.

There have been multiple studies on the classic timing mistake made by investors, in that they often allocate money to strategies after they performed well and pull the money out when they have performed poorly. Even a vast amount of professional investors fall into this particularly dangerous trap. The reality is that every strategy, no matter how good it is in the long run, has strong and weak periods of performance. Despite this obvious fact, most people tend to invest in a strategy after it just had a few really strong years, and once it has a long streak they pull the money back. The strategy as such may have shown gain, but despite this it is entirely possible that a new dollar amount was lost. This is an investment paradox which we see all the time in the hedge fund business.

Even though trend following as such is based on following recent price trends, it makes sense to invest in trend following after a bad run, not after a great one. A case in point here is the relatively mediocre performance of trend following from 2015 to 2019. During these years the strategy was declared dead more times than Mark Twain, and few people wanted to even hear about it. But then, in 2020, the strategy came back strong, followed by an even stronger 2021. For practical reasons, I set the end of 2021 as the cut-off date for analysis for this book, but as of writing this in July of 2022, we're seeing yet another very strong year.

Table 5.1 shows the monthly performance, which is usually an easier way to get a feel for a strategy or fund's long-term performance than a graph. I would suggest that you take a moment to study this table, and that you do the same with your own backtests and strategies. The monthly frequency does hide some of the action, but you get the general idea. Take 2020, for instance, where we ended the year at +24%. Sounds like a great year! But then you see that we started with −14% in January. That's a serious setback and you need to ask yourself if you can really handle such moves. If you can't, and there's nothing wrong with that, you need to dial down the risk.

■ Crisis Alpha

A much-touted aspect of trend following is the so-called crisis alpha effect, the tendency of the strategy to perform well when traditional markets do not. This is arguably the most important feature of a strategy such as trend

													Year
Year	Jan	Feb	Mar	Apr	May	Jun	Jul	Aug	Sept	Oct	Nov	Dec	total
1991	1.6	−0.8	0.1	0.4	0.9	3.6	−9.4	5.1	5.5	7.4	−2.1	11.9	25.2
1992	−7.7	−4.2	−4.9	−2.6	2.3	6.3	10.5	2.4	−2.7	−5.1	5.2	2.4	0.4
1993	2.9	6.7	1.7	3.3	−1.5	-0.5	4.4	−0.3	−6.5	−1.8	9.1	7.3	26.6
1994	−4.6	−5.4	5.3	4.7	11.9	13.9	-0.3	0.4	6.1	−4.3	7.2	−1.6	35.8
1995	−1.8	3.0	−0.3	0.4	3.7	−0.3	−5.2	−2.4	5.4	4.1	2.0	18.7	28.8
1996	0.2	−1.6	9.1	12.5	−3.5	−1.4	−6.1	2.2	8.2	10.5	4.7	−0.9	37.0
1997	0.2	4.7	−0.4	0.3	1.9	−6.0	2.7	−6.5	−1.0	2.4	−3.2	7.8	2.0
1998	0.6	5.6	3.6	3.9	−0.1	−3.6	7.0	15.1	−2.6	−5.9	−2.7	4.0	25.8
1999	1.8	9.4	−11.2	9.9	−4.9	2.7	0.0	−1.7	2.9	−6.8	7.9	11.8	20.8
2000	0.1	10.9	−3.2	−3.0	1.1	1.5	0.1	10.4	−3.6	1.4	8.3	11.2	38.9
2001	−1.5	6.6	10.8	−14.2	2.5	0.0	−0.9	2.7	18.3	7.3	−8.6	−1.0	19.6
2002	−4.9	0.9	2.2	−3.3	2.9	5.9	17.7	5.5	12.9	−9.1	−4.9	1.2	26.7
2003	11.5	8.7	−13.5	2.5	8.4	−5.9	−3.5	2.9	−3.4	15.1	1.1	2.2	24.9
2004	4.3	15.6	5.7	−10.0	−11.0	0.5	3.8	−6.8	4.0	6.3	5.9	−0.1	16.0
2005	−3.1	−1.6	−4.8	−7.1	−0.2	0.8	1.7	−0.6	4.9	−3.4	9.4	4.0	−1.2
2006	12.5	−0.9	15.6	13.1	−5.2	−6.6	−9.5	−0.9	2.6	−0.8	4.7	−2.3	20.5
2007	2.3	−7.3	−3.7	3.7	6.7	−0.2	−10.1	−9.6	11.1	5.5	−0.1	7.9	3.5
2008	27.8	30.2	−8.5	−1.7	6.0	1.2	−12.2	−0.7	26.6	47.2	11.5	5.7	207.4
2009	0.2	3.5	-0.9	−2.6	10.6	−8.0	4.4	5.9	6.5	−4.6	14.3	−5.4	23.8
2010	−2.9	2.0	5.7	1.6	−8.8	−0.6	−5.7	5.0	8.9	18.7	−11.3	19.2	30.5
2011	8.5	4.4	−5.3	8.0	−10.6	−7.7	10.8	−0.4	8.8	−18.9	10.9	−0.1	3.1
2012	0.5	2.3	−2.2	−0.6	−2.4	−11.4	7.8	−9.5	−3.8	−5.7	−0.6	2.5	−22.2
2013	0.8	−4.1	3.7	−0.5	0.9	−2.2	−1.4	−4.5	1.7	5.7	−0.6	1.1	0.1
2014	1.6	3.4	−1.5	4.9	−1.3	3.3	2.1	7.3	16.8	−5.8	9.9	8.6	59.1
2015	13.9	−2.5	0.5	−1.5	−0.3	−8.7	−5.1	−2.0	9.1	−14.4	7.8	−2.2	−8.4
2016	0.0	10.1	−8.6	−0.4	−3.8	8.8	0.3	−4.4	3.9	−6.3	7.2	2.6	7.7
2017	−7.0	2.0	−1.9	1.9	4.7	−2.8	0.1	−1.0	−6.6	7.3	2.5	1.3	−0.4
2018	6.5	−12.4	−1.2	6.0	−7.2	−1.6	−1.0	4.5	−3.3	−9.0	−0.2	8.7	−11.9
2019	−9.2	−0.3	1.9	6.0	−5.6	3.7	3.5	10.9	−14.3	−1.9	2.4	4.5	−1.4
2020	−14.2	−1.8	25.5	−1.2	−6.4	−4.1	3.9	4.8	−2.7	1.4	3.5	19.1	24.1
2021	6.7	21.0	2.6	12.1	−1.5	−4.1	6.5	−0.9	0.8	10.5	−16.0	7.4	48.8

TABLE 5.1 Monthly performance: core trend model (%)

following and far too often overlooked in the chase for pure returns. What is often forgotten is just how valuable it can be to simply not lose money at the same time as traditional investments do. As we'll see later on, such a feature can greatly help overall portfolio diversification and improve risk adjusted returns in the long run.

Let's have a look at a few specific points where the markets struggled and see if our simple little trend model managed to live up to the hype of crisis alpha. First, look at Figure 5.3, where we see the quickly forgotten bear market of 1990. Did you honestly remember that there was a bear market in 1990? Well, in the second part of that year, the S&P 500 lost almost 20% in a few months and that was a dramatic event back then. While this happened, while the regular equity investors lost 20%, the trend model gained double that, for a return of 40% during this difficult time.

Next up we have the events of late 1998. Do you at least remember this one? This was when the supposedly smartest people in the world, who won the Nobel Prize for figuring out how options should be valued, failed to properly value options and lost a ridiculous amount of money when a nuclear power defaulted on their bond payments. Yes, that was an interesting ride. Figure 5.4 shows how our trend model handled that situation, and, as you see there, we were already correctly positioned and when the markets tanked, trend following boomed. At the same time, equity markets lost 20% and trend following gained nearly 30.

One bear market you surely haven't forgotten about is the dot.com crash. When reality hit, the inflated tech valuations fell hard from 2000 to 2003 (Figure 5.5). This was a multi-year bear market where it was very difficult

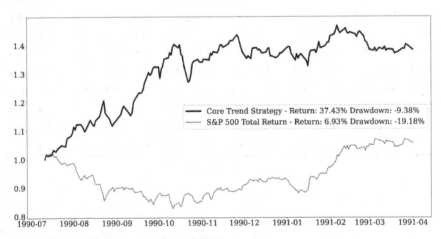

FIGURE 5.3 The bear market of 1990.

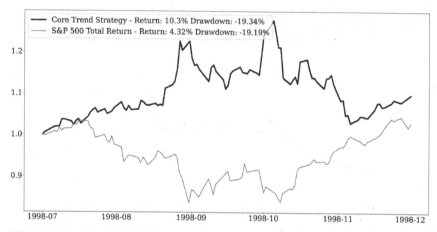

FIGURE 5.4 The LTCM blow-up of 1998.

FIGURE 5.5 The dot.com crash.

to make money from anything. But once again, trend following to the rescue. When the stock markets started falling in earnest, trend following did the opposite. The model was already short stocks, long bonds, and ready to profit from further declines. All in all, the stock markets lost nearly half its value during this phase, at -47.5%. At the same time, during all of this blood on the street, the trend-following model managed to double the money. That's right, while stock markets lost half, trend following doubled.

But there is of course a more recent market crash, one which most readers of this book likely traded through and still have traumatic memories of, the so-called Global Financial Crisis (GFC) of 2008. Well, Figure 5.6 speaks for itself. This was a horrible year for almost anything, but trend following

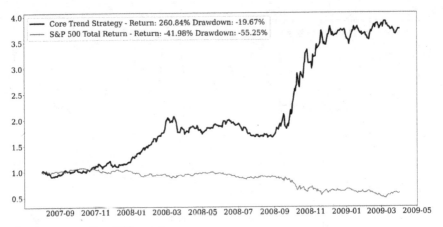

FIGURE 5.6 The GFC crash.

had record returns. This was a remarkable year, and we'll return to it in much more detail in Chapter 6. It was the best year ever for trend followers, with shockingly strong returns.

Lastly, let's see how the strategy faired during March of 2020. If you don't know what I'm talking about this time, I have plenty of sympathy for that. We've all tried our best to forget about Covid (Figure 5.7). The impact on the financial system was swift and shocking, and markets fell hard on this new and unpredictable event. Even though the stock markets recovered fairly quickly, surprisingly quickly to most, it was a very scary event at the time. Yet again, trend-following models were already well positioned and as the markets fell hard, trend followers gained. In that first scary month, the

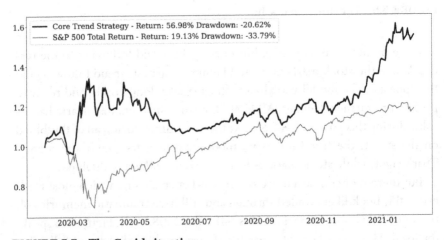

FIGURE 5.7 The Covid situation.

stock markets fell by about a third, all while trend models gained about the same amount.

The conclusion of all of this must be that trend following really does live up to its promise of crisis alpha. When the stock markets are in trouble, more often than not, trend following is gaining. That makes for excellent possibilities to use trend following to diversify a traditional portfolio, to achieve better risk-adjusted returns on the overall portfolio.

■ Trading Direction

The strategy we have arrived at is direction agnostic, using symmetrical rules for longs and shorts both in terms of entry and exit and in position sizing. So far we have only looked at the overview aggregated results and they seem to hold up well against the benchmarks, but we have not dug into the details of performance attribution yet. The first point we need to look into is how the long and the short side fare against each other and whether there are any differences between the two. For those who previously have not done these simulations themselves, the result of such an investigation may be a bit of a shock.

Figure 5.8 shows the yearly performance for the core trend model, divided on long and short sides. The long performance, shown in black, clearly dominates the picture. We see that the long side has a positive performance for most, almost all years, while the short side has plenty of losing

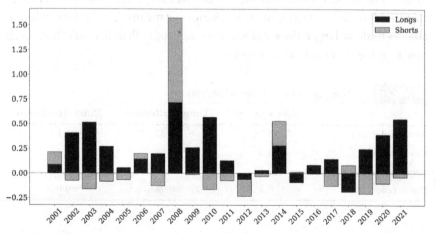

FIGURE 5.8 Yearly results longs versus shorts.

years. But you can also see how the short side had a large contribution in 2008, and was quite nice in 2014 as well.

The short side of trend-following strategies is quite a problem to deal with and it requires some counter-intuitive thinking to tackle it. To start by demonstrating the problem, I present in Table 5.2 the results of using the same core strategy that we have arrived at so far when trading both sides, taking only the long trades and taking only the short trades.

The compound return on the short side of −2.13% is not a typo. Neither is the worst drawdown of over half the capital. This tells us that the short side of the strategy, at least as a stand-alone strategy, looks quite abysmal.

One thing is certain; trading only the short side is a very bad idea. It may seem as if the obvious conclusion is to trade only the long side, but things are not as simple as they seem here. For the long-only version, you would have made a return of 20% for a maximum drawdown of 32%, making it appear even more attractive than the long/short version. Looking at standard optimisation techniques, it would appear as if the long-only strategy is the most desirable, with a higher Sharpe ratio, higher Sortino ratio, and so on. But standard optimisation techniques more often than not lead to strategies that fail in reality, so don't stop analysing the results just because a couple of ratios ended up slightly higher.

Such premature conclusions also ignore a key factor, which may not be as obvious. What you are looking at here, in Table 5.2, is data showing the attribution of the long and the short side of the full strategy. It does not show the results of only taking long trades or only short sides. It makes a difference, as the compound returns include the interaction of the two sides. The fact that the short side acts as a volatility dampener means that the long side was able to trade at larger sizes and make more profits than it would have been able to if the short side wasn't there.

TABLE 5.2 Long versus short, since 2001 (%)

	Core strategy	Long attribution	Short attribution
Annualised return	18.24	20.37	−2.13
Max drawdown	−43.30	−32.58	−54.27
Annualised volatility	27.52	21.02	15.90
Sharpe ratio	0.722	0.988	−0.056

Looking at Figure 5.9 shows that the long-only version moves up in a reasonable smooth pattern, showing solid results and matching the long/short version quite well. The short-only strategy has an odder pattern and does not move up anywhere near as much as the long version. This distinction is not the important piece of information, however, which comes when you compare the results of the short-only strategy to that of the MSCI World Index. Note that when the world equity markets suffer, the short side of the strategy tends to do very well. Don't underestimate the value of this effect. During equity bear markets, very few strategies do well and the help that the short side of this strategy can provide during these times makes a big difference. Even more importantly though, during the times of serious market distress, when things are getting really scary for most market participants and there are few places to hide, the short side of the strategy tends to spike up and show excellent profits. It is not necessarily short equity index futures that yield the big profits in these bearish years, it may also be short energies and similar. The rather extreme performance of trend-following futures in 2008 was in a large part accomplished by the short side and those managers who had chosen to forgo the shorts only had long rates left to save the year.

It is tempting for a strategy developer to follow the easy path and just 'optimise' the short side away. It looks like a no-brainer, giving higher volatility adjusted ratios, decreasing trading, and lowering overall exposure. Still, you should take some more time to think through whether you do

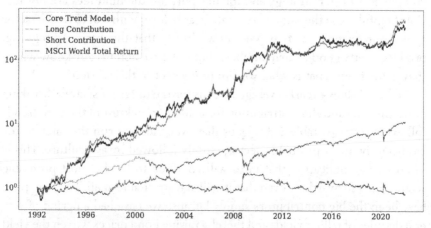

FIGURE 5.9 Comparing long versus short.

want to cut out the short side: it may make your strategy less competitive and may create some major problems for you in the case of a volatile financial environment.

The reason it may decrease the competitiveness of your strategy is simple. The more you lean towards long-only, even if you still trade all asset classes, the higher the correlation is to the world stock markets. One of the core benefits of managed futures is the ability to decouple from the stock markets and make money in up and down years, regardless of the equity crowd's mood swings. To be an attractive complement to the ubiquitous equity portfolio, our managed-futures strategy should have clear positive expected returns while having low to slightly negative correlations to the world stock markets. If we can achieve that, there are great diversification gains for a stock market investor to buy our product and that is a key sales argument. The reason is that with low or negative correlation along with positive returns, we would push the investor's overall portfolio to a more attractive point on the efficient frontier curve.

■ Sector Impact

When doing the attribution calculations in this section, I ignore the effects of management fees and performance fees, as well as the interest effect, because it would make little sense in breaking it down on the sectors. The information we are looking for here is the relative performance of the subcomponents of our strategy and for this purpose the fund fees are not terribly helpful. I use the same core strategy as before, with a 0.15% risk factor as per our original strategy. We know already that this basic strategy can produce pretty good return numbers, but so far we don't really know where they come from. That is what we aim to uncover in this section.

Table 5.3 shows yearly average returns for the different sectors, breaking down the long and short attribution for a 30-year backtest of the core trend-following strategy. Table 5.3 tells us that over the long run the rates sector has been the most profitable sector, closely followed by agriculture. This is in no way an indication that rates will continue to be the most profitable sector going forward, or even that it will stay profitable at all. The long rates have been the big contributors simply because we have had a period of several decades of falling yields and thereby raising bond prices. Given the yield levels in most of the developed world at the moment, there are likely to be limited possibilities in long rates for a while.

	Currencies	Agriculture	Non-Agriculture	Equities	Rates	All sectors
Long	−0.18	6.43	−0.41	5.44	9.10	20.37
Short	0.51	−0.84	0.67	−1.33	−1.13	−2.13
Total	0.33	5.58	0.26	4.11	7.97	18.24

TABLE 5.3 Sector comparison: annualised returns before fees (%)

Both the commodity buckets produced positive returns over time, with agriculture showing a clear lead. That shouldn't be terribly surprising, as the agricultural space is perhaps the most interesting for a trend follower. In this sector, we can find a variety of uncorrelated markets, assets which are not directly interrelated. That makes it a very valuable sector. The non-agricultural sector, energies and metals, also performed quite well, contributing on the short side of the game.

As you may notice in Table 5.3, the short side looks rather mediocre. In fact, if you look at just the short side, it looks downright terrible. Over a 20-year time horizon, we would have ended up losing 2% per year, on average. In fact, only two sectors showed a positive return on the short side over this 20-year span: currencies and non-agriculture. With the former, currencies, you could very well argue that there is no such thing as long and short. It's an academic argument, but completely valid. The long versus shorts in that sector is about mathematics, not behaviour of the market. An equity bear market is a very different animal from an equity bull market, but in the currency world there is no distinction. Long or short depends on the direction in which you quote the cross.

Equities did well on the long side but not so much on the short side. Equities used to be much easier for these types of strategies a decade or two earlier and one can only speculate about what, if anything, made the equity markets change and become more erratic and less prone to sustained trending. What comes to mind, of course, would be not only the increased amount of electronic trading and high frequency algorithmic trading, but also the increasingly globalised world in which all equity futures across the world tend to see a remarkably high level of correlation to each other. In particular, when the markets are experiencing high levels of fear, such as the crises during 2000, 2008 and 2011, the correlation between indices with seemingly very different sector or geographic compositions quickly approaches one. High correlation between instruments in our investment universe is undesirable and although it sometimes means quick profits, it more often than not means sudden and simultaneous reversals in a large number of positions, causing painful losses in a very short time.

As usual, the yearly charts get distorted by the outsized returns in 2008 but try to look beyond that. The extreme profitability, along with the equally extreme volatility that year, seem to be somewhat of an anomaly and not very likely, or even desirable, to be repeated any time soon. Still, these figures with the average sector returns for the strategy, along with the long and short side should help clarify where the profits and losses come from.

Looking at the sector results in Figure 5.10, the following can be observed:

- Rates show an overwhelming amount of positive years and quite a few outsized returns on the positive side.

- Equities play a relatively minor role in comparison to rates and commodities. The most eye-catching year for equities should be 2008, which I will return to later.

- Non-agricultural commodities had a generally positive contribution, with two truly outsized positive years, in 1996 and 2008.

- Agricultural commodities sector shows strong overall performance with multiple stellar years.

- Currencies rarely make big waves and have about half of the years in the black, but tend to win more on good years than they lose in bad years.

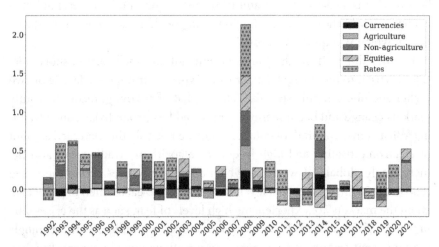

FIGURE 5.10 Yearly sector attribution.

■ Putting Leverage into Context

That trend-following futures trading need to be leveraged is hardly a shocking revelation, but you may perhaps wonder just how leveraged we have to be. Both mainstream and financial media like to use leverage terminology to make a point about how risky a fund or other investment is and you often hear outsized numbers about how leveraged traders are. The problem is that leverage and risk are two completely different concepts and they are not necessarily related. A higher leverage could mean higher risk but it by no means has to imply this. Of course, if you only hold one asset, such as stocks in IBM, then your risk is double if you have US$100,000 exposure compared to having US$50,000 exposure, but when dealing with derivatives and cross-asset instruments, the picture is not that simple.

To put leverage into proper context and perspective, let's take a look at a typical portfolio for our core strategy. If you have an account size of about US$5 million and trade the core strategy with a risk factor of 0.15% as described above, your portfolio would hold 40 positions covering all sectors on 21 May 2009. This date is chosen rather arbitrarily, and for the point I am making here pretty much any randomly chosen date would be just fine. Let's start with the funny number and then I demonstrate why this seemingly ridiculous number is of little to no value to us: On this randomly chosen day, we had a total gross exposure of 1353%. If we at that time were trading a portfolio worth US$10 million, that means that we would have investments worth over US$135 million. How's that for leveraged?

Large numbers at times are hard to relate to, so imagine having a personal trading account at your local broker worth $10,000. Now imagine using that account to enter positions worth $135,000. Most people would see this as an absolutely insane risk, and in most cases, rightly so. But this is not most cases. You're probably wondering what the trick is. Perhaps you think it's that term I used in the last paragraph, about gross exposure. The gross exposure is the total of longs and shorts, adding it up instead of netting longs against shorts. So if we would be long 10% and short 10%, that's a net exposure of zero and a gross exposure of 20%. But no, in this case, that is the trick. While our gross exposure is 1353%, the net exposure is still a whopping 1233%. Yes, for those of you who just did that maths, that means that we have long positions of 1295% and short positions of just 62%. These ratios may change dramatically over time, but this is how it looked on this particular day.

The trick, if there is such a thing, should already be clear to you if you paid attention earlier about how the position sizing works for this type of strategy. We don't care about notional exposure; we size positions according to volatility. If a market normally moves only 0.1% in a regular trading day and another market usually has daily moves of 3% up or down per day, then clearly you need to allocate more to the former. If you don't, the portfolio would be entirely driven by the volatile markets.

If you work in finance, or studied finance at university, there should be no doubt which sector is the least volatile and which sector is clearly responsible for our seemingly ridiculously high exposure. Yes, it's the rates sector, and more specifically the shorter-term side of that sector.

Table 5.4 shows you the positions which we had on for this particular day, along with some details. You can see which exact contract we had and which sector it belongs to. You can also see the exposure in USD along with this value divided by the total portfolio value, which gives us the exposure in percent. The USD exposure amount is calculated by multiplying the number of contracts held by the most current price, multiplied by the point value for the corresponding market, and in case of foreign markets, adjusted to USD.

TABLE 5.4 Portfolio composition, 21 May 2009

Contract	Sector	Exposure US$	Exposure (%)
Live Cattle June 2009	Agriculture	−429,130	−4.3
White Sugar August 2009	Agriculture	808,080	8.1
Lean Hogs June 2009	Agriculture	−260,900	−2.6
Robusta Coffee 10 Tonne July 2009	Agriculture	−215,460	−2.2
Soybean Meal July 2009	Agriculture	606,720	6.1
Soybean July 2009	Agriculture	587,500	5.9
Frozen Concentrated Orange Juice Grade A July 2009	Agriculture	513,570	5.1
Cotton No. 2 July 2009	Agriculture	482,630	4.8
Sugar No. 11 July 2009	Agriculture	507,338	5.1
Soybean Oil July 2009	Agriculture	478,548	4.8
Canola July 2009	Agriculture	879,152	8.8
Coffee C July 2009	Agriculture	611,100	6.1
Feeder Cattle August 2009	Agriculture	864,238	8.6
Japanese Yen June 2009	Currencies	−795,750	−8.0
Australian Dollar June 2009	Currencies	696,600	7.0

(Continued)

Table 5.4 (Continued)

Contract	Sector	Exposure US$	Exposure (%)
Canadian Dollar June 2009	Currencies	1,052,400	10.5
New Zealand Dollar June 2009	Currencies	666,600	6.7
British Pound June 2009	Currencies	990,000	9.9
US Dollar Index June 2009	Currencies	−1,209,600	−12.1
E-mini Nasdaq-100 June 2009	Equities	437,600	4.4
S&P/TSX 60 Index June 2009	Equities	483,760	4.8
Hang Seng Index − Mini May 2009	Equities	510,690	5.1
E-mini S&P MidCap 400 June 2009	Equities	388,990	3.9
Hang Seng Index May 2009	Equities	851,150	8.5
Nikkei 225 Dollar June 2009	Equities	502,150	5.0
E-mini Russell 2000 June 2009	Equities	361,350	3.6
CBOE Volatility Index June 2009	Equities	−225,400	−2.3
Platinum July 2009	Non-Agriculture	519,615	5.2
Palladium June 2009	Non-Agriculture	353,250	3.5
Henry Hub Natural Gas June 2009	Non-Agriculture	−144,120	−1.4
Copper July 2009	Non-Agriculture	358,925	3.6
RBOB Gasoline June 2009	Non-Agriculture	378,000	3.8
Brent Crude Oil July 2009	Non-Agriculture	359,580	3.6
Canadian Bankers Acceptance June 2009	Rates	7,222,088	72.2
2-Year U.S. T-Note June 2009	Rates	6,970,496	69.7
Euribor June 2009	Rates	26,429,000	264.3
30 Day Federal Funds May 2009	Rates	49,496,555	495.0
U.S. T-Bond June 2009	Rates	−842,296	−8.4
Euro-Bund June 2009	Rates	−2,060,060	−20.6
Eurodollar June 2009	Rates	24,092,375	240.9

To further demonstrate the rather extreme proportions involved in the differences in notional exposure of the five sectors, take a look at Figure 5.11. The rates sector has such large positions that they make the rest look like rounding errors. This is not something strange, it's not surprising and it really has nothing to do with the risk involved. It merely reflects the low volatility of the sector, which forces us to take on larger notional position sizes to achieve the same risk level. What we're aiming for is an approximate equal risk per position.

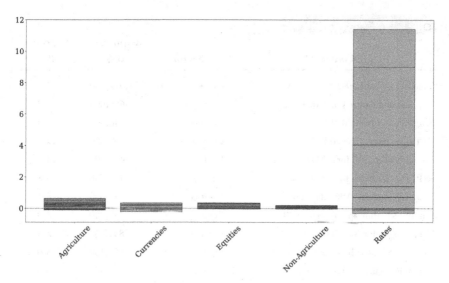

FIGURE 5.11 Portfolio composition: notional weights.

Figure 5.11 will give you quite a distorted view of the actual risk picture. Since each position is sized according to volatility, with the aim of having about the same risk, we could easily make another figure of the same portfolio. In Figure 5.12, each position is shown as an equal size box, reflecting the risk parity position approach. Now you see that the rates sector wasn't the heaviest weighted sector at this time, as the notional approach in Figure 5.11 might have led you to believe. It is rather the agricultural sector which holds the highest risk.

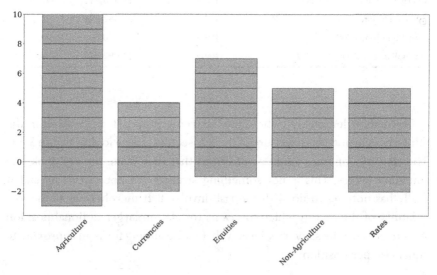

FIGURE 5.12 Portfolio composition: equal weights.

I hope this way of looking at risk can help you approach portfolio composition in a different manner.

■ As a Complement to an Equity Portfolio

Most investors, institutional as well as individual, prefer to hold a large part of their money in the equities market, that is, they want to be long stocks for the long term. I attribute this attitude mostly to the indoctrination from schools and governments about the conventional wisdom that 'the equity markets always go up in the long run', which in a manner of speaking is absolutely true, if you live long enough. Between 1992 and 2021, the S&P 500 returned around 10% per year on average, including dividends. And this period covers some extraordinary bull markets which are unlikely to last. During the same time, it showed three drawdowns in the 35–55% range. So if you happen to buy at the peak just before that drawdown, you can expect over a decade to recover your initial investment. To add insult to injury, if you had your money invested with an indexed mutual fund, you would with overwhelming probability end up with an even lower annual return while you pay the bank to keep underperforming.

Now, before I get beaten over the head with a stick for writing off a whole asset class, let me explain my position a bit further. I have nothing against stocks and, in fact, I trade several profitable stock strategies and even some that are long only. My objection is only to the standard approach to the stock market of buying a basket of stocks, most likely whatever happens to be in a specific index, and just holding it for year after year. This is indeed a very risky strategy which can easily be seen from the numbers just mentioned, but the marketing effort of certain universities, governments, and banks has been massively successful and people seem quite content to get their single, digit return for taking the risk of losing over half their assets. There are many viable strategies for participating in the long-term bull markets in equities, which tend to be very profitable when they come along, but simply buying and sitting on stocks for decades does not make much sense to me. Still, many investors like doing this and so let's have a closer look at how their overall returns can be improved by holding part of their money in the equities market and part of it in a strategy, such as the ones I discuss in this book.

The question that we need to ask here, and which ultimately we would like our potential investors to ask themselves, is: 'Can a standard long-only equity portfolio be improved by adding managed futures to the mix?' This problem could be approached from a strict Markowitz methodology of building covariance matrices, Lagrange multipliers, and other equally fun things to arrive at an exact optimal asset mix to the tenth decimal, but frankly I find this a waste of everyone's time, including the valued reader of this book. There are many interesting concepts coming out of Modern Portfolio Theory, but the vast majority of the methods have absolutely no bearing on reality and should probably not be used very much outside of classrooms.

Still, the core concept of the efficient frontier is reasonably valid, even though some assumptions and methods surrounding it may not be, so I'm going to make a very simplified variant just to prove my point regarding diversification. In the following analysis, I have two assets to choose from: one is our core trend-following futures strategy with all costs loaded, and the other is the S&P 500 Total Return Index net of dividends. The question is how much we should buy of each to get the best volatility adjusted results for the overall portfolio.

To test this, I ran a 100-iteration efficient frontier calculation for combinations of these two assets, shown in Figure 5.13. The rebalancing is done monthly to make sure that the much higher long-term yield of the futures strategy does not result in an overwhelming amount of the assets in that strategy after a good period.

We already know that the futures strategy has a much higher expected return, so there is no surprise that the highest returns are achieved with a maximum allocation to futures, but that is not what we are looking for here. Figure 5.13 shows the equivalent of a so-called efficient frontier for the two assets in our portfolio, with annual compound return on the y-axis and

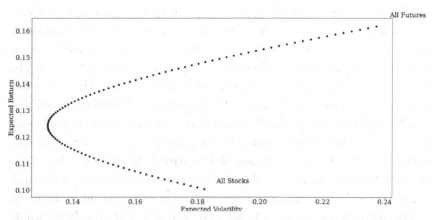

FIGURE 5.13 Diversified futures as an enhancement to an equity portfolio.

standard deviation, as a proxy of risk, on the x-axis. The idea is simple; we want to achieve as high an annual return as possible at the expense of as low a volatility as we can. The volatility is essentially the currency in which we pay for returns.

Figure 5.13 tells us right away that if we start with a portfolio of only the stock index and keep gradually adding allocation to the futures strategy, we get a lower and lower standard deviation while at the same time the annual compound return rises. The obvious conclusion from a quick inspection of this chart is that it does not make sense to have less than 30–40% futures and the remaining part in equities, because anything less means a lower return at a higher or equal risk level.

Table 5.5 shows the same data as in Figure 5.13 but it also has an additional column with the Sharpe ratio for each point in the curve. Even though 100% allocation to the futures gives the best overall return, the Sharpe ratio of the strategy can be enhanced by adding stocks to the mix.

Naturally, in a real-world scenario, you have more than two assets to choose from and there are other real-life complications as well, which makes it tricky to determine an exact optimal amount to buy of each asset class. Therefore, view this as a guideline approach and a way of demonstrating a concept more than exact numbers.

TABLE 5.5   Adding diversified futures to an equity portfolio

Percent futures	Return	Volatility	Sharpe ratio
100	16.16	23.71	0.68
90	15.55	21.10	0.74
80	14.94	18.69	0.80
70	14.33	16.56	0.87
60	13.72	14.84	0.92
50	13.10	13.66	0.96
40	12.49	13.19	0.95
30	11.88	13.50	0.88
20	11.27	14.54	0.78
10	10.65	16.16	0.66
0	10.04	18.22	0.55

CHAPTER 6

A Year-by-Year Review

The strategy we have arrived at is already on a par with what most CTA funds and futures managers are able to produce. In its current shape it is quite usable for managing money, although it is certainly possible to improve upon it further. What we have now is a core strategy that is very similar to the base strategy of most trend-following managed futures funds and, as such, it has its merits. To be able to make intelligent decisions regarding what should be further enhanced with this strategy you need to properly understand how it really behaves and this is an extremely tough insight to build. There is no substitute for experience in this regard and having seen a strategy perform in the wild is the only way to gain a complete understanding of what it is capable of. But in lieu of that, in this chapter I try to paint as clear a picture as I can of what it would have been like to manage this strategy as it stands over a longer period of time.

It is clear that certain years are more interesting than others. Some years everything is just plain old business as usual with not much action, but in other years there may be large swings and important analytical conclusions to be drawn. I go over the 20 years from 2002 to 2021 and explain what happened, what went right and what went wrong. If things looked easy when you saw the overview simulation data in the previous chapters, this chapter will highlight where the difficulties can arise.

In the following analyses I always take commissions and slippage into account to keep things realistic and I assume a 1.5% management fee and 15% performance fee, with the management fee paid out quarterly and the performance fee yearly. That's the most common set-up for professionals trading these kinds of strategies on behalf of others.

As a general market comparison, I use the global equity index MSCI World Total Return, which includes reinvested dividends. This is certainly not a strategy that attempts to mimic or beat the equity indices and as a benchmark it is not really a fair comparison because they are very different animals, but it is my experience that investors, individual and institutional alike, are very focused on the overall state of the equity market and that the pressure on a futures manager thereby goes up as equities go up and declines when equity markets are doing poorly. Even if your strategy is completely unrelated to equities, this tends to be the case. The only explanation I can offer is that it is human nature to want to gain when everyone else is gaining and that a loss does not feel so bad when everyone else is also losing. For most investors, a loss hurts much more if their neighbours are gaining at the same time. This phenomenon never ceases to amaze me, but it seems a fact of life for our industry.

■ How to Read This Chapter

This is the longest chapter of the book and as it goes through the behaviour and performance of the strategy over the course of 20 years, it may feel like ancient history and cause you to wonder whether this is just a page filler. I can assure you that nothing is further from the truth. In my view, this chapter is by far the most valuable learning opportunity in the book and if you want to understand trend trading in depth, you should reflect on each year, looking at the details in the performance charts and trying to imagine what life is like for a professional trend trader.

What you are normally told in books and marketing material is that trend trading is easy and highly profitable. The study of the year-by-year behaviour and breakdowns on sectors and directions shows that although it is profitable in the long run and the trading rules are theoretically simple, it is far from easy to accomplish the results in real life. Consider this chapter as a reality check. It is my way of showing the real side of this business, the good and the bad, without overselling or overhyping. If you want to enter the field of trend trading, read the book through once first. Then go back and study the details of this chapter again.

When you have settled on your own trading strategy, whether by constructing your own or modifying my core strategy, make realistic simulations and compare the details to this chapter, year by year and month by month, to see how your strategy would have handled things differently and whether it is still a viable way forward.

You simply cannot base your strategy selection process just on simulation summary statistics or a long-term equity curve.

After this year-by-year review, in the next chapters I look more closely at how to replicate and reverse engineer existing futures hedge funds as well as how to further improve upon the core strategy.

■ 2002

So, imagine that we are back in late 2001 and we're about to embark on a 20-year trading journey. In the first edition of this book, I started the year-by-year review in 1990 and made some offhand jokes about Bon Jovi, fading pastel colours, and Tiananmen Square, which was just the first things that came to mind from remembering 1989. Of course, when writing that, I hadn't expected this book to be such a big success, and I certainly hadn't expected it to be translated into Chinese. Writing this update, I just had to find out how my off-the-cuff remarks were handled in those versions. As it turns out, the Simplified Chinese, which was translated in Beijing, kept Bon Jovi but cut any references to pastel colours and tanks in Tiananmen Square. In the Traditional Chinese version, translated in Taipei, they kept all three, and added a clarification about said tanks being part of the Chinese People's Liberation Army. In retrospect, I'm not sure if I should be worried or proud of having accidentally wandered into a geopolitical minefield, and now I seem to have gone and done it again.

Well, this time around we're starting off at the end of 2001, which is a year I also have very vivid memories of, but find it harder to crack jokes about.

Anyhow, it's the morning of 2 January 2002 and you're all set to begin your adventure. You were in luck because you had just received US$10 million committed from investors for your new managed futures fund and you had all your infrastructure set up, ready to go. You start off by running your backtest to get your starting positions, your list of long and short futures positions which you're supposed to hold on that day. The number of positions held will vary quite a bit over time, and depends on how many trends are available at the moment.

A very common question I've heard so many times over the years is about how you actually start off, and which positions you take. There are two ways of looking at this, where one is clearly wrong. You could take the view of entering only new signals from the time you go live. That is, you don't actually take any positions on the first day you launch your strategy, but rather wait for new entry signals. The problem with this is that we're dealing with a portfolio strategy here, one which relies on position interaction and diversification. The backtest and research are all based on having a fully loaded portfolio. Taking only new positions would greatly deviate from the plan and could result in highly unpredictable results. That's why we'll go with option number two, replicating the current state of the backtest on the first day, entering into all the positions right away.

An important thing to remember is that all position sizes are adjusted for volatility, so that in theory they have the same approximate daily impact on the bottom line of our whole strategy. You can find the details of this process in previous chapters, but the importance of taking that part seriously cannot be overstressed. Without proper position sizing, your strategy will fail.

The initial portfolio for this strategy at the start of January 2002 is shown in Table 6.1.

Given that each position has the same volatility adjusted size, we can easily sum up each sector to see how the overall allocation of the fund looked (see Table 6.2). This is naturally always an approximation, because the volatility adjusting sizing relies on the flawed assumption that the volatility of the respective instruments will remain constant. As the pie chart in Figure 6.1 shows, our initial portfolio is quite commodity heavy, with over 60% of the allocation between the two commodity sectors.

In the rates section, we hold a mixed long and short exposure, over the long and short side of the curve. Now that may sound a little confusing if you're not used to the interest rates sector, as the words long and short are used in different contexts. The long end of the curve refers to treasuries or bonds maturing a long time from the present, such as a US 30-year bond, while the short end of the curve would be things like shorter-term money market instruments, like the 30-day Fed funds or 90-day Eurodollar.

In the remaining two sectors we carry very little exposure at this point. There really weren't many trends to speak of in the currency and equity sectors by the end of 2001.

Figure 6.2 shows how our strategy performed compared to the MSCI World Total Return Index this year. Early on in the year the strategy was

TABLE 6.1 Initial portfolio 2002

Market	Direction	Sector
Cocoa	Long	Agriculture
Coffee C	Short	Agriculture
KC HRW Wheat	Short	Agriculture
Corn	Short	Agriculture
Lean Hogs	Short	Agriculture
Soybean Meal	Short	Agriculture
Soybean	Short	Agriculture
Robusta Coffee	Short	Agriculture
US Dollar Index	Long	Currencies
Japanese Yen	Short	Currencies
E-mini Russell 2000	Long	Equities
Crude Oil – Light Sweet	Short	Non-Agriculture
Henry Hub Natural Gas	Short	Non-Agriculture
Brent	Short	Non-Agriculture
NY Harbor ULSD	Short	Non-Agriculture
Gas Oil	Short	Non-Agriculture
Platinum	Long	Non-Agriculture
Euro-Bund	Short	Rates
Eurodollar	Long	Rates
Euribor	Long	Rates
U.S. T-Bond	Short	Rates
Long Gilt	Short	Rates

TABLE 6.2 Initial sector allocation 2002

	Long	Short	Total
Rates	2	3	5
Agriculture	1	7	8
Non-Agriculture	1	5	6
Currencies	1	1	2
Equities	1	0	1
Total	6	16	22

struggling sideways with a maximum loss on the year of nearly 10%. During this period, the strategy really didn't stray far from the equity markets, which were equally sideways in the first half of the year. This was a calm

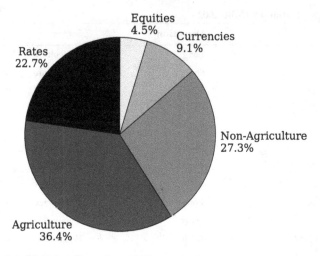

FIGURE 6.1   Sector allocation 2002.

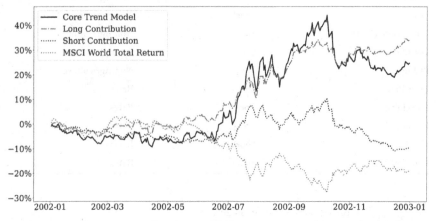

FIGURE 6.2   Strategy performance 2002.

phase, where there were really quite a few trends around. That would change quite quickly by mid-year.

Starting in July, we saw a sudden jump in the profits of the strategy. If you had started your trading journey at the beginning of this year, you certainly has an interesting start. Looking at a long-term graph simply doesn't do this experience justice. After finally launching your live strategy in January, you're trading day in and day out, seeing almost nothing for it. Not much up, not much down. You're probably starting to wonder about this whole idea, and starting to question what you do for a living. And then, all of a sudden, it moves. And it moves a lot. You've been so used to slow, uneventful days and now it just fires on all cylinders at once.

About the same time, the stock markets start declining as well. We go from having a flat year for stocks to seeing losses of nearly 30% in the global index, and this is while our strategy is gaining handsomely. What looked like a boring, perhaps even failed, year quickly turned into a great success. Even though little profits were given up before the year was up, we still had a great first year.

In this part of finance, success can come quickly and unexpectedly, but remember, so can failure. Starting this adventure in 2002 would have been lucky indeed. Yes, luck is very much a factor in long-term success. Any trading strategy, no matter how brilliant, will have good years and bad years, and you won't know when they will arrive. If your first year happens to be a bad one, odds are that you won't continue or that your investors will pull their money, even if the strategy is absolutely fine.

To find out what really happened in the second part of the year, a good start would be to look at the sector attribution. Figure 6.3 shows this attribution over time and how each sector impacted the bottom line results this year. Looking at the July to August period, when the strategy returns took off for the upside, we see that three sectors were responsible for the effect. We see that currencies, equities, and rates all helped at almost the same time.

Going one step further, we can compare the longs versus the shorts in Figures 6.4 and 6.5. From the long side, we can see that the number one contributor was the rates sector, adding about 20% to our bottom line all by itself. On the short side, we see an overwhelming effect from a different sector, and given that this is during the post dot.com bear

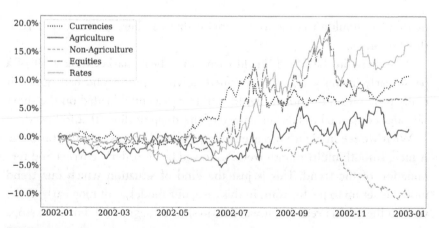

FIGURE 6.3 Sector performance 2002.

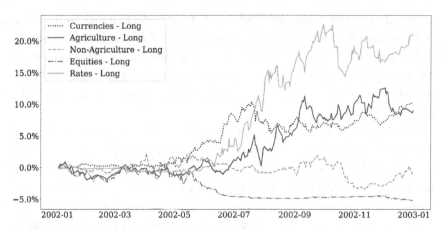

FIGURE 6.4 Long sector performance 2002.

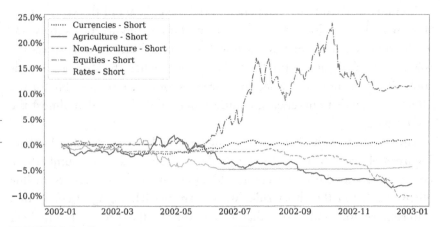

FIGURE 6.5 Short sector performance 2002.

market, it shouldn't come as a surprise that the hero performer here is short equities.

As we saw in the MSCI World earlier, the bear market took a bit of a pause early in the year, and continued down in the second half. Once it really took off on the downside, the strategy was fully loaded on the short side and positioned to take advantage of the steep declines that followed.

What we see in Figure 6.6 is exactly what we like to see in this business. A nice, smooth multi-month trend followed by an orderly correct and termination of the trend. This is just the kind of situation which our trend model is set up to profit from. In this case, our model went long early in the year on the initial breakout. It was a little slow to begin with, but as no stops

FIGURE 6.6 Long trend in the Euro.

were hit, we stayed on the long side. By April, the Euro futures price took off and we saw a powerful trend from 1.02 all the way up to 1.16. This greatly contributed to the bottom line profits of the strategy, and we saw a very similar pattern in other currency markets during this time. The effect of this can clearly be seen in Figure 6.3, where we could see the currency sector adding about 10% to the strategy from May to August. Dollar weakness was a general theme this year, with the dollar falling throughout the year, giving us profits in almost all currency markets.

By the end of our first year, we managed to score a success of 27% return on our capital (Table 6.3). That is an incredibly strong year. If you believe that a near 30% return is somehow too low, then you should stay away from trading. Despite what influencers and self-proclaimed trading gurus might claim, such an extreme return is unsustainable in real life and over longer time periods, practically no one has ever realized such gains over time. In any given year, anything can happen, and you can occasionally see much larger gains, but you will also see much lower as well as negative years.

TABLE 6.3 Sector results 2002

	Currencies	Agriculture	Non-Agriculture	Equities	Rates	All sectors
Long	10.3	9.0	−1.1	−5.2	21.1	34.0
Short	1.0	−7.6	−10.0	11.5	−4.4	−9.5
Total	10.8	1.4	−10.6	6.7	16.4	24.7

The story of this year doesn't end with the 27% trading gains, of course. There is some good news and there is some bad news. The good news is that we also got some free money from Uncle Sam for stashing our capital reserves with him. For futures trading we only need a small portion of the total capital for margin, so the rest we put in short-term treasuries. The income on this depends very much on how high is the interest the government is paying. Some years we get quite a nice contribution, other years it's marginal. This particular year, we got 1.8% added to the bottom line of the portfolio.

In the bad news category, there are fees to be paid. We're charging a 1.5% management fee and a 15% performance fee to the portfolio. The silver lining is that this money goes to you, dear trader, and is paid by your investors.

The management fees for this year totalled 1.8%, by chance, the same amount as the interest income (Table 6.4). How, you ask, is this possible when we just agreed on a 1.5% management fee? Welcome to finance. The fee is 1.5% of capital under management, and this is calculated and accrued each day, and paid on a quarterly basis. As we've seen gains over the year, the basis of this calculation is growing along with the portfolio's total value. If you then divide the actual management fees for the entire year by the starting value of the portfolio, you'll end up with a number greater than the nominal 1.5%. This is the real beauty of asset management. Your fee is expressed as a percentage of assets managed, and if you grow those assets, your fee grows automatically.

The management fees are your base pay as an asset manager, your salary, if you like. This money you'll get regardless of your performance, and thus you need to make sure that you and your trading business can survive on it.

TABLE 6.4	Results 2002	
	US$	**Percentage**
Starting NAV	10,000,000	100.00
Trading result	2,468,651	24.70
Interest income	180,566	1.80
Management fee	184,107	1.80
Performance fee	369,767	3.70
Net result	2,095,344	21.00
Ending NAV	12,095,344	121.00

The real juice, however, is in the performance fees. You won't get rich on management fees, but the performance fees can do the trick. If the management fee is your salary, then the performance fee is your bonus. In this case, after a stellar performance year, this bonus amounted to nearly 4% of the asset base.

If you had started off with a US$10 million portfolio, and didn't see any inflows or outflows during the year, it's quite easy to figure out the economics involved. You got paid US$184,000 for showing up to work this year, and you got a bonus of US$370,000 for doing a good job, a total compensation of over US$550,000. If you think that sounds like a good pay, you should try managing a hundred million, rather than just ten.

■ 2003

Going into our second year, we're already riding high. We had a great start of our new managed futures fund and 2002 turned out to be a brilliant time to start. Don't get cocky, kid. There's a significant element of luck in starting timing of any strategy. In this particular case, I chose to start the year-by-year review chapter in 2002 just to get a full twenty years. In the business, most get nervous after a great year, since they're so often followed by a bad year. There's no statistical significance to that statement of course, but that's "what if" often feels like.

Our portfolio composition looks a little different at the start of 2003. Most notably, we have twice the number of positions in the portfolio (Table 6.5). And if you recall, with each position approximately the same risk size, that means we have doubled the amount of risk from last year. We still have a large number of commodities, about half of the portfolio risk exposure. We're now long across the rates curve, with a tiny, mixed exposure in equities (Table 6.6, Figure 6.7). Those of you who have been around the markets a while already know that 2003 is when we started seeing the stock markets returning after the dot.com crash, and the return of the bull market trends, but at the start of the year, there wasn't any sign of that just yet.

Figure 6.8 shows the performance of our little strategy over the course of 2003, along with the long and short contribution to that performance, and a comparison with MSCI World Total Return Index. There's more than one thing that stands out here. Whether you first notice that the strategy ended

TABLE 6.5	Initial portfolio 2003		
Market	**Direction**		**Sector**
Sugar No. 11	Long		Agriculture
Cotton No. 2	Long		Agriculture
Lean Hogs	Long		Agriculture
KC HRW Wheat	Short		Agriculture
Soybean	Long		Agriculture
Live Cattle	Long		Agriculture
Corn	Short		Agriculture
Coffee C	Long		Agriculture
Feeder Cattle	Long		Agriculture
White Sugar	Long		Agriculture
Lumber	Short		Agriculture
Soybean Oil	Long		Agriculture
Robusta Coffee	Long		Agriculture
Australian Dollar	Long		Currencies
US Dollar Index	Short		Currencies
Canadian Dollar	Long		Currencies
Swiss Franc	Long		Currencies
British Pound	Long		Currencies
Euro FX	Long		Currencies
DAX	Short		Equities
Nikkei 225 Dollar	Short		Equities
E-mini Nasdaq-100	Long		Equities
NY Harbor ULSD	Long		Non-Agriculture
Brent	Long		Non-Agriculture
Crude Oil – Light Sweet	Long		Non-Agriculture
Gold	Long		Non-Agriculture
Platinum	Long		Non-Agriculture
Palladium	Short		Non-Agriculture
Gas Oil	Long		Non-Agriculture
Silver	Long		Non-Agriculture
2-Year U.S. T-Note	Long		Rates
Euribor	Long		Rates
10-Year Govt. of Canada Bond	Long		Rates
Euro-Bund	Long		Rates
Euro-Bobl	Long		Rates
Eurodollar	Long		Rates

(Continued)

TABLE 6.5	(Continued)	
Market	**Direction**	**Sector**
Euro-Schatz	Long	Rates
Long Gilt	Long	Rates
10-Year U.S. T-Note	Long	Rates
5-Year U.S. T-Note	Long	Rates

TABLE 6.6 Initial sector allocation 2003

	Long	**Short**	**Total**
Agriculture	10	3	13
Rates	10	0	10
Non-Agriculture	7	1	8
Equities	1	2	3
Currencies	5	1	6
Total	33	7	40

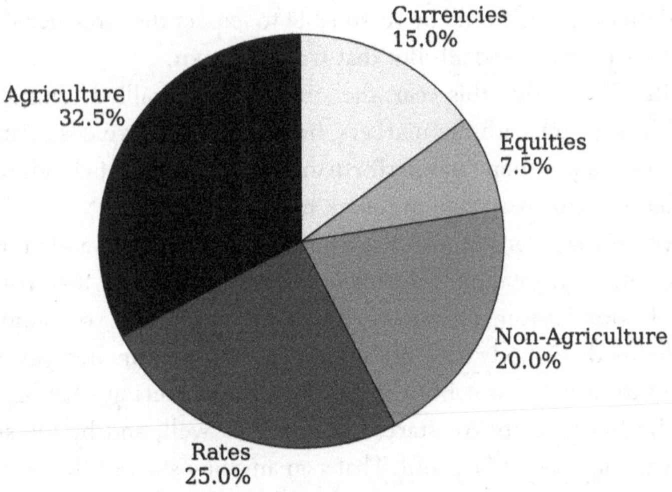

FIGURE 6.7 Sector allocation 2003.

up with another impressive profit, or that the strategy took a very worrying hit in the first part of the year, probably says a lot about your experience in

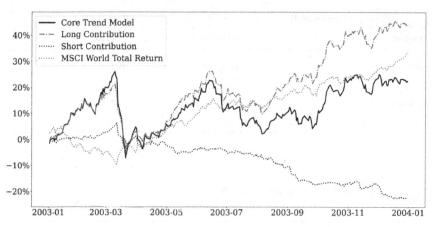

FIGURE 6.8 Strategy performance 2003.

the market. While a novice trader might focus on the performance, the experienced trader would wonder about that drop.

The strategy did end up quite well, with trading gains before costs nearly as high as last year. If you're new to the managed futures space, or the hedge fund space for that matter, you're in for an interesting surprise at the end of this year. Last year you were the big hero, returning nearly 25% while the stock markets were tanking. This year, you finish at about the same performance numbers, and it would be reasonable to expect the same hero's treatment, victory parades, and all. But that won't happen.

The difference is that this year, the stock markets rallied. Our strategy more or less kept up with the markets, but that was before cost. After you get paid your management and performance fees, you'll be behind. You will have yielded less this year than the stock markets.

Why would that matter? You don't buy and hold stocks, and you never claimed to return more money during bull markets. None of that matters in reality, and your customers may very well be upset that you supposedly underperformed. Nobody said life is supposed to be fair. But you do get paid, and quite well to boot. But I'm sure you're wondering what happened with that big scary drop. We started the year so well, and by the start of March we already had 30% profit. That's an amazing start of the year. After such an extreme start, most of us start making the mistake of calculating what the year would end like if we continue on that path, making 30% a quarter and what that would mean for your performance fees. We've all been there.

Then the real action starts, and not in a good way. From our +30% on the year in March, we find ourselves dropping fast until we hit a low of −5% a month later (Figures 6.9 and 6.10). This doesn't look so big in the graph perhaps, but when it happens, it feels like the end. At the numbers you held in March, you would have had another half a million dollars payday to look forward to. Then in a matter of weeks, that's all gone. This is what really messes with your head when you manage money.

It shouldn't be surprising that the main losses came from the long side, given that we've already seen in Figure 6.9 that the long side is the only

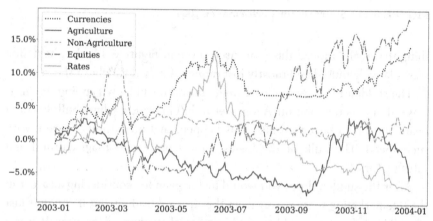

FIGURE 6.9 Sector performance 2003.

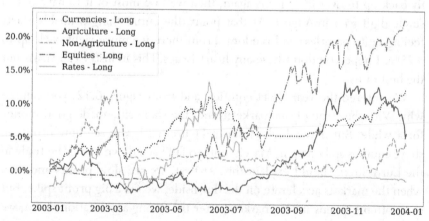

FIGURE 6.10 Long sector performance 2003.

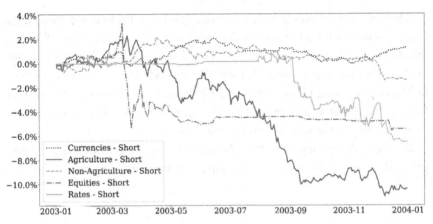

FIGURE 6.11 Short sector performance 2003.

thing that really moved this year. As you see in Figure 6.11, the short side was relatively muted and mostly lost money slowly throughout the year.

The sudden losses were not a single position suddenly gapping down, it was rather a sector rotation. A long-term shift in trends, where bulls become bears and bears become bulls. This happens at times, though rarely with such speed. The bulk of the losses came from the non-agricultural and rates sectors.

After the sudden drop, you would be forgiven for considering a career in the telemarketing sector, away from the stress of trading. But if you quit just after that drop, you would miss the drama of the rest of the year. It was a wild ride, that's for sure. In the next few months, we move slowly but steadily back up to over 20% gains again, then we lose most of it to have only a single-digit gain in August. At that point, the entire thing probably starts feeling quite pointless and random. From there we move right back up to +25%. I hope you don't have any heart issues. This industry can stress out the best of us.

We entered the year short equities, and from Figure 6.12, you can see why. With the strong bear market trend, the short side made good money for a while. But if you look closer at Figure 6.12, you see how profits in short equities spiked up in March, only to fall back down hard. The trade in the Euro Stoxx should explain this. At first, we see slow profits and then when the markets accelerate on the downside, we see a big profit spike. But as so often happens in the markets, after the strong acceleration down, we get an even strong rebound. As the markets turn up in late February, we get

FIGURE 6.12 Short trade in the Euro Stoxx.

hit on short equities across the board until stops are hit, and we eventually go long later in the year.

After this rollercoaster ride of a year, we finally ended up with money on the table. In this case, all the money came from the long side while the shorts showed nothing but losses (Tables 6.7 and 6.8). We gained 44% on the longs, where half of that came from riding the brand new equity rally. The short side lost 22% all in all, spread out on agriculture, equities and rates. All in all, a nice ending to a pretty horrible year.

TABLE 6.7 Sector results 2003

	Currencies	Agriculture	Non-Agriculture	Equities	Rates	All sectors
Long	12.5	5.9	4.1	22.7	−1.2	44.0
Short	1.4	−10.4	−1.4	−5.5	−6.5	−22.4
Total	14.2	−5.1	2.6	18.1	−7.3	22.5

TABLE 6.8 Results 2003

	US$	Percentage
Starting NAV	12,095,344	120.95
Trading result	2,719,802	22.50
Interest income	144,105	1.20
Management fee	218,755	1.80
Performance fee	396,773	3.30
Net result	2,248,379	18.60
Ending NAV	14,343,723	143.40

In retrospect, just looking at the results in Table 6.8, this looks like another success year. And sure, you got paid quite well and probably had some well-deserved champagne at the end of the year, but it was not an easy year. But, of course, even though you probably didn't sleep much during the first half of the year, things worked out in the end. You scored another victory, cashed in on over US$600,000 for yourself and your investors made two and a quarter million dollars net profits. From when they first entrusted you with managing US$10 million, they now have nearly an additional five million in their pockets.

To give you a sense of the actual money growth, I have assumed in this chapter that there are no money flows in or out of your new fund. No new investments coming in and no redemptions going out. You started out with U$10 million, as mentioned earlier, and this is the money that you have to manage. After two years, over a million of this pot has become yours, while the pot after those fees has grown to close to US$15 million. Not too bad so far.

■ 2004

So far it looks like we had amazing luck with the launch of our fund. The first two years were stressful but returned substantial money, both for the investors and for you as a manager of their assets. We start out our third year with a heavy exposure to equities, which shouldn't be a surprise to anyone knowing their market history. After the markets turned for the upside in 2003, trend followers built up a significant long exposure. We're now also heavily into long metals and energies, but there's not much rates positions in the portfolio.

The recovery rally in the stock markets is still ongoing and we should be well positioned to take advantage of further advances. The long equity index positions we have on are spread across all major geographical regions, including Europe and Asia (Tables 6.9 and 6.10, and Figure 6.13). This bull market wasn't limited to the United States and our investment universe is diversified to cover all major markets.

This year was yet another difficult experience. In Chapter 5, you saw long-term graphs of the performance of our trend-following strategy over decades. It looks so easy, like such a nice, smooth ride to victory. That's what long-term charts do for you; obscure the shorter-term and the real-life experience. On such a long scale, you can barely see the little wiggles that were 2004.

TABLE 6.9 Initial portfolio 2004

Market	Direction	Sector
Coffee	Short	Agriculture
Soybean Meal	Long	Agriculture
Soybean Oil	Long	Agriculture
Canola	Long	Agriculture
Soybean	Long	Agriculture
Sugar No. 11	Short	Agriculture
Corn	Long	Agriculture
KC HRW Wheat	Long	Agriculture
Lean Hogs	Short	Agriculture
Canadian Dollar	Long	Currencies
Australian Dollar	Long	Currencies
Euro FX	Long	Currencies
Swiss Franc	Long	Currencies
British Pound	Long	Currencies
Japanese Yen	Long	Currencies
US Dollar Index	Short	Currencies
CAC 40	Long	Equities
DAX	Long	Equities
FTSE 100	Long	Equities
EURO STOXX 50	Long	Equities
HS China E	Long	Equities
E-mini Nasdaq-100	Long	Equities
E-mini Russell 2000	Long	Equities
S&P/TSX 60 Index	Long	Equities
E-mini S&P MidCap 400	Long	Equities
Hang Seng Index	Long	Equities
E-mini Dow	Long	Equities
E-mini S&P 500	Long	Equities
Henry Hub Natural Gas	Long	Non-Agriculture
Gas Oil	Long	Non-Agriculture
Crude Oil – Light Sweet	Long	Non-Agriculture
NY Harbor ULSD	Long	Non-Agriculture
Gold	Long	Non-Agriculture
Brent	Long	Non-Agriculture
Copper	Long	Non-Agriculture
Platinum	Long	Non-Agriculture
10-Year Govt. of Canada Bond	Long	Rates
U.S. T-Bond	Long	Rates

TABLE 6.10	Initial sector allocation 2004		
	Long	Short	Total
Agriculture	6	3	9
Non-Agriculture	8	0	8
Currencies	6	1	7
Equities	12	0	12
Rates	2	0	2
Total	34	4	38

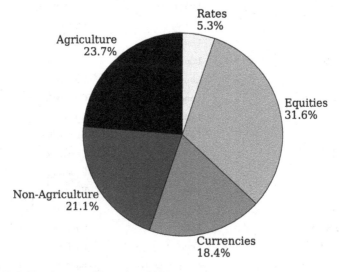

FIGURE 6.13 Sector allocation 2004.

Our third year started well enough, with a sudden gain of 15% by mid-February. This is when you would start doing the really unhelpful maths on how much money you would make if you continue like that the whole year, and you'll probably start picking out your BWM and your Rolex. But the markets are rarely that cooperative and by the end of February, you lost all your profits in just a matter of days.

After that emotional ride, you suddenly see profits once more, and fast. From being back at the zero line, we see the gains take off like a rocket ship, and after only brief pauses we reach a high of nearly +30% on the year by April. Thirty per cent in four months. If we compound at that rate, we'll end up at 120% on the year, and get paid millions in performance fees. It looks like yet another success year!

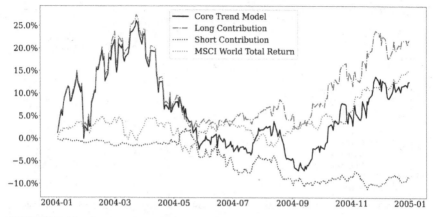

FIGURE 6.14 Strategy performance 2004.

That's, of course, the time that the markets decide to teach you another lesson in humility, because, of course, it will drop. From having this amazing near 30% profit, we see loss after loss, week after week, month after month, and half a year later, we have a negative performance of −5% (Figure 6.14). What you will learn at that point is that your investors won't call and congratulate you on the +30% in April, but they will call you and demand answers when you're at −5%. Worst case, they will lose faith in you and start withdrawing their money.

Lucky for you, the fortunes turn again by September and you slowly move up for the rest of the year, finishing at +16%. Yes, another profitable year, but at a terrible cost of drawdowns and volatility. It's a respectable double digit return, but a prudent investor would question if this kind of volatility would not warrant a higher return.

Often when we see fast gains or losses, it's driven by a single sector or at times two sectors together. The move early this year, the one that brought us up to nearly +15%, was a joint operation across sectors. We saw smaller gains on all sectors and it added up nicely. More interestingly is what happened during that powerful phase that took us from the zero line up to nearly +30% in a short period of time. Starting from March, we saw primarily two sectors take off, at about the same time. One was the agricultural complex, which showed fast gains and managed to hold onto them for the entire year. The other was rates, which didn't fare as well in the long run. The rates sector provided strong returns up until April,

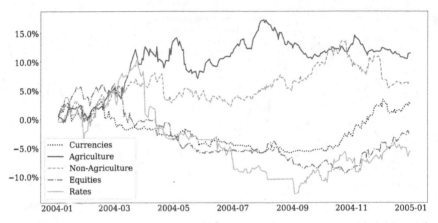

FIGURE 6.15 Sector performance 2004.

only to keep losing for the rest of the year and end up deep in the red (Figure 6.15).

As often is the case, the action this year was mostly on the long side (Figure 6.16). In fact, we had very few short positions on until about mid-year, and we gained quite well on the short side all in all, but we ended up losing money on the shorts (Figure 6.17). This happens more often than not, and the short side can be seen a sort of insurance policy. It ends up costing money most of the time, but once in a while it pays out really well.

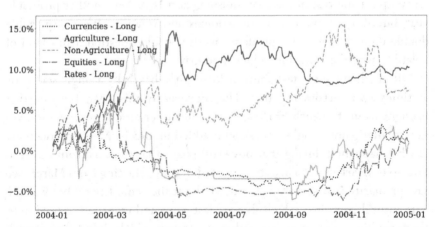

FIGURE 6.16 Long sector performance 2004.

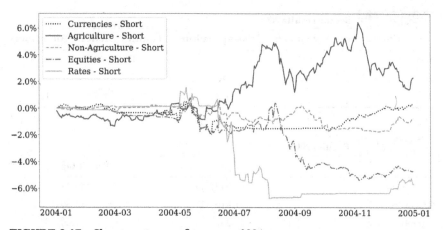

FIGURE 6.17   Short sector performance 2004.

The Long Gilt chart in Figure 6.18 is a good example of the weakness of our overall approach, and the risk that we face with every trade we enter. In this case, the price shot up in early March and our trend model entered a new long position just at the highs of March. From there, the price fell down, first a little bit, not enough to trigger stops. Then a sudden large move down, we took a painful loss. This head-fake move in the rates sector is clearly visible in the sector charts, where the long rates sector took a double digit hit during the same time.

FIGURE 6.18   Costly trade in the Gilt.

TABLE 6.11	Sector results 2004					
	Currencies	Agriculture	Non-Agriculture	Equities	Rates	All sectors
Long	2.4	10.2	7.3	1.1	0.9	21.8
Short	0.2	2.3	−0.8	−4.7	−5.7	−8.7
Total	2.7	11.6	6.4	−2.5	−5.6	12.6

TABLE 6.12	Results 2004	
	US$	Percentage
Starting NAV	14,343,723	143.44
Trading result	1,810,357	12.60
Interest income	232,280	1.60
Management fee	238,525	1.70
Performance fee	270,617	1.90
Net result	1,533,495	10.70
Ending NAV	15,877,218	158.80

At the end of this year the gross trading gains were a little over 12% (Tables 6.11 and 6.12). Taken out of context, that sounds just fine. That's a good return on a trading portfolio, but given what a volatile and risky ride we had, it can hardly be called a success. Your investors will not tell you how happy they are to have 11% more money after paying fees. They would prefer to have the 30% more money that they saw in April.

As for our little trading business, we end up making a little money again of course. Around US$240,000 in management fees and nearly US$300,000 in performance fees. Compounding is a nice effect, not only for investors. We had lower profits than earlier years, but a larger asset base due to that early success, and the fees increase proportionally. Three years after we start out, the initial investor money has grown from US$10 million to almost US$16 million.

■ 2005

It's 2005 and the bear market of 2000 to 2003 is long forgotten. Happy days are back, Wall Street is booming and risk is definitely on again. Our trading business has made decent money over the past three years, even if we really had to work for it. So far, this probably feels very little like what you may have expected from that long-term performance illustration in Figure 4.10, but at least we have been making money, both for ourselves and for our investors.

The initial portfolio in January 2005 is heavy long equity indices, with mixed agricultural commodities exposure, and a significant long rates exposure (Tables 6.13 and 6.14, and Figure 6.19).

TABLE 6.13	Initial portfolio 2005	
Market	**Direction**	**Sector**
Lean Hogs	Long	Agriculture
Class III Milk	Long	Agriculture
Soybean	Short	Agriculture
Soybean Oil	Short	Agriculture
Corn	Short	Agriculture
Canola	Short	Agriculture
Cotton No. 2	Short	Agriculture
Coffee C	Long	Agriculture
Feeder Cattle	Short	Agriculture
KC HRW Wheat	Short	Agriculture
British Pound	Long	Currencies
US Dollar Index	Short	Currencies
Canadian Dollar	Long	Currencies
Australian Dollar	Long	Currencies
Euro FX	Long	Currencies
FTSE 100	Long	Equities
EURO STOXX 50	Long	Equities
S&P/TSX 60 Index	Long	Equities
E-mini Nasdaq-100	Long	Equities
E-mini Dow	Long	Equities
E-mini S&P MidCap 400	Long	Equities
DAX	Long	Equities
E-mini Russell 2000	Long	Equities
HS China E	Long	Equities
Nikkei 225 Dollar	Long	Equities
CBOE Volatility Index	Short	Equities
E-mini S&P 500	Long	Equities
Henry Hub Natural Gas	Short	Non-Agriculture

(Continued)

TABLE 6.13	(Continued)	
Market	**Direction**	**Sector**
Palladium	Short	Non-Agriculture
Gold	Long	Non-Agriculture
Copper	Long	Non-Agriculture
Euribor	Long	Rates
Euro-Bobl	Long	Rates
Long Gilt	Long	Rates
Euro-Schatz	Long	Rates
Euro-Bund	Long	Rates
10-Year Govt. of Canada Bond	Long	Rates
U.S. T-Bond	Long	Rates
Eurodollar	Short	Rates

TABLE 6.14	Initial sector allocation 2005		
	Long	**Short**	**Total**
Rates	7	1	8
Agriculture	3	7	10
Equities	11	1	12
Non-Agriculture	2	2	4
Currencies	4	1	5
Total	27	12	39

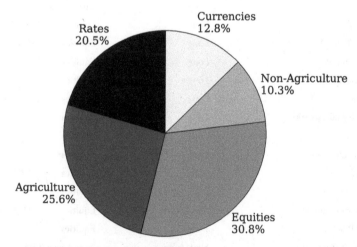

FIGURE 6.19 Sector allocation 2005.

At the end of 2004, we had finally recovered from what looked like a disaster of a year, and we just had a few months of positive performance. This warm and fuzzy feeling won't last for long. In the very first week of 2005, we take a hit. Six per cent lost in a single week can ruin anyone's weekend. This will be a bumpy ride, that's for sure. After that disastrous week, we spend a few months in the −6% to −2% range, in fast and choppy moves. Then, in April, just when we think we have had a really bad year, the true trouble starts. We start losing, and we start losing fast. Did you think this would be all roses and sunshine? Welcome to finance.

After a fast drop, we are down 12% on the year, and after a brief pause we free-fall down to nearly −20% (Figure 6.20). That's a fifth of the assets. Congratulations, you just lost over US$ 3 million! How does that feel? It's half-way through our fourth year of operations, and the first meaningful loss just reared its ugly head. It may very well be mostly other people's money, but that first time you find yourself responsible for losing millions of dollars, it will hit you hard. What could you do with US$ 3 million? That money you just burnt could have been life-changing for almost anyone on the planet, and you've just blown it on your irresponsible speculation. I hope you didn't plan on sleeping much during the summer of 2005.

In late October we are no better off and you probably dread the sound of the phone ringing. Nobody likes to talk to investors after having just lost them substantial amounts of money, but it needs to be done nonetheless. From the darkest hour of the autumn, we finally start to recover somewhat. Starting off at nearly −20%, we see some gains for the final

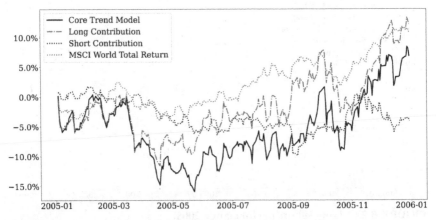

FIGURE 6.20 Strategy performance 2005.

months of the year and even manage to move into positive territory, in the single digits.

Not all sectors contributed to the horrible performance of 2005, but none of them were stellar in any way. The worst offender this year was the agricultural sector, which just kept on falling practically throughout the year. While this was the big negative factor, most other sectors contributed at least in part to the declines (Figures 6.21–6.23). The metals and energies were losing money until late summer, at which point they started to recover, and only the rates sector remained positive for the duration of the year, which ultimately saved us from utter disaster.

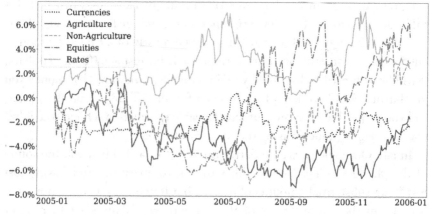

FIGURE 6.21   Sector performance 2005.

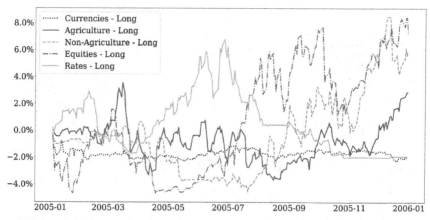

FIGURE 6.22   Long sector performance 2005.

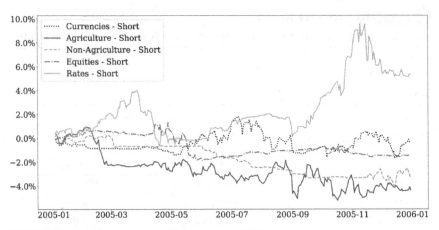

FIGURE 6.23 Short sector performance 2005.

There was a very welcome bull market happening in the global stock markets, from around mid-year, and what you see in the Nikkei in Figure 6.24 is an illustration of this. From a somewhat struggling profile, the market moves up from the lows of May and the trend model enters soon after. This trend continued throughout the year and only ended at the start of 2006. A strong bull market lasting half a year can make a whole lot of difference to a year's performance, and that's just what happened in 2005.

At the end of another Pyrrhic victory, we close the year with trading gains of a little shy of 7%. For the entire year, we have been behind the

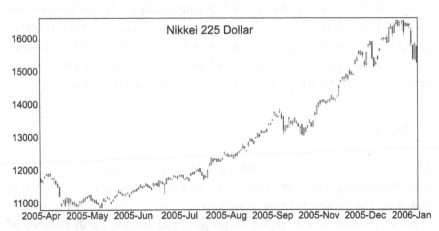

FIGURE 6.24 Bull trend in the Nikkei.

TABLE 6.15 Sector results 2005

	Currencies	Agriculture	Non-Agriculture	Equities	Rates	All sectors
Long	−1.9	2.9	5.9	7.2	−1.9	12.1
Short	−0.3	−4.4	−3.4	−1.4	5.4	−4.1
Total	−2.2	−1.6	2.6	5.1	3.0	6.9

TABLE 6.16 Results 2005

	US$	Percentage
Starting NAV	15,877,218	158.77
Trading result	1,093,525	6.90
Interest income	377,066	2.40
Management fee	250,584	1.60
Performance fee	183,001	1.20
Net result	1,037,006	6.50
Ending NAV	16,914,224	169.10

equity markets and we saw deep drawdowns. A year like this will shake the confidence of your investors and it certainly won't make it easy to raise additional investments for your little trading business. We really dodged the bullet here, with that end of year rally that at least put us back in black for the year again (Tables 6.15 and 6.16).

After this nightmare of a year, you can expect quite a few worried or even angry investors. They probably won't get much happier about the fact that you still make a quarter of a million in management fees and US$180,000 in performance fee. The interest on excess capital was a nice addition this year, and as it happens, it pays for nearly all our management and performance fees, letting us close the year at a net profit to investors of 6.5%.

■ 2006

As you've seen to this point, making money can be a very painful experience. We had four profitable years in a row, but it probably won't really feel that way. The reason for this year-by-year chapter should now hopefully become quite clear. I'm trying to prepare you for the harsh realities of money management, and show you just how difficult it can be to trade even a profitable trading model. You've made good money to this point, and your investors saw profits year after year. But don't expect happy investors, certainly not after last year. You can also expect your own confidence in what you're doing to be in doubt. At this point, you probably start wondering if you're just a gambler, if you just had some random luck. Can't we just get a really nice and smooth profitable year, just once? Let's see what 2006 can bring.

We go into 2006 heavily long stocks with a massive 29% risk exposure, and we're quite heavily loaded with commodities as well (Table 6.17, Figure 6.25). Quite a risky portfolio, but trend following is all about taking risk when risk is good. For all the diversification potential, when the trends are really on, these kinds of trading models tend to build concentrated exposure to a single or a few themes and right now the bet is on a continued bull market (Table 6.18).

TABLE 6.17 Initial portfolio 2006

Market	Direction	Sector
Sugar No. 11	Long	Agriculture
Lean Hogs	Long	Agriculture
White Sugar	Long	Agriculture
Corn	Short	Agriculture
Live Cattle	Long	Agriculture
Lumber	Long	Agriculture
Feeder Cattle	Long	Agriculture
Canola	Short	Agriculture
Soybean Oil	Short	Agriculture
Swiss Franc	Short	Currencies
Australian Dollar	Short	Currencies
US Dollar Index	Long	Currencies
British Pound	Short	Currencies
Euro FX	Short	Currencies
Japanese Yen	Short	Currencies
Canadian Dollar	Long	Currencies
DAX	Long	Equities
EURO STOXX 50	Long	Equities
E-mini Nasdaq-100	Long	Equities
E-mini Dow	Long	Equities
E-mini S&P MidCap 400	Long	Equities

(Continued)

TABLE 6.17 (Continued)

Market	Direction	Sector
Nikkei 225 Dollar	Long	Equities
S&P/TSX 60 Index	Long	Equities
FTSE 100	Long	Equities
CBOE Volatility Index	Short	Equities
E-mini S&P 500	Long	Equities
CAC 40	Long	Equities
Crude Oil – Light Sweet	Short	Non-Agriculture
Platinum	Long	Non-Agriculture
NY Harbor ULSD	Short	Non-Agriculture
Gas Oil	Short	Non-Agriculture
Silver	Long	Non-Agriculture
Copper	Long	Non-Agriculture
Gold	Long	Non-Agriculture
Palladium	Long	Non-Agriculture
Brent	Short	Non-Agriculture
Euribor	Short	Rates
Eurodollar	Short	Rates

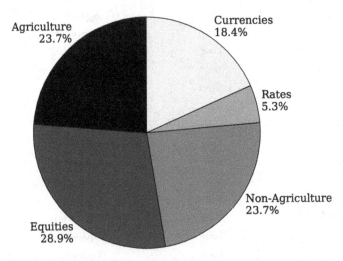

FIGURE 6.25 Sector allocation 2006.

We leave the dreaded zero line right away at the start of January and we never see it again for the remainder of the year. That's the good part. Even better, we move up into double digit gains in February and hit 20% already

TABLE 6.18   Initial sector allocation 2006

	Long	Short	Total
Agriculture	6	3	9
Equities	10	1	11
Non-Agriculture	5	4	9
Rates	0	2	2
Currencies	2	5	7
Total	23	15	38

in April. If you had doubts about what you do for a living a few months ago, they're probably long gone after seeing the profits shoot up to 30 then to 40 and 50 and an amazing 60% return. A 60% return!! On a starting year portfolio worth US$17 million. Consider that for a moment. You just created US$10 million in less than half a year. That's a one followed by seven zeros.

But I'm sure by now you've come to realize that the Gods of Trading have a mean sense of humour and that nothing lasts forever. Wouldn't it have been nice if you simply took the money off the table in late May and sat back for the rest of the year? Sure, but you have no way of knowing when these peaks, or bottoms, occur. The losses from that May peak were swift, a large part of the gains gone by July before the strategy returns stabilized (Figure 6.26). It's all part of the game and now, in your fifth year in the market, you should be getting used to it. If anything, this business tends to turn you into a cynic and a pessimist, even if you end up successful.

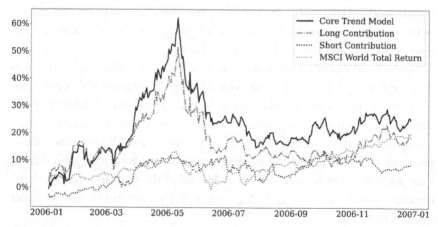

FIGURE 6.26   Strategy performance 2006.

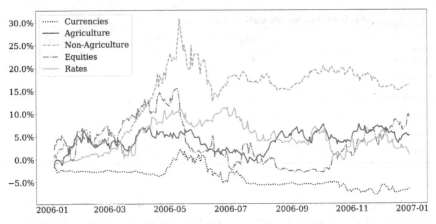

FIGURE 6.27 Sector performance 2006.

Remember how great it felt to gain US$10 million? Now imagine how it feels to lose US$6 million. Some may think that this isn't a loss, it's merely giving up some excess profits. But, no, that's not how finance works. You don't pick arbitrary points to calculate profits and losses. At one point, this portfolio had gained US$10 million and was worth US$27 million, and that was then the market-to-market value (Figure 6.27). That's the basis of calculating your loss. Never fall into the amateur trap of using gambling terminology such as "playing with the bank's money". This loss was very real.

The rocket ride up to +60% was primarily fuelled by the long non-agricultural sector, which was responsible for about half of this gain all by itself (Figure 6.28). The bet on the continued stock market bull trend paid off as well, up until the stock markets briefly turned down in June (Figure 6.29). Having concentrated bets like this can pay off greatly as long as the trends continue the way they were going, but they can also rack up losses very fast, and that's what happened here.

Figure 6.30 shows two distinct phases of the market this year, and in this case we managed to profit from both. The market started off rather sideways, but as the prices started falling in May, the trend model entered on the short side. Much of these profits were given up when the markets did a V-shaped turn in July and headed up, but some were still kept when those positions were exited. As the markets powered on, we soon entered fresh long positions, which were still on at the end of the year. In other markets, the short positions ended up losing money and net we lost money on short equities this year.

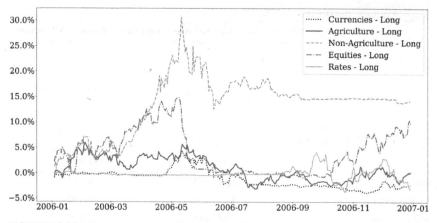

FIGURE 6.28 Long sector performance 2006.

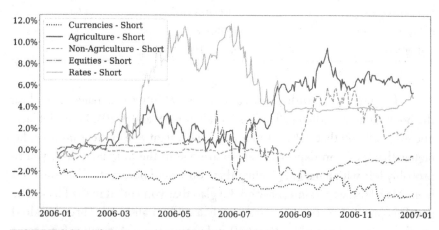

FIGURE 6.29 Short sector performance 2006.

FIGURE 6.30 Nasdaq V-shape of 2006.

TABLE 6.19 Sector results 2006

	Currencies	Agriculture	Non-Agriculture	Equities	Rates	All sectors
Long	−2.4	0.1	14.1	9.7	−3.2	18.4
Short	−4.0	5.4	2.6	−0.5	4.9	8.4
Total	−6.5	5.2	16.2	9.1	1.0	24.9

TABLE 6.20 Results 2006

	US$	Percentage
Starting NAV	16,914,224	169.14
Trading result	4,214,597	24.90
Interest income	649,648	3.80
Management fee	310,742	1.80
Performance fee	683,026	4.00
Net result	3,870,478	22.90
Ending NAV	20,784,702	207.80

At the end of your fifth year as a professional futures manager, you close the books with a trading gain of 25% (Tables 6.19 and 6.20). Don't let anyone ever tell you that 25% is too low. It's a brilliant end-of-year number, far higher than you can expect to see on average in the long run. Still, you're probably left with a nagging feeling that you would have rather had the 60% from May. Hey, easy come, easy go. Be glad that you ended in the black. The payoff is pretty OK this year too, nearly a million all in all. Three hundred on management fee and another 680 and change on performance fee. Don't do the maths of how much money you would have made if you closed at +60%. It won't help you sleep.

■ 2007

After six years, you're probably staring to see a pattern. Tough years, sharp gains, sharp losses but ending up with profits and getting paid well. You probably start getting a bit jaded and you're able to shake off the intra-year volatility and trust in the long-term plan. Trust in the plan, have faith, and keep on swimming. Well, let's see if you're able to keep the faith after this year. The initial US$10 million have now doubled and we start off trading

US$21 million. This is investor money, after having paid you quite a bit in fees over these years. And how much have you been paid in the first five years? All in all, about US$3.5 million have ended up in your own pocket.

If you still wonder why you would want to trade other people's money rather than your own, there's your answer. You could have traded your own money, taking all the risk and all the upside, but this way you made millions while taking very little risk, all while also making a great return for your investors. Everyone's happy.

Tables 6.21 and 6.22 show the initial allocation for 2007, and, as you see, long equities is the main theme. We're fairly balanced on most other sectors except for the non-agricultural commodities, where we are short.

TABLE 6.21	Initial portfolio 2007	
Market	**Direction**	**Sector**
Sugar No. 11	Short	Agriculture
Lean Hogs	Short	Agriculture
Soybean Oil	Long	Agriculture
Soybean	Long	Agriculture
Canola	Long	Agriculture
Cocoa	Long	Agriculture
Live Cattle	Short	Agriculture
Class III Milk	Long	Agriculture
Corn	Long	Agriculture
Lumber	Short	Agriculture
Feeder Cattle	Short	Agriculture
Coffee C	Long	Agriculture
Australian Dollar	Long	Currencies
Japanese Yen	Short	Currencies
Canadian Dollar	Short	Currencies
US Dollar Index	Short	Currencies
New Zealand Dollar	Long	Currencies
Hang Seng Index	Long	Equities
HS China E	Long	Equities
CBOE Volatility Index	Short	Equities
CAC 40	Long	Equities
Nikkei 225 Dollar	Long	Equities
DAX	Long	Equities
S&P/TSX 60 Index	Long	Equities

(Continued)

TABLE 6.21   (Continued)

Market	Direction	Sector
E-mini Dow	Long	Equities
E-mini Nasdaq-100	Long	Equities
E-mini S&P 500	Long	Equities
EURO STOXX 50	Long	Equities
E-mini S&P MidCap 400	Long	Equities
E-mini Russell 2000	Long	Equities
Gas Oil	Short	Non-Agriculture
Silver	Long	Non-Agriculture
Henry Hub Natural Gas	Short	Non-Agriculture
NY Harbor ULSD	Short	Non-Agriculture
Crude Oil – Light Sweet	Short	Non-Agriculture
Brent	Short	Non-Agriculture
Copper	Short	Non-Agriculture
Long Gilt	Short	Rates
Euro-Schatz	Short	Rates
Euribor	Short	Rates
U.S. T-Bond	Long	Rates
5-Year U.S. T-Note	Long	Rates
10-Year U.S. T-Note	Long	Rates
10-Year Govt. of Canada Bond	Long	Rates
Eurodollar	Long	Rates
Euro-Bobl	Short	Rates

TABLE 6.22   Initial sector allocation 2007

	Long	Short	Total
Agriculture	7	5	12
Rates	5	4	9
Non-Agriculture	1	6	7
Equities	12	1	13
Currencies	2	3	5
Total	27	19	46

While you were probably prepared for a choppy year, as we've seen before, 2007 is the most horrific year so far on our trading journey. It starts well enough with a gain of about 6% by February, but then we see a shocking drop from that level all the way down to −12% in a matter of days (Figures 6.31 and 6.32). Such swift losses are extremely painful and they can quickly shake the confidence of your investors. You'll have some explaining to do.

This this substantial loss isn't the worst thing that'll happen to you this year. From that bottom in March, we move slowly but steadily and even manage to not only climb above zero, but all the way up to over 10% gain on

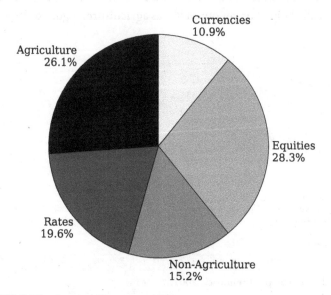

FIGURE 6.31 Sector allocation 2007.

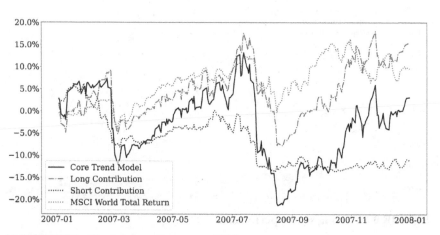

FIGURE 6.32 Strategy performance 2007.

the year. That's when it happens. From having trading gains of over US$2 million, we step on land mine after land mine, and not only do we lose the US$2 million but an additional four! Yes, in a single month, you're responsible for losing US$6 million! That stuff hurts. In an oddly familiar routine, the strategy gains again by the third quarter, and you very barely manage to recover the worst losses and end the year at a measly +3%. Another gain, but at what price? You saw very high volatility and a drawdown of 30%, and all you have to show for it is 3% (Figures 6.33–6.35).

When we found ourselves in that scary 20% hole in August, one of the sectors that really helped us get out of it was agriculture. Figure 6.36 showed

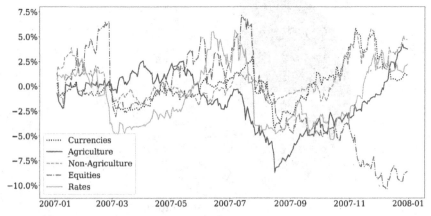

FIGURE 6.33   **Sector performance 2007.**

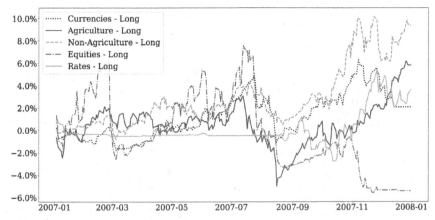

FIGURE 6.34   **Long sector performance 2007.**

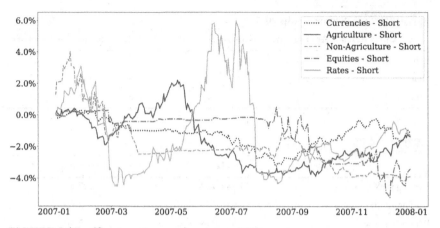

FIGURE 6.35 Short sector performance 2007.

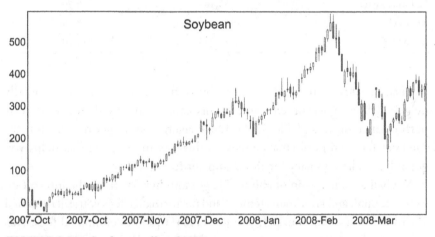

FIGURE 6.36 Soybean rally of 2007.

one of several positions which greatly helped in our dire situation. We saw a solid bull market trend, taking off in October and powering on fall the way into February of 2008.

Once again, we see that the gains were on the long side of the portfolio and the losses on the short side (Table 6.23). Why do we even bother trading the short side? Why don't we just tweak the model and remove the shorts all together? Those are questions which not only you, but also your investors, will start asking. While I have seen successful trend followers who only trade the long side, they are missing some of the really big values in this type of approach. Just trust me for now.

TABLE 6.23 Sector results 2007

	Currencies	Agriculture	Non-Agriculture	Equities	Rates	All sectors
Long	2.1	5.8	9.4	−5.4	3.6	15.5
Short	−1.1	−1.4	−3.9	−3.4	−1.3	−11.2
Total	1.1	3.7	4.7	−8.6	2.2	3.1

TABLE 6.24 Results 2007

	US$	Percentage
Starting NAV	20,784,702	207.85
Trading result	646,307	3.10
Interest income	570,098	2.70
Management fee	315,187	1.50
Performance fee	135,183	0.70
Net result	766,036	3.70
Ending NAV	21,550,738	215.50

Back in 2007, you could still get a bit of free money from your friendly neighbourhood government, and in this case we nearly doubled our tiny performance on this (Table 6.24). Once again, you do get paid both management fees and performance fees on this free money, and that helps you get at least a living salary for this dumpster fire of a year.

We had a trading gain of about 3%, got another 3% from the interest on excess capital, and after management and performance fees you still returned 4% to investors. For yourself, you got US$450,000 in combined fees. This being a trading business, you have probably started building a cost structure around you by now, perhaps with offices and employees, and so it's not like this is just money in the pocket. Still, you're making money and so are your investors, and that's the main thing.

■ 2008

You underperformed the equity markets a few years and now your investors are likely asking you why they should pay you millions of dollars to gamble their money, when they could have simply bought a lost cost passive ETF, tracking the stock markets. You might even start wondering the same thing. If you've been around the markets long enough, you should know that in a strong bull market, stocks are king. But you should also know that it never lasts.

The year of 2008 is arguably the year that truly proved trend following and made this industry balloon from a fringe strategy to a giant half a trillion dollar affair. If this year doesn't mean anything special to you, then you're probably quite young or you're new to finance. Most of us can be pushed to the point of a nervous breakdown simply by hearing this combination of those four cursed digits.

For those of you who have been living under a rock, or failed to watch *The Big Short*, here's a quick recap of why this year was a little different. After the stock market crash of 1929 and the ensuing Great Depression, a pretty important law was imposed which essentially said that banks can't go around taking massive gambles with savers' money, which was the big reason why we had such a severe crash in the first place. By 1999, following substantial lobbying, this law was quietly repealed, allowing banks to operate as giant casinos once again. For nearly a decade there was no world-threatening consequences of this, but by that time the casino mentality had built up a five trillion dollar business of repackaging worthless mortgage loans, risking not only bank money but pretty much everybody's money. Predictably, this situation blew up and blew up good, and practically everybody but the bankers behind the situation lost a lot of money. They got their bonuses as usual, because, of course, they did.

Anyhow, I digress. The first warning shot across the bow this year was when prestigious investment bank Bear Sterns quite suddenly blew up in March of 2008. It was a pretty big deal at the time, but it wasn't until nearly half a year later when the true horror started. Wall Street fixture Lehman Brothers, founded in 1850 and with 26,000 employees, blew up in September, nearly bringing the rest of the financial world down with it in a massive chain reaction. There were a few weeks in autumn of 2008 where it really looked as if any bank could blow up any day. Like watching popcorn in the pot, trying to predict which one will pop next.

I remember spending hours each day trying to analyse which banks were least likely to go bankrupt in the next 24 hours, and moving cash to the safest place overnight. It was a time like no other. It was also the most profitable year ever seen in trend following, but despite that, I hope never again to see a year like it.

Entering this year, you can see that the market action of 2007 has already started to push the portfolio allocation into a bear mode (Tables 6.25 and 6.26, and Figure 6.37). We're already somewhat short equities and have a few long rates positions. It's not a very big exposure yet, but we're seeing a tilt in the bearish direction.

TABLE 6.25	Initial portfolio 2008	
Market	**Direction**	**Sector**
Feeder Cattle	Short	Agriculture
Soybean Meal	Long	Agriculture
Soybean Oil	Long	Agriculture
Class III Milk	Long	Agriculture
Soybean	Long	Agriculture
Robusta Coffee	Long	Agriculture
Sugar No. 11	Long	Agriculture
Canola	Long	Agriculture
KC HRW Wheat	Long	Agriculture
Lean Hogs	Short	Agriculture
Cocoa	Long	Agriculture
Corn	Long	Agriculture
Lumber	Short	Agriculture
Live Cattle	Short	Agriculture
Coffee C	Long	Agriculture
US Dollar Index	Short	Currencies
Nikkei 225 Dollar	Short	Equities
E-mini Dow	Short	Equities
E-mini S&P MidCap 400	Short	Equities
E-mini S&P 500	Short	Equities
E-mini Russell 2000	Short	Equities
RBOB Gasoline	Long	Non-Agriculture
NY Harbor ULSD	Long	Non-Agriculture
Copper	Short	Non-Agriculture
Gas Oil	Long	Non-Agriculture
Crude Oil – Light Sweet	Long	Non-Agriculture
Brent	Long	Non-Agriculture
Platinum	Long	Non-Agriculture
10-Year U.S. T-Note	Long	Rates
Long Gilt	Long	Rates
10-Year Govt. of Canada Bond	Long	Rates
Euribor	Short	Rates
5-Year U.S. T-Note	Long	Rates
Eurodollar	Short	Rates
2-Year U.S. T-Note	Long	Rates

TABLE 6.26	Initial sector allocation 2008		
	Long	Short	Total
Agriculture	11	4	15
Rates	5	2	7
Non-Agriculture	6	1	7
Currencies	0	1	1
Equities	0	5	5
Total	22	13	35

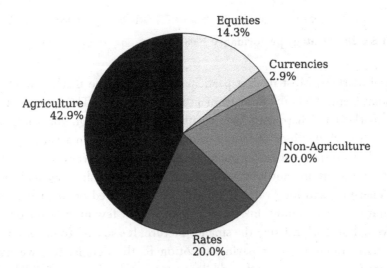

FIGURE 6.37   Sector allocation 2008.

Take a look at the scale of Figure 6.38. That's something we haven't seen before. So once again, we have a nice start of the year, and not too different from what we saw back in 2006. By April, we stand at +60%, and given your previous experiences, perhaps you're now inclined to just take that profit and run. To take the bets down, sit back for the rest of the year and cash in on performance fees on 60%. Well, this year has barely even begun.

From the highs of April, we lose a bit, but remain in the 20–40% gain range for much of the year. It was actually surprisingly calm up until end of summer, despite the canary in the coal mine that was Bear Sterns. Then we get to September and the near nuclear level obliteration of the global

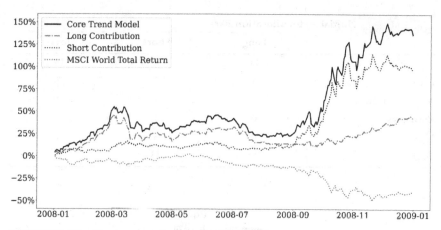

FIGURE 6.38 Strategy performance 2008.

financial markets. Most market participants would agree that we were at one point just mere hours away from a cataclysmic event. This is where the stock markets fell hard and fast, volatility spiked through the roof, oil crashed through the floor and money flowed into the bond markets.

All of these things were in our favour, as trend followers. Going into this absolutely insane autumn, we were short equities, short agriculture, short energies, and long rates (Figure 6.39). We gained on all sides, and we did it fast. You would think this was then an easy few months for trend followers, but that's missing the smaller picture. It's so easy to just see the long-term graphs without paying attention to the details. Yes, we had enormous gains these months, while everyone else in the world kept

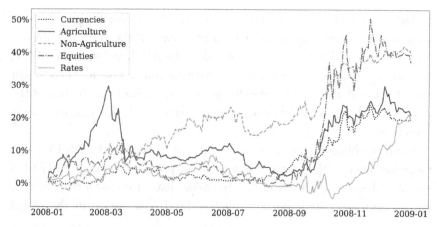

FIGURE 6.39 Sector performance 2008.

losing money. But we had ridiculously volatile returns, and if you didn't adjust your strategy, you might have seen daily moves in the portfolio of 20% or more. In a single day!

How to handle situations like this is a controversial subject. You would clearly have made the most money by simply sticking to your rules and ignoring the noise. But there's good reason why most trend followers didn't do this, why they overrode their models. This situation, this type of market, was something totally new. No amount of planning or backtesting could have prepared you for this, and your models simply weren't made for this market regime. Allowing daily swings of 20% or more is simply irresponsible, and even if luck now puts you on the winning side, as an asset manager you have a fiduciary responsibility towards your investors. They never signed up for this kind of insane ride.

For this book and this chapter, I will assume that you followed the rules nonetheless. But, personally, I would advocate for overriding the model and greatly reducing risk if something like this ever happens again. Better still, have a plan in place for unthinkable events.

Remember how we kept losing on the short side for all this time? Almost every year, we see all the gains on the long side and all the losses on the short. Well, this is the year to show you why you need to trade both. We did see a respectable gain of 40-odd% on the long side (Figure 6.40), but it was the near 100% return on the short side that really made a difference. We made some money on long non-agricultural, mostly gold, early in the year. After that, there were no more bullish trends in that space, and the only thing that made money on the long side late in the year was long rates.

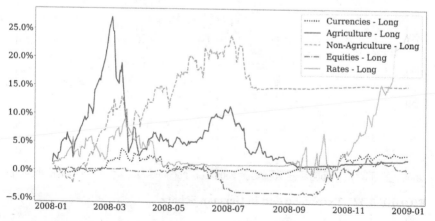

FIGURE 6.40 Long sector performance 2008.

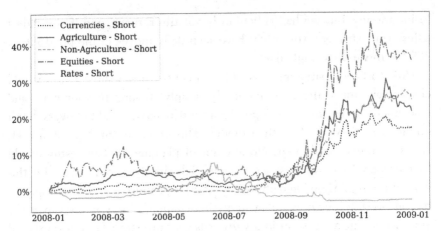

FIGURE 6.41 Short sector performance 2008.

The short side is where the action was, and from September on, we saw an absolute bonanza on the short side (Figure 6.41). The rates sector, quite obviously, was the only one not participating, but all other sectors showed outsized gains for us.

The bond markets were skyrocketing this year, and the German Schatz was no exception (Figure 6.42). This was just one of many highly profitable long trades in the sector, and the trend model went long by mid-year and stayed long. The bulk of the gains were made on that amazing September to February period, where the prices just kept moving up.

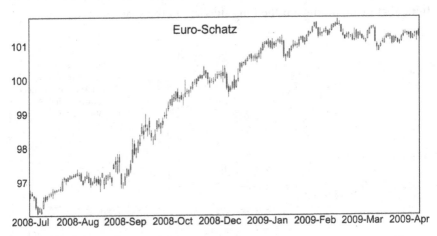

FIGURE 6.42 Extreme trend in German Schatz.

At first glance, that Euro Stoxx chart in Figure 6.43 looks like an easy ride on the short side. It was profitable for sure, but not easy and not as profitable as it may seem. If you take a closer look at the scale, you see this was a period of insane volatility and you run the risk of getting whipsawed on this huge swings. The main money was made on the initial drop, from August to October, and after that it was very tough for trend models to squeeze out any more money.

This is the year where your tiny little trading business is moving into the big leagues (Tables 6.27 and 6.28). From managing less than US$22 million in January, your investors are now closing in on nearly US$50 million with you. The best part of it is that while you had your strongest year ever, most people in the world had their worst year ever. You're now so far ahead of the benchmark index that it's not likely that it will ever catch up. In the inspiring words of the great visionary Lex Luthor, "It is not enough that I win; everyone else must lose."

FIGURE 6.43 Extreme volatility in the Euro Stoxx 50.

TABLE 6.27	Sector results 2008				
Currencies	Agriculture	Non-Agriculture	Equities	Rates	All sectors
2.8	2.1	15.1	0.0	23.0	43.0
16.9	21.6	24.7	35.6	−2.9	95.9
19.5	21.1	39.4	37.2	19.7	136.8

TABLE 6.28 Results 2008

	US$	Percentage
Starting NAV	21,550,738	215.51
Trading result	29,484,929	136.80
Interest income	403,937	1.90
Management fee	756,564	3.50
Performance fee	4,369,845	20.30
Net result	24,762,456	114.90
Ending NAV	46,313,195	463.10

Well, the world almost went under, millions of average people lost all their savings, hundreds of thousands lost their homes, but at least you got paid five million and change and profited nicely from the whole situation.

■ 2009

If your investors were getting worried about your performance and considered pulling their money from you by December of 2007, after 2008, they would trust you to watch their kids over the weekend. I mentioned earlier that you will be compared to the stock markets, whether you like it or not. In a bull market, you won't like it, mostly because you'll probably fail to keep up. That's normal. Few things manage to keep up with stocks in a bull market. But in a bear market, you'll love being compared to the equity index.

After the spectacular bear market of 2008, we're still heavily short stocks of course (Tables 6.29 and 6.30, and Figure 6.44). It takes time to turn that ship around. We're also very much long rates, and that's also a bear market position. The bear market continued into the first part of 2009 and we were well positioned for it. By March, the stock markets are down over 20%, while we have a gain of 10%. Even as the markets recover from there, we handle it quite well and we only lost what we gained during the declines.

For much of the year, we continued in the plus or minus 5–10% range, and it was really quite uneventful until the second half of the year. If you look closely at Figure 6.45, you can see clearly how our exposure turned from mainly short equities to mainly long equities. You won't need to do any maths to notice how the correlation turns from negative to positive, and

| TABLE 6.29 | Initial portfolio 2009 |

Market	Direction	Sector
Sugar No. 11	Short	Agriculture
Canola	Short	Agriculture
Robusta Coffee	Short	Agriculture
Class III Milk	Short	Agriculture
Lean Hogs	Short	Agriculture
Live Cattle	Short	Agriculture
Corn	Short	Agriculture
Soybean Oil	Short	Agriculture
Feeder Cattle	Short	Agriculture
Lumber	Short	Agriculture
Coffee C	Short	Agriculture
White Sugar	Short	Agriculture
Cotton No. 2	Short	Agriculture
British Pound	Short	Currencies
Japanese Yen	Long	Currencies
Canadian Dollar	Short	Currencies
E-mini Dow	Short	Equities
E-mini Nasdaq-100	Short	Equities
E-mini S&P MidCap 400	Short	Equities
Nikkei 225 Dollar	Short	Equities
CBOE Volatility Index	Long	Equities
S&P/TSX 60 Index	Short	Equities
EURO STOXX 50	Short	Equities
E-mini Russell 2000	Short	Equities
E-mini S&P 500	Short	Equities
Crude Oil – Light Sweet	Short	Non-Agriculture
NY Harbor ULSD	Short	Non-Agriculture
Brent	Short	Non-Agriculture
RBOB Gasoline	Short	Non-Agriculture
Gas Oil	Short	Non-Agriculture
Copper	Short	Non-Agriculture
Palladium	Short	Non-Agriculture
Euribor	Long	Rates
Eurodollar	Long	Rates
Euro-Bund	Long	Rates

(Continued)

TABLE 6.29	(Continued)	
Market	**Direction**	**Sector**
Euro-Schatz	Long	Rates
Euro-Bobl	Long	Rates
2-Year U.S. T-Note	Long	Rates
U.S. T-Bond	Long	Rates
5-Year U.S. T-Note	Long	Rates
10-Year U.S. T-Note	Long	Rates
10-Year Govt. of Canada Bond	Long	Rates
Long Gilt	Long	Rates

TABLE 6.30	Initial sector allocation 2009		
	Long	**Short**	**Total**
Agriculture	0	13	13
Rates	11	0	11
Non-Agriculture	0	7	7
Equities	1	8	9
Currencies	1	2	3
Total	13	30	43

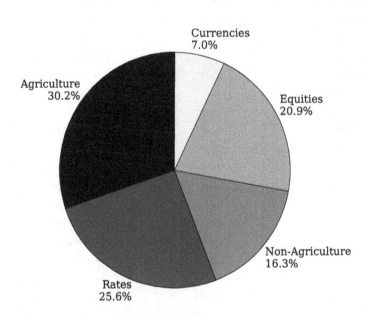

FIGURE 6.44 Sector allocation 2009.

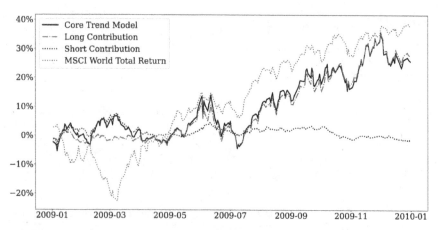

FIGURE 6.45 Strategy performance 2009.

how closely we track the index once we turned the ship around to bull mode. From around July on, we time our peaks and troughs with the market, and that shows that we now have a bullish portfolio on.

That worked out just fine, as the market turned bullish once more in 2009 (Figures 6.46–6.48). The markets can be really odd at times. We had a massive bull market up until early 2008. Then it turns out that much of the bull market is in large part based on what amounts to near fraudulent banking behaviour and that the financial world as we know it nearly ended. After a brief but sharp bear market, here we are a year later, back in full bull market again!

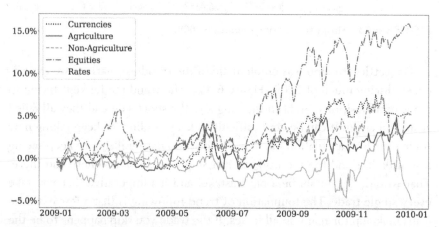

FIGURE 6.46 Sector performance 2009.

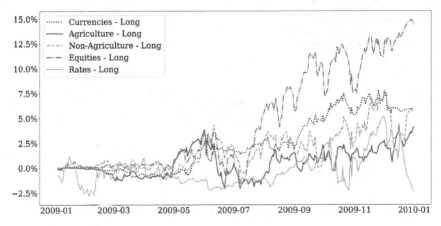

FIGURE 6.47 Long sector performance 2009.

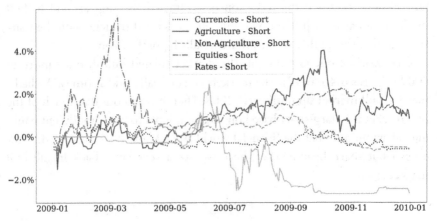

FIGURE 6.48 Short sector performance 2009.

The cattle situation was emblematic of the trendless markets we experienced during much of 2009 (Figure 6.49). The trend model kept trying to enter new positions, on both the long and the short side and they all failed again and again. It can be very difficult to keep trading, to keep taking new trade signals in a situation like this. It's just too demoralising to keep seeing loss after loss and too tempting to just skip a trade or two here and there. That would, of course, be a big mistake, and it's imperative that you take every single trade. The foundation of trend following is that a few extreme gains make up for many small losses. If the trade you skip happens to be the one that finally pays off, your entire year may be ruined.

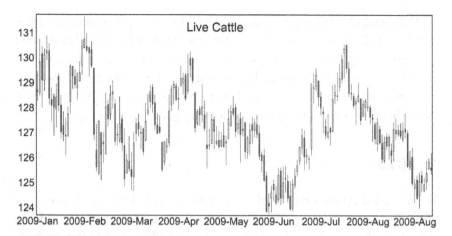

FIGURE 6.49 Lack of trends in Live Cattle.

2009 turned out to be a pretty fun year. No major drama, and ending with a substantial payoff both to our investors and to us. The major contributor was long equities, but all sectors except for rates contributed to the success of this year (Tables 6.31 and 6.32).

TABLE 6.31 Sector results 2009

	Currencies	Agriculture	Non-Agriculture	Equities	Rates	All sectors
Long	5.9	4.1	6.0	14.4	−2.4	27.9
Short	−0.6	0.8	−0.6	1.0	−2.7	−2.0
Total	5.3	4.1	5.7	15.4	−4.8	25.7

TABLE 6.32 Results 2009

	US$	Percentage
Starting NAV	46,313,195	463.13
Trading result	11,915,454	25.70
Interest income	313,684	0.70
Management fee	859,782	1.90
Performance fee	1,705,403	3.70
Net result	9,663,952	20.90
Ending NAV	55,977,147	559.80

At the end of 2009, we close the books with a trading gain of nearly 26%. Not bad at all. The interest income is down significantly, now that interest rates are getting really low. But at least we had nice gains from trading, and after fees we added US$10 million to our investors' coffers and, perhaps even more importantly, we got paid over US$2.5 million for this year. With the higher asset base of the portfolio, fees are getting interesting.

■ 2010

We're loaded up on a bull market portfolio, heavily long the equity complex. The bet on long stocks is quite substantial, with longs on most indexes as well as a short on the VIX index to add to the bull posture. In fact, we have very much a long portfolio across the board this year, over rates, agriculture, energies and metals (Tables 6.33 and 6.34, and Figure 6.50). Quite a risky portfolio, but risk is part of the game and after the previous couple of years, we're flying high and probably getting more than a little cocky.

TABLE 6.33 Initial portfolio 2010

Market	Direction	Sector
Soybean Oil	Long	Agriculture
Soybean Meal	Long	Agriculture
Robusta Coffee	Short	Agriculture
Live Cattle	Short	Agriculture
Coffee C	Long	Agriculture
Lean Hogs	Long	Agriculture
Cotton No. 2	Long	Agriculture
Soybean	Long	Agriculture
Feeder Cattle	Short	Agriculture
Cocoa	Long	Agriculture
White Sugar	Long	Agriculture
Sugar No. 11	Long	Agriculture
Lumber	Long	Agriculture
Canadian Dollar	Long	Currencies
E-mini S&P MidCap 400	Long	Equities
S&P/TSX 60 Index	Long	Equities
E-mini Russell 2000	Long	Equities
E-mini Dow	Long	Equities

(Continued)

TABLE 6.33 (Continued)

Market	Direction	Sector
E-mini S&P 500	Long	Equities
FTSE 100	Long	Equities
E-mini Nasdaq-100	Long	Equities
CBOE Volatility Index	Short	Equities
DAX	Long	Equities
EURO STOXX 50	Long	Equities
CAC 40	Long	Equities
Platinum	Long	Non-Agriculture
Silver	Long	Non-Agriculture
Copper	Long	Non-Agriculture
Gold	Long	Non-Agriculture
Brent	Long	Non-Agriculture
NY Harbor ULSD	Long	Non-Agriculture
Palladium	Long	Non-Agriculture
RBOB Gasoline	Long	Non-Agriculture
Gas Oil	Long	Non-Agriculture
Eurodollar	Long	Rates
Euro-Bobl	Long	Rates
Euro-BTP Long-Term	Long	Rates
Euro-Schatz	Long	Rates
5-Year U.S. T-Note	Long	Rates
2-Year U.S. T-Note	Long	Rates
Euribor	Long	Rates
Euro-Bund	Long	Rates
Long Gilt	Short	Rates

TABLE 6.34 Initial sector allocation 2010

	Long	Short	Total
Rates	8	1	9
Agriculture	10	3	13
Non-Agriculture	9	0	9
Equities	10	1	11
Currencies	1	0	1
Total	38	5	43

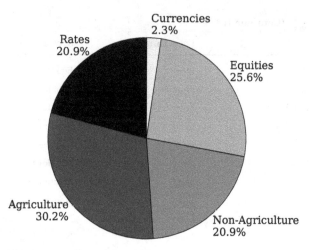

FIGURE 6.50 Sector allocation 2010.

After nine years of trading futures models, you're probably also starting to get a bit jaded. Perhaps the ups and downs of everyday life as a futures manager isn't getting to you as much any more. After all, it always worked out in the past. Even when there were stomach-turning losses, we always recovered them. So when this year starts to wobble up and down, from an initial +8% to −5% by February, it might not bother you as much. Even when the profits are back up to +10%, only to drop down to −15% in August, you might have learned to shrug it off.

We are, once more, saved by the second half of the year, and profits move up from the double digits negative, up to +35% in November. A sharp loss, a partial recovery and we end the year with trading gains of +30% for 2011 (Figures 6.51–6.53). It was another year not too different from what we've already seen. Eventful, plenty of nail-biting episodes, mixing between uneventful slow moves to sharp losses, to swift gains, but all's well that ends well. Nine years and clear sailing! I bet you could get used to this.

The one sector which worked out for us during the whole year was the rates. These guys took off at the start and never really looked back. More troublesome were the equity markets, where we saw loss after loss and failed to make any money. The non-agricultural space as well showed us nothing but losses. In terms of action, we saw some interesting moves in the agricultural space, where we had losses up until late in the year, but it was the turnaround in this sector which saved our bacon in the end. That sharp drop and recovery late in the year, that was all the agricultural sector as well (Figure 6.54).

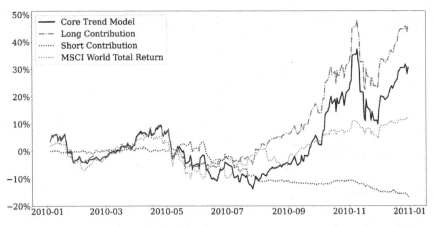

FIGURE 6.51   Strategy performance 2010.

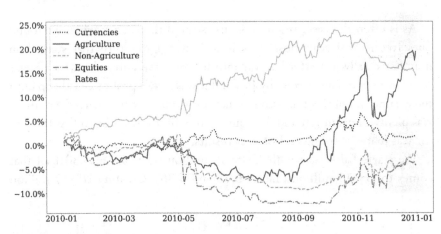

FIGURE 6.52   Sector performance 2010.

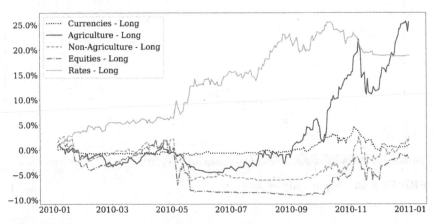

FIGURE 6.53   Long sector performance 2010.

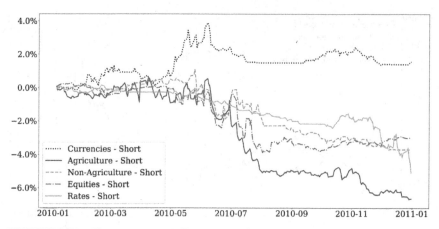

FIGURE 6.54 Short sector performance 2010.

As is often the case, rescue was just around the corner when we found ourselves in that scary loss. This time it was agriculture that started an impressive rally just after halfway into the year. We entered into the Sugar trend, shown in Figure 6.55 by July and it was a very profitable ride up until the abrupt end of this bull run in October. Even after the sharp drop, there was plenty of profit left and the contribution of this trade as well as the sector was material to the end-of-year results.

We started the year with a US$56 million portfolio and 30% of that comes to US$17 million (Tables 6.35 and 6.36). Creating US$17 million

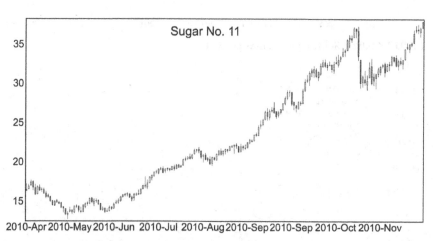

FIGURE 6.55 Sugar rally of 2010.

TABLE 6.35	Sector results 2010					
	Currencies	Agriculture	Non-Agriculture	Equities	Rates	All sectors
Long	1.0	25.5	2.6	−2.0	18.9	46.0
Short	1.6	−6.6	−3.7	−3.0	−5.1	−16.8
Total	2.1	19.4	−1.2	−4.2	14.4	30.5

TABLE 6.36	Results 2010	
	US$	Percentage
Starting NAV	55,977,147	559.77
Trading result	17,077,542	30.50
Interest income	258,194	0.50
Management fee	1,078,698	1.90
Performance fee	2,438,556	4.40
Net result	13,818,482	24.70
Ending NAV	69,795,629	698.00

from proverbial thin air feels pretty good, doesn't it? The interest rates are starting to get quite low, so we won't get much help from that side, but perhaps it doesn't matter so much with the amount of trading gains we're making. After this nice year, we end up charging US$3.5 million to the fund, and after this the investors still have a profit on their capital of nearly US$14 million. The initial US$10 million that they entrusted to your care in late 2001 is now worth nearly US$70 million.

■ 2011

Despite struggling with the equity markets last year, we're still fully loaded on the bullish side at the start of 2011. It's another high-risk portfolio composition, with concentrated bets on long equities, long agriculture, and in a reversal from last year, short rates (Tables 6.37 and 6.38, and Figure 6.56). What could possibly go wrong with being fully loaded on stocks in early 2011? Those of us who were in the market at that time, or who were in Asia, are probably a little concerned over this allocation. As someone who had a big bet on long Japanese stocks on at the time, this is not a year that I remember fondly.

TABLE 6.37	Initial portfolio 2011	
Market	**Direction**	**Sector**
Sugar No. 11	Long	Agriculture
Lumber	Long	Agriculture
White Sugar	Long	Agriculture
Cotton No. 2	Long	Agriculture
Coffee C	Long	Agriculture
Feeder Cattle	Long	Agriculture
Corn	Long	Agriculture
Live Cattle	Long	Agriculture
KC HRW Wheat	Long	Agriculture
Soybean Meal	Long	Agriculture
Soybean Oil	Long	Agriculture
Soybean	Long	Agriculture
Canola	Long	Agriculture
Robusta Coffee	Long	Agriculture
Australian Dollar	Long	Currencies
Canadian Dollar	Long	Currencies
Swiss Franc	Long	Currencies
E-mini S&P 500	Long	Equities
Nikkei 225 Dollar	Long	Equities
FTSE 100	Long	Equities
DAX	Long	Equities
S&P/TSX 60 Index	Long	Equities
CBOE Volatility Index	Short	Equities
E-mini S&P MidCap 400	Long	Equities
E-mini Russell 2000	Long	Equities
E-mini Dow	Long	Equities
E-mini Nasdaq-100	Long	Equities
CAC 40	Long	Equities
NY Harbor ULSD	Long	Non-Agriculture
Gold	Long	Non-Agriculture
Gas Oil	Long	Non-Agriculture
Silver	Long	Non-Agriculture
Palladium	Long	Non-Agriculture
RBOB Gasoline	Long	Non-Agriculture
Copper	Long	Non-Agriculture
Crude Oil – Light Sweet	Long	Non-Agriculture
Brent	Long	Non-Agriculture

(Continued)

TABLE 6.37 (Continued)

Market	Direction	Sector
Platinum	Long	Non-Agriculture
2-Year U.S. T-Note	Short	Rates
Euro-BTP Long-Term	Short	Rates
5-Year U.S. T-Note	Short	Rates
Euro-Bobl	Short	Rates
U.S. T-Bond	Short	Rates
10-Year U.S. T-Note	Short	Rates
Euro-Schatz	Short	Rates
Euro-Bund	Short	Rates
Long Gilt	Short	Rates

TABLE 6.38 Initial sector allocation 2011

	Long	Short	Total
Agriculture	14	0	14
Non-Agriculture	10	0	10
Rates	0	9	9
Equities	10	1	11
Currencies	3	0	3
Total	37	10	47

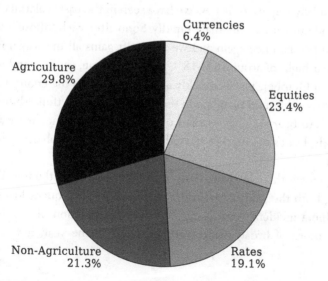

FIGURE 6.56 Sector allocation 2011.

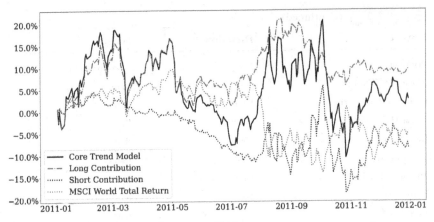

FIGURE 6.57 Strategy performance 2011.

There was nothing wrong with the start of the year, and by early March we already hold a 17% trading gain (Figure 6.57). So far, it looked like another really strong year. But that's when an earthquake caused a tsunami which caused a nuclear accident which caused a market crash. This little surprise caused a general market shock and most sectors, except for currencies, moved against us quickly. After that, uncertainty dominated the markets and we saw a more risk-averse stance among market participants.

After the initial hit from the Japanese disaster, we recovered almost all the gains before losing them again. Yes, this is shaping up to be another sleepless, rollercoaster of year. From having seen that initial 17% gain, we're in a 10% hole in July (Figure 6.58). As we have seen in the past, volatility begets volatility and our returns fluctuate rapidly. Soon after we hit those lows, the trading winds turn once again and we see swift gains all the way up to the previous year highs of around 15–18%. But easy come, easy go, and we lose it all again in October, just as quickly as we made it. As the equity markets took a sharp southbound turn late in the summer, our portfolio shifted tack from bullish to bearish. That worked out during the decline, as we flipped quite quickly, but as the market started rebounding in October, we lost the gains again.

The big moves this year were concentrated in just a few themes. The initial moves, both the gains early in the year and the subsequent losses after the Fukushima incident were generated by a combination of sectors, and they were more of broad market events. Later in the year, however, we

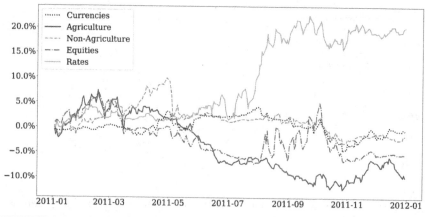

FIGURE 6.58 Sector performance 2011.

started seeing a wider dispersion in sector behaviour. The hard drop in May was primarily caused by exposure to long metals and energies (Figure 6.59), and the rather dramatic moves in the second half of the year were mostly an effect of short positions in equity indexes (Figure 6.60). The one saving grace this year was the long rates positions, which ended up yielding a substantial profit. This sector alone provided a positive contribution of over 20% to the portfolio, and without it we would have ended the year with a disaster of our own.

The heating oil chart in Figure 6.61 shows one of the dangers with our kind of trading models. We were in this bull trend for multiple months, all

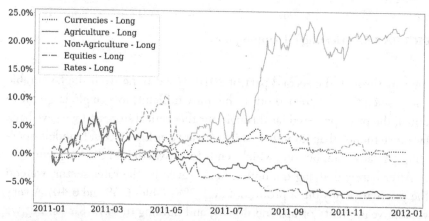

FIGURE 6.59 Long sector performance 2011.

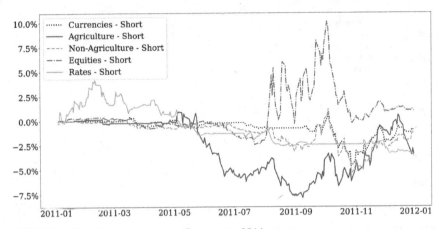

FIGURE 6.60 Short sector performance 2011.

FIGURE 6.61 Heating oil gapping down.

the way through the second part of 2010. Good thing we had a favourable entry, since the exit turned out to be quite difficult. In a single large move down, the price powered far through our theoretical stop, and we gave back far more money than intended. This is always a risk with trend models operating on daily data, but one which tends to be worth it in the long run.

After barely dodging the bullet, being saved by the rates sector, we end the year with a tiny bit of profit, not even 3% (Tables 6.39 and 6.40). A very volatile year, plenty of ups and downs, and nothing to show for us. But we do have something to cheer for this year, a reason why you probably won't

TABLE 6.39 Sector results 2011

	Currencies	Agriculture	Non-Agriculture	Equities	Rates	All sectors
Long	1.0	−6.7	−0.7	−7.2	23.1	9.5
Short	−1.2	−3.4	−1.3	1.0	−3.6	− 8.5
Total	−0.6	−9.8	−1.6	−5.5	20.1	2.7

TABLE 6.40 Results 2011

	US$	Percentage
Starting NAV	69,795,629	697.96
Trading result	1,870,674	2.70
Interest income	212,375	0.30
Management fee	1,058,198	1.50
Performance fee	153,728	0.20
Net result	871,123	1.20
Ending NAV	70,666,752	706.70

hear many complaints from investors, despite the poor performance. We ended up, and the stock markets didn't.

Now that we've grown the asset base to around US$70 million, we still got a million for ourselves in basic management fees, a slight comfort for a tough year. You may notice that the trading profits were merely 2.7% and we got paid 1.5% in just management fees. Well, that's how the business works. We would have been paid that even without a profit, or with a loss. Now, since we did make an admittedly tiny bit of profit, we also get a tiny bit of performance fee, of about US$150,000 and change. Not a great year, but at least we gained while the market lost.

■ 2012

Congratulations, you've completed the first decade of your trading business and you've performed quite well. That last year, 2011, might not have been so stellar, but on average it was a very strong decade. Well, I hope you're ready for another decade! As we enter our eleventh year, we have already closed most of the bear market exposure and only have a short left on one single index. We've also built a very steep exposure to short commodities.

That is in fact the largest bet we've got on at the start of 2012. We're short 13 different agricultural markets and 5 non-agricultural, from coffee and soybeans to gold and oil, all short (Tables 6.41 and 6.42, and Figure 6.62).

TABLE 6.41	Initial portfolio 2012	
Market	**Direction**	**Sector**
Lumber	Short	Agriculture
Corn	Short	Agriculture
Canola	Short	Agriculture
Robusta Coffee	Short	Agriculture
Soybean Meal	Short	Agriculture
Soybean Oil	Short	Agriculture
Soybean	Short	Agriculture
White Sugar	Short	Agriculture
Sugar No. 11	Short	Agriculture
Coffee C	Short	Agriculture
Cotton No. 2	Short	Agriculture
Cocoa	Short	Agriculture
KC HRW Wheat	Short	Agriculture
Euro FX	Short	Currencies
British Pound	Short	Currencies
Canadian Dollar	Short	Currencies
S&P/TSX 60 Index	Short	Equities
E-mini Dow	Long	Equities
Henry Hub Natural Gas	Short	Non-Agriculture
RBOB Gasoline	Short	Non-Agriculture
Silver	Short	Non-Agriculture
Gold	Short	Non-Agriculture
Platinum	Short	Non-Agriculture
10-Year U.S. T-Note	Long	Rates
Euribor	Short	Rates
Eurodollar	Short	Rates
10-Year Govt. of Canada Bond	Long	Rates
Euro-Schatz	Long	Rates
5-Year U.S. T-Note	Long	Rates
Euro-Bobl	Long	Rates
Long Gilt	Long	Rates
U.S. T-Bond	Long	Rates

TABLE 6.42	Initial sector allocation 2012		
	Long	Short	Total
Agriculture	0	13	13
Rates	7	2	9
Equities	1	1	2
Non-Agriculture	0	5	5
Currencies	0	3	3
Total	8	24	32

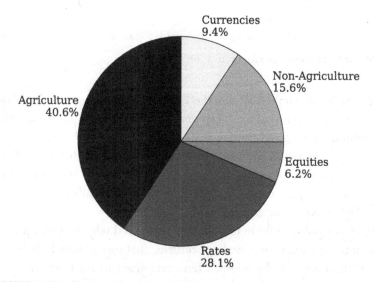

FIGURE 6.62 Sector allocation 2012.

In ten years, we've seen it all, and this year doesn't look any different, at least not in the first few months. We gain a bit, lose a bit, but generally stay around zero up until April. This is when we start seeing something that we just haven't seen in the first ten years. We lose, and we keep losing. Loss after loss, month after month. After each month, you'll probably expect to see a bounce right back up to the highs, just as we've seen so many times before. But there also comes a point where you stop believing in magic and start getting seriously pessimistic. We were only over the zero line for a brief period early in the year, and then we hit −10%, −20%, −25% and finally end a horror of a year after a small bump at a cool −20%. Our first serious loss (Figure 6.63).

I can tell you, very much from experience, that losses of this magnitude are very painful. In this book and this chapter, the start of your trading

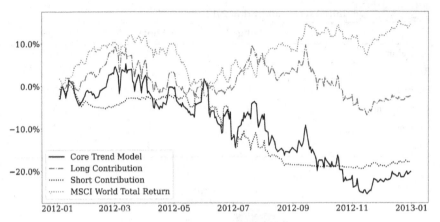

FIGURE 6.63 Strategy performance 2012.

venture was in January 2002, for the only reason that I wanted to cover twenty years of performance. But imagine if you just got your initial US$10 million and started trading at the beginning of 2012. Your very first year, starting with a 20% loss. Now that can be a career killer. Even if your trading strategy is absolutely sound and likely to produce strong results in the long run, the entry timing and the luck that this entails can be the one deciding factor over your career and your business.

If you at any point so far in this chapter wondered why we don't just dial the risk factor up, and cash in on huge returns, that should hopefully be very clear now. If you got lucky and had ten great years to start off with, then sure, having twice the risk on would have made you a ton of money. But what if you get an initial bad year? Or three of them?

This was a year where everything went wrong. There was no big single disaster, no single sector or position that blew up in our faces. It was just a slow bleed, across everything (Figures 6.64 and 6.65). For a while, the equity markets cushioned the blow somewhat, but that didn't last. We lost on both the long side and the short, though more on the short side (Figure 6.66). The commodity sector was particularly painful, and nothing really helped in the end.

A year like this can easily kill not only your business but your confidence in your trading model and in yourself. It's not easy to continue to execute trade after trade, when you see how they all end up losing money. The risk is that sooner or later, you decide to skip a trade, or a few trades. Perhaps those were the trades which would have rescued you. There just isn't any way of knowing in advance which trades will pay off and which will not.

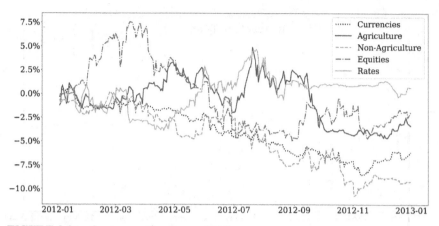

FIGURE 6.64 Sector performance 2012.

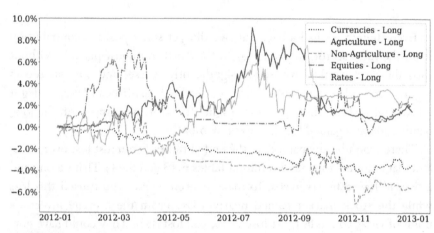

FIGURE 6.65 Long sector performance 2012.

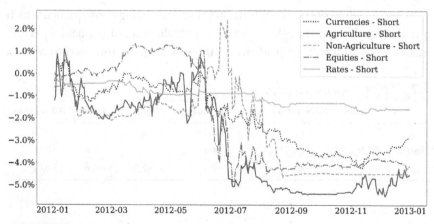

FIGURE 6.66 Short sector performance 2012.

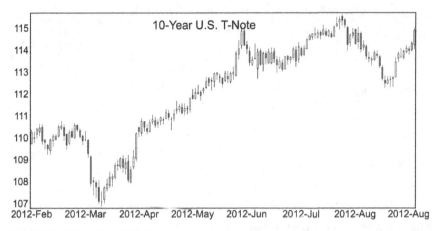

FIGURE 6.67 US 10Y Treasury.

Even though we had a bad year, we did get some positive contribution from the rates sector, in particular in the April to August period. Without this, the year would have ended significantly worse, and we can see in Figure 6.67 what happened. First, we had a bearish head-fake, and got tricked into a brief short position. Right after that, we jumped on the long bandwagon and gained for the next few months.

There won't be any parades at the end of this one. You just lost over 20%, and that amounts to US$15 million (Tables 6.43 and 6.44). That's a one and a five, followed by six zeros. To make it even worse, you caused this loss while the stock market gained nearly 15%. From the average investor's point of view, you didn't just lose 20%, you lost 35%. They could have gotten the 15% for free in the stock markets. You're in the doghouse, that's for sure.

Being in a drawdown like this has another interesting consequence which you perhaps haven't thought of yet. Not only do you not get paid a performance fee, you won't get paid any on the way back up. You need to make a

TABLE 6.43 Sector results 2012

	Currencies	Agriculture	Non-Agriculture	Equities	Rates	All sectors
Long	−3.4	1.5	−5.5	2.3	2.8	−2.3
Short	−2.9	−4.6	−4.5	−4.1	−1.6	−17.6
Total	−6.2	−3.4	−9.3	−2.0	0.6	−20.1

TABLE 6.44   Results 2012

	US$	Percentage
Starting NAV	70,666,752	706.67
Trading result	−14,226,173	−20.10
Interest income	112,764	0.20
Management fee	826,766	1.20
Performance fee	−14,940,175	0.00
Net result	—	−21.10
Ending NAV	55,726,577	557.30

new high on the portfolio value before you get paid a performance fee. So now that you're down 21%, you need to trade the portfolio up 27% before you get paid any serious money. Why 27 and not 21? If you ask that question, you need a basic maths refresh. If we started with 100, we would have 79 after the loss of 21%. To get back up to the old high-water mark of 100, we need to multiply 79 by 1.27.

So we get no performance fee, and only US$820,000 in management fees. That may sound huge, but you need to put it in context. We're now managing US$70 million, we probably have offices, staff, and overheads. This is a business, and 800k won't keep us above the waterline.

■ 2013

It's January 2013 and we have a 27% hike up to get paid performance fee again. That's a very tough spot to be in, and without a doubt very demoralising. As you've seen, the interesting money comes from performance fees and at this point we can be quite sure that we have a least one year ahead of us where we work almost for free. This is the reason why some hedge funds simply choose to close down once they are in a deep hole. But we're not quitters, are we?

The portfolio we're sitting on at this time is betting on a renewed bull market. We're long equities across the board as well as long rates (Tables 6.45 and 6.46 and Figure 6.68). Our largest exposure is to the agricultural space, with a mix of longs and shorts. This is often a comfortable sector to be exposed to, as it tends to be less correlated to the often binary risk-on, risk-off types of themes that often dominate the financial markets. Unusual as it is, we only carry one single position in the non-agricultural sector, which is a long in palladium.

TABLE 6.45 Initial portfolio 2013

Market	Direction	Sector
Sugar No. 11	Short	Agriculture
Class III Milk	Short	Agriculture
Feeder Cattle	Long	Agriculture
Robusta Coffee	Short	Agriculture
KC HRW Wheat	Short	Agriculture
Corn	Short	Agriculture
Live Cattle	Long	Agriculture
Cocoa	Short	Agriculture
Soybean	Short	Agriculture
Soybean Oil	Short	Agriculture
Lean Hogs	Long	Agriculture
Coffee C	Short	Agriculture
White Sugar	Short	Agriculture
Lumber	Long	Agriculture
Canola	Short	Agriculture
Japanese Yen	Short	Currencies
British Pound	Long	Currencies
Swiss Franc	Long	Currencies
Euro FX	Long	Currencies
Australian Dollar	Long	Currencies
New Zealand Dollar	Long	Currencies
Hang Seng Index	Long	Equities
HS China E	Long	Equities
EURO STOXX 50	Long	Equities
DAX	Long	Equities
CAC 40	Long	Equities
S&P/TSX 60 Index	Long	Equities
E-mini S&P MidCap 400	Long	Equities
Nikkei 225 Dollar	Long	Equities
Palladium	Long	Non-Agriculture
10-Year U.S. T-Note	Long	Rates
Euro-Bund	Long	Rates
Euro-BTP Long-Term	Long	Rates
5-Year U.S. T-Note	Long	Rates
Euro-Bobl	Long	Rates
Euro-Schatz	Long	Rates

TABLE 6.46	Initial sector allocation 2013		
	Long	Short	Total
Agriculture	4	11	15
Rates	6	0	6
Non-Agriculture	1	0	1
Equities	8	0	8
Currencies	5	1	6
Total	24	12	36

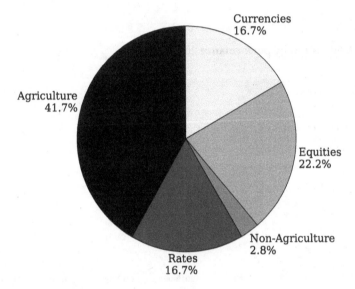

FIGURE 6.68 Sector allocation 2013.

This year, the stock markets performed quite well throughout the year. Given that we went into the year heavily long stocks, we should be in a good position to profit. While we do end up making strong returns in that sector, we also lose money in all other sectors this year. Whatever we're making on equities, we lose in other areas (Figure 6.69). The result is a choppy year, up a bit, down a bit, rarely straying from the $+/-5\%$ area. While the stock markets just kept climbing the whole year, we remain flat. After the disaster of last year, this will be a very tough experience.

Not only do you fail to make money this year, but you do this while most average investors make a 20% return on the stock markets. This kind of year can threaten your entire business and there's a risk that your investors pull their money. At the end of the year, we have a trading profit of about 2%, nearly 20% behind the MSCI World Index.

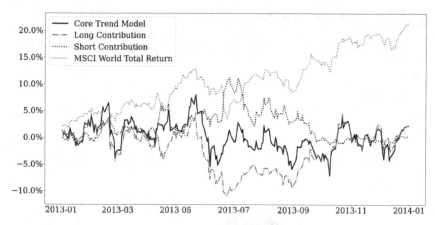

FIGURE 6.69 Strategy performance 2013.

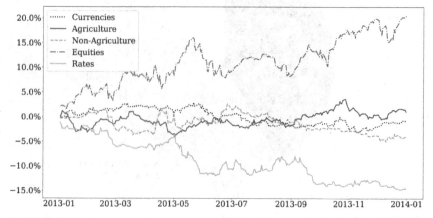

FIGURE 6.70 Sector performance 2013.

As you see in the sector performance graph in Figure 6.70, the equity index futures did just fine throughout the year. We ended up with a 20% profit in that sector. But we also lost 15% on the rates sector, and together with the poor performance on the other sectors, there really wasn't much left over for this year (Figures 6.71 and 6.72).

The one sector which really performed this year was the equities, specifically on the long side. From the profile you see in Figure 6.73, you can see why. We stayed long most equity indexes the entire year and it added up to some serious profits. All in all, the sector added nearly 20% to the bottom line; it's just a shame that we lost about as much on the other sectors.

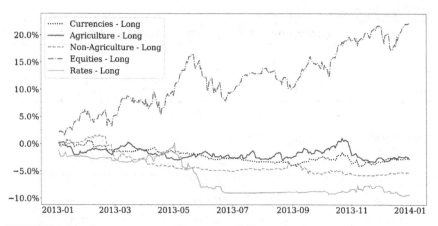

FIGURE 6.71   Long sector performance 2013.

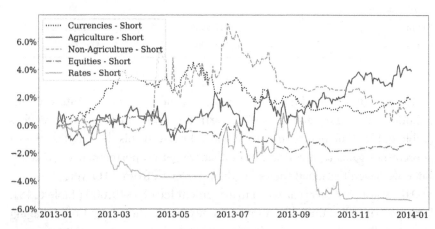

FIGURE 6.72   Short sector performance 2013.

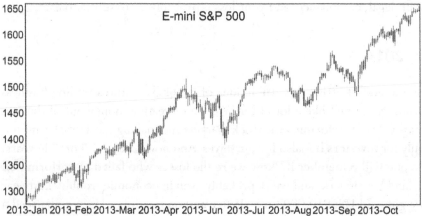

FIGURE 6.73   S&P 500 bullish trend.

TABLE 6.47 Sector results 2013

	Currencies	Agriculture	Non-Agriculture	Equities	Rates	All sectors
Long	−2.6	−2.8	−5.3	22.4	−9.4	2.3
Short	1.9	3.9	1.0	−1.4	−5.4	0.1
Total	−0.8	1.1	−4.0	20.6	−14.6	2.2

TABLE 6.48 Results 2013

	US$	Percentage
Starting NAV	55,726,577	557.27
Trading result	1,238,093	2.20
Interest income	108,578	0.20
Management fee	841,119	1.50
Performance fee	—	0.00
Net result	505,553	0.90
Ending NAV	56,232,130	562.30

The end-of-year trading gains were 2.2%, and we got a tiny interest contribution of 0.2%, for a 2.4% portfolio value increase before fees (Table 6.47). Our management fee eats up most of this, leaving less than a percent net gains to investors. Note that we get no performance fee at all, since we haven't reached the old high-water mark from 2011 yet.

All we got paid this year was a management fee of $840,000 (Table 6.48). Perhaps that still sounds like a lot of money, but in the context of managing US$55 million, it's really tiny. Imagine if you had managed only US$5.5 million, and got paid US$84,000. Now pay the office rent, the market data, the staff, legal, compliance, and your loss is probably quite substantial.

■ 2014

By the end of 2012, this whole idea of running a futures trading business probably seemed like a lot of fun. We were creating money out of thin air, massively outperforming the stock markets and making substantial gains not only for investors but also for ourselves. And now, after two horrible years, no one will remember it. Now we're the losers who failed to perform, fell behind benchmark, and we're probably even in economic trouble. Last year we got paid US$840,000 on a US$55 million portfolio. Having managed a successful trading business for a decade, we've probably built up quite a bit of overhead costs and it's not exactly like that's just clean profits.

There's an old expression in the businesses, one which used to be a lot truer than it is today. We used to say that there is no such thing as a third bad year for a hedge fund. The point being that after two bad years, you're done. Investors pull their money and your fund is closed. That's not necessarily true any more and it's really up to marketing, investor relations and expectation management. Still, you're in a really bad spot here at the start of 2014 and you're probably considering giving up.

The bull market is still here and we're still very much long stock market indexes. The large allocation we had a year ago to the rates sector is now nearly completely gone, and overall we're running a mixed and not terribly aggressive portfolio (Tables 6.49 and 6.50, and Figure 6.74). This is it, if we fail this year, it would be exceedingly difficult to continue operations.

TABLE 6.49	Initial portfolio 2014	
Market	Direction	Sector
Feeder Cattle	Long	Agriculture
Canola	Short	Agriculture
Soybean Oil	Short	Agriculture
KC HRW Wheat	Short	Agriculture
Soybean Meal	Long	Agriculture
White Sugar	Short	Agriculture
Sugar No. 11	Short	Agriculture
Corn	Short	Agriculture
Coffee C	Short	Agriculture
Cocoa	Long	Agriculture
Live Cattle	Long	Agriculture
British Pound	Long	Currencies
Japanese Yen	Short	Currencies
Swiss Franc	Long	Currencies
Canadian Dollar	Short	Currencies
FTSE 100	Long	Equities
DAX	Long	Equities
EURO STOXX 50	Long	Equities
S&P/TSX 60 Index	Long	Equities
E-mini S&P 500	Long	Equities
E-mini Nasdaq-100	Long	Equities

TABLE 6.49	(Continued)	
Market	**Direction**	**Sector**
E-mini Dow	Long	Equities
E-mini Russell 2000	Long	Equities
E-mini S&P MidCap 400	Long	Equities
Nikkei 225 Dollar	Long	Equities
CBOE Volatility Index	Short	Equities
Copper	Long	Non-Agriculture
Silver	Short	Non-Agriculture
Gold	Short	Non-Agriculture
Platinum	Short	Non-Agriculture
Long Gilt	Short	Rates
Euro-BTP Long-Term	Long	Rates

TABLE 6.50	Initial sector allocation 2014		
	Long	**Short**	**Total**
Agriculture	4	7	11
Non-Agriculture	1	3	4
Rates	1	1	2
Equities	10	1	11
Currencies	2	2	4
Total	18	14	32

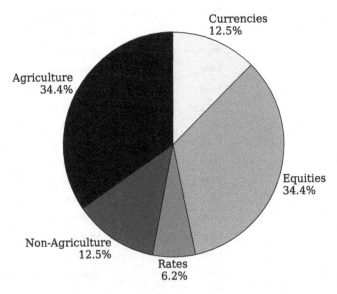

FIGURE 6.74 Sector allocation 2014.

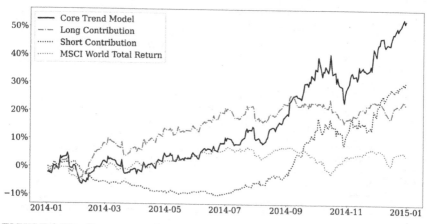

FIGURE 6.75 Strategy performance 2014.

Given what's at stake here, we have real nail biter of a start of the year. First, we swiftly move up 5%, and then we lose it and more (Figure 6.75). By February, we're down about 5% on the year, and you would be forgiven for updating your LinkedIn profile and browsing job ads. But from there, things slowly improve. We track the equity index quite well all the way up to +10% in late summer, when something really interesting starts happening. We start outperforming in a big way. While the stock market index continues sideways, we move up and we move up fast. There was a brief scare in October when we had a couple of weeks of sharp losses, but they were quickly recovered and then some. At the end of this year, we gained over 50% and this is during a nearly flat year in the stock markets. We're back! It was a scary couple of years, but after this 50% return, we've proved not only that we can generate strong absolute return, but that we can be uncorrelated to the stock markets. As much as investors dislike it when you fail to perform in a bull market, they love it even more when you do perform in a bear market.

Since the stock markets didn't perform well this year, clearly other sectors were driving our returns. We did in fact lose quite a lot on our equity sector trades, but all other sectors performed remarkably well (Figures 6.76–6.78). We lost 20% on stocks, but gained enough on the rest for a total of +53% on the year. The agricultural sector performed well all year, but it was in the second half of the year when currencies and non-agricultural positions really took off.

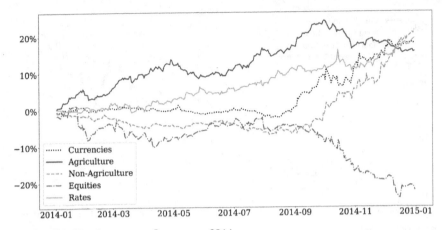

FIGURE 6.76 Sector performance 2014.

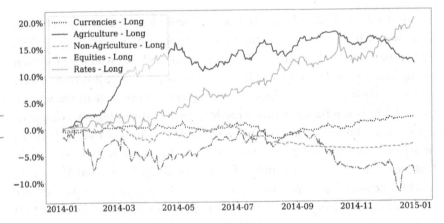

FIGURE 6.77 Long sector performance 2014.

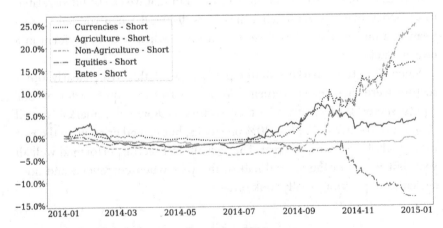

FIGURE 6.78 Short sector performance 2014.

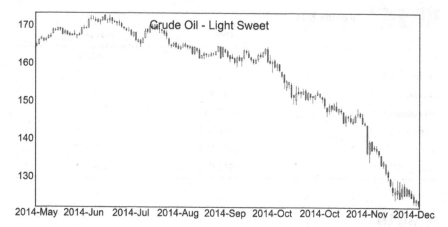

FIGURE 6.79 Short Crude Oil.

A major contributor to the success of 2014 was the bear market in the energies. A quick look at Figure 6.79 shows you why. After the oil price started falling in June, it just didn't stop. Month after month, it just kept falling, and that's just the kind of situation we're set up to profit from.

Making such a huge gain and with a substantial asset base, we should see some welcome revenue this year. But bear in mind that we don't get paid performance fee until we exceed the previous high-water mark, so about half of the performance does not get us any money. Luckily we make more than the 25% or so we need to return to the HWM and we do get a fair chunk of performance fees this year.

The interest rates contribution is really low still and can almost be approximated to zero (Tables 6.51 and 6.52). But with 53% return, even after deducting our fees, investors get to keep 47% and they probably have a renewed confidence in our abilities to generate strong long-term results. If only every year could be like this one.

TABLE 6.51 Sector results 2014

	Currencies	Agriculture	Non-Agriculture	Equities	Rates	All sectors
Long	2.0	12.0	−3.2	−8.7	20.4	22.5
Short	16.3	3.9	25.2	−13.6	−0.8	30.9
Total	18.3	15.8	21.5	−22.3	19.3	52.6

TABLE 6.52 Results 2014

	US$	Percentage
Starting NAV	56,232,130	562.32
Trading result	29,585,729	52.60
Interest income	192,835	0.30
Management fee	1,267,154	2.30
Performance fee	2,111,518	3.80
Net result	26,399,891	46.90
Ending NAV	82,632,021	826.30

■ 2015

We start 2015 in a fairly comfortable position, having just had a stellar year behind us. The risk level of the portfolio at this point is quite high with 43 positions across all sectors, and while we're still long stocks, it's not an overwhelming part of the allocation (Table 6.53). We have a significant portion of the portfolio exposed to the agricultural sector, with a healthy mix of longs and shorts (Table 6.54). The metals and energies are all short at this point (Figure 6.80).

TABLE 6.53 Initial portfolio 2015

Market	Direction	Sector
Sugar No. 11	Short	Agriculture
Soybean Oil	Short	Agriculture
Soybean Meal	Long	Agriculture
Robusta Coffee	Short	Agriculture
KC HRW Wheat	Long	Agriculture
Corn	Long	Agriculture
Coffee C	Short	Agriculture
Lean Hogs	Short	Agriculture
Canola	Long	Agriculture
Cotton No. 2	Short	Agriculture
White Sugar	Short	Agriculture
Cocoa	Short	Agriculture
Lumber	Short	Agriculture
Euro FX	Short	Currencies
British Pound	Short	Currencies
Swiss Franc	Short	Currencies

(Continued)

TABLE 6.53   (Continued)

Market	Direction	Sector
Australian Dollar	Short	Currencies
Canadian Dollar	Short	Currencies
US Dollar Index	Long	Currencies
Nikkei 225 Dollar	Long	Equities
E-mini Nasdaq-100	Long	Equities
E-mini S&P 500	Long	Equities
E-mini Dow	Long	Equities
E-mini Russell 2000	Long	Equities
S&P/TSX 60 Index	Short	Equities
E-mini S&P MidCap 400	Long	Equities
Henry Hub Natural Gas	Short	Non-Agriculture
NY Harbor ULSD	Short	Non-Agriculture
Crude Oil – Light Sweet	Short	Non-Agriculture
RBOB Gasoline	Short	Non-Agriculture
Gas Oil	Short	Non-Agriculture
Platinum	Short	Non-Agriculture
Brent	Short	Non-Agriculture
Copper	Short	Non-Agriculture
10-Year Govt. of Canada Bond	Long	Rates
Euribor	Long	Rates
Euro-Schatz	Long	Rates
Long Gilt	Long	Rates
U.S. T-Bond	Long	Rates
Euro-Bund	Long	Rates
Euro-Bobl	Long	Rates
Euro-BTP Long-Term	Long	Rates
Eurodollar	Short	Rates

TABLE 6.54   Initial sector allocation 2015

	Long	Short	Total
Agriculture	4	9	13
Rates	8	1	9
Non-Agriculture	0	8	8
Equities	6	1	7
Currencies	1	5	6
Total	19	24	43

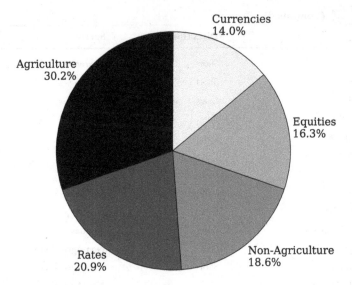

FIGURE 6.80 Sector allocation 2015.

The first few months of the year went really well. We gain on most sectors but we gain the most on the long equity index part, and by May we're nearly 20% up on the year (Figure 6.81). That would be a brilliant continuation after last year's success. This first part of the year, we saw losses in metals and energies only, but after that peak in May, we start seeing losses in other sectors. Not only do we give up the gains on the stocks, we also start losing on rates and agriculture. The result is that we move from our near 20% gain, down to a loss of over 10% in November. After recovering a bit of that, we close the year at a -6% (Figures 6.82–6.84).

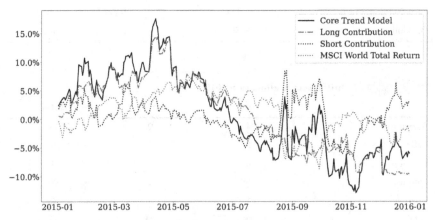

FIGURE 6.81 Strategy performance 2015.

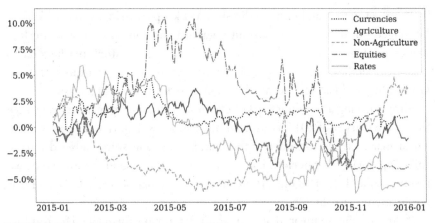

FIGURE 6.82   Sector performance 2015.

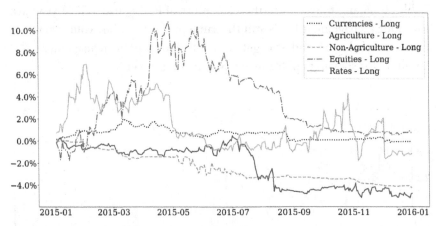

FIGURE 6.83   Long sector performance 2015.

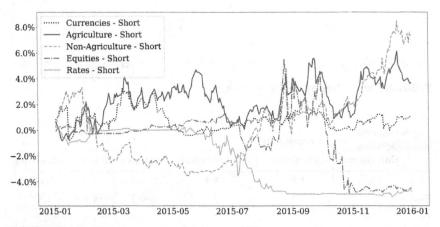

FIGURE 6.84   Short sector performance 2015.

It was a tough year, but not a disaster. As I keep stressing, you are likely to be judged not only on your absolute performance but also on your performance relative to the stock markets. In this case, the stock markets had a weak year, ending only a couple of percent better than your futures strategy. Given how well last year went, this slight loss isn't much of an issue.

Simply having a trending market may not be enough to make money. Take the coffee market of 2015 as an example. You see in Figure 6.85 how we had a bear market trend for much of the year, but also saw some rather dramatic spikes up during that period. Each time we got those sudden moves out, we lost money and stopped out. All in all, this particular bear market trend was not in any way profitable.

It does of course mean that you won't get any performance fee. You lost nearly 6%, or US$5 million, and after fees, the net loss was about 7% (Tables 6.55 and 6.56). Note the nice effect of having had a 50% year just now. Your management fee is still the same percentage, but your asset base is now much higher and you get over a million just in management fee. A million for showing up. It's nice work, if you can get it.

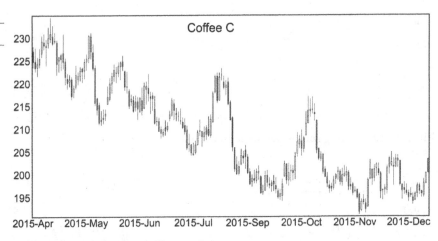

FIGURE 6.85 Choppy coffee market.

TABLE 6.55	Sector results 2015					
	Currencies	Agriculture	Non-Agriculture	Equities	Rates	All sectors
Long	−0.1	−4.8	−4.3	0.7	−1.2	−9.6
Short	1.1	3.7	7.3	−4.5	−4.8	2.8
Total	1.0	−1.1	3.7	−3.9	−5.6	−5.9

TABLE 6.56 | **Results 2015**

	US$	Percentage
Starting NAV	82,632,021	826.32
Trading result	−4,894,486	−5.90
Interest income	364,724	0.40
Management fee	1,147,843	1.40
Performance fee	—	0.00
Net result	−5,677,605	−6.90
Ending NAV	76,954,416	769.50

■ 2016

The largest exposure in early 2016 us once again in agriculture. A mix of longs and shorts (Tables 6.57 and 6.58, and Figure 6.86). We hold practically no exposure to equities after the recent volatility, and there's no clear story in the rates sector either. On the metals and energies, we're short across the board though, betting on a decline in both metals and energies.

TABLE 6.57 | **Initial portfolio 2016**

Market	Direction	Sector
Sugar No. 11	Long	Agriculture
Lumber	Long	Agriculture
Lean Hogs	Short	Agriculture
Robusta Coffee	Short	Agriculture
Cocoa	Long	Agriculture
Soybean	Short	Agriculture
Canola	Short	Agriculture
Live Cattle	Short	Agriculture
Corn	Short	Agriculture
KC HRW Wheat	Short	Agriculture
Cotton No. 2	Short	Agriculture
Feeder Cattle	Short	Agriculture
Coffee C	Short	Agriculture
White Sugar	Long	Agriculture
Soybean Meal	Short	Agriculture
New Zealand Dollar	Long	Currencies
British Pound	Short	Currencies

(Continued)

TABLE 6.57   (Continued)

Market	Direction	Sector
Canadian Dollar	Short	Currencies
E-mini Nasdaq-100	Long	Equities
S&P/TSX 60 Index	Short	Equities
RBOB Gasoline	Short	Non-Agriculture
NY Harbor ULSD	Short	Non-Agriculture
Crude Oil – Light Sweet	Short	Non-Agriculture
Platinum	Short	Non-Agriculture
Gas Oil	Short	Non-Agriculture
Palladium	Short	Non-Agriculture
Copper	Short	Non-Agriculture
Silver	Short	Non-Agriculture
Gold	Short	Non-Agriculture
Brent	Short	Non-Agriculture
5-Year U.S. T-Note	Short	Rates
Euro-Schatz	Long	Rates
Eurodollar	Short	Rates
2-Year U.S. T-Note	Short	Rates
U.S. T-Bond	Long	Rates
Euribor	Long	Rates

TABLE 6.58   Initial sector allocation 2016

	Long	Short	Total
Agriculture	4	11	15
Rates	3	3	6
Non-Agriculture	0	10	10
Currencies	1	2	3
Equities	1	1	2
Total	9	27	36

Early on in the year, we see a bit of drama. An initial spike up in performance to over 10%. A swift loss of this gain, and then even faster move back up to nearly +20%. Big swings, but we return back to around plus/minus zero on the year again and remain close to that line for much of the year. Thanks to a bump both in the agriculture sector returns and the rates, we do see a bit of a profit on the year, even it's modest (Figure 6.87).

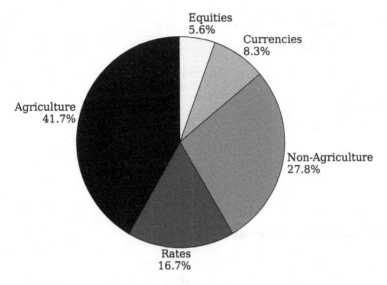

FIGURE 6.86 Sector allocation 2016.

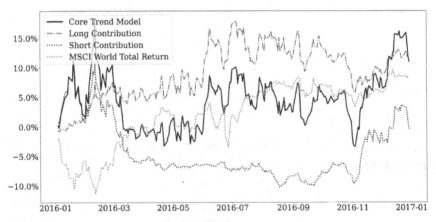

FIGURE 6.87 Strategy performance 2016.

Compared to some of the really dramatic years we've seen so far, this was reasonably quiet and walking away with a trading gain of 11% without any really scary moments was a welcome change (Figures 6.88–6.90).

During this tough year, we saw plenty of both gaining and losing positions. One which did quite well was the Arabica coffee, which we held on the long side for much of the year (Figure 6.91). It was a choppy ride, but not enough to kick us out of the position, and we stayed in until the trend ended in November.

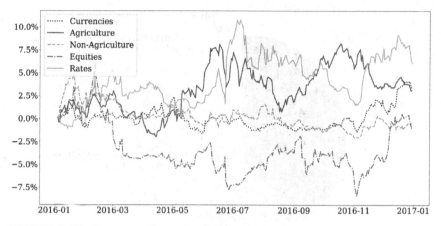

FIGURE 6.88 Sector performance 2016.

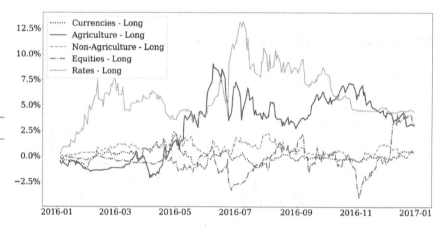

FIGURE 6.89 Long sector performance 2016.

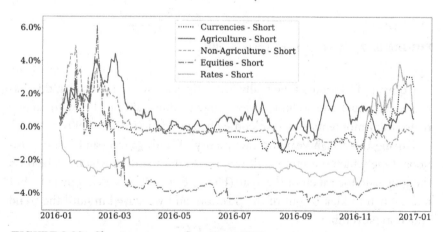

FIGURE 6.90 Short sector performance 2016.

FIGURE 6.91 Arabica coffee.

We've now completed 15 years of trading, and the original investment of US$10 million has turned in almost US$85 million. The power of compounding can do amazing things. This is just the investor part of course and you have been paid quite a few millions over the years. If you compare the adventure so far to having just put up a few hundred thousand of your own money, dialling the risk level to 11 and hoping for the best, the winning way to go should be quite clear.

This year we didn't really get much performance fee (Tables 6.59 and 6.60). Remember that we had a loss of 7% last year, and this year we only gained 11% before fees. We did set a new high-water mark here, but most of the year's trading gains were spent getting back up to that line, and we don't get paid for that. Still, we get one and a quarter million in base fees, and another three hundred in performance fee. Now that we are at the high-water mark, we can start making money again.

TABLE 6.59 Sector results 2016

	Currencies	Agriculture	Non-Agriculture	Equities	Rates	All sectors
Long	0.3	3.1	0.6	3.0	4.4	11.4
Short	2.5	0.5	−0.3	−4.0	0.9	−0.4
Total	3.3	3.1	−0.4	−1.2	6.1	11.0

TABLE 6.60 Results 2016

	US$	Percentage
Starting NAV	76,954,416	769.54
Trading result	8,472,094	11.00
Interest income	435,309	0.60
Management fee	1,261,376	1.60
Performance fee	295,263	0.40
Net result	7,350,763	9.60
Ending NAV	84,305,179	843.10

■ 2017

At the start of 2017, there was an abundance of trends available. We have a portfolio of 54 positions, which is far more than normal. Under the current rules, we don't adapt risk on a portfolio level, but rather keep each position risk static, and therefore this is a very risky portfolio. Given how many positions we have on, it's also a surprisingly diverse portfolio. We have 26 long positions and 28 short, and we're quite evenly spread across sectors (Tables 6.61 and 6.62, and Figure 6.92). Usually when there are many trends around, they tend to be of the same theme, but in this case we have a broad exposure. One theme that we do see is long stocks, but we also see a mix of longs and shorts in metals, rates, and agriculture.

TABLE 6.61 Initial portfolio 2017

Market	Direction	Sector
Cocoa	Short	Agriculture
Lean Hogs	Long	Agriculture
Live Cattle	Long	Agriculture
Coffee C	Short	Agriculture
Robusta Coffee	Long	Agriculture
White Sugar	Short	Agriculture
Sugar No. 11	Short	Agriculture
Lumber	Short	Agriculture
Canola	Long	Agriculture
KC HRW Wheat	Short	Agriculture
Soybean Meal	Short	Agriculture
Soybean Oil	Long	Agriculture
New Zealand Dollar	Short	Currencies
Japanese Yen	Short	Currencies
Australian Dollar	Short	Currencies

(Continued)

TABLE 6.61 (Continued)

Market	Direction	Sector
British Pound	Short	Currencies
US Dollar Index	Long	Currencies
Canadian Dollar	Short	Currencies
Euro FX	Short	Currencies
CAC 40	Long	Equities
HS China E	Short	Equities
CBOE Volatility Index	Short	Equities
Nikkei 225 Dollar	Long	Equities
EURO STOXX 50	Long	Equities
DAX	Long	Equities
FTSE 100	Long	Equities
E-mini S&P 500	Long	Equities
E-mini Nasdaq-100	Long	Equities
E-mini S&P MidCap 400	Long	Equities
Hang Seng Index	Short	Equities
E-mini Russell 2000	Long	Equities
E-mini Dow	Long	Equities
S&P/TSX 60 Index	Long	Equities
Crude Oil – Light Sweet	Long	Non-Agriculture
NY Harbor ULSD	Long	Non-Agriculture
RBOB Gasoline	Long	Non-Agriculture
Brent	Long	Non-Agriculture
Silver	Short	Non-Agriculture
Gas Oil	Long	Non-Agriculture
Copper	Long	Non-Agriculture
Gold	Short	Non-Agriculture
Palladium	Long	Non-Agriculture
Platinum	Short	Non-Agriculture
Euro-Schatz	Long	Rates
Euro-Bund	Short	Rates
Euro-BTP Long-Term	Short	Rates
5-Year U.S. T-Note	Short	Rates
2-Year U.S. T-Note	Short	Rates
U.S. T-Bond	Short	Rates
Euro-Bobl	Long	Rates
10-Year U.S. T-Note	Short	Rates
Long Gilt	Short	Rates
10-Year Govt. of Canada Bond	Short	Rates
Eurodollar	Short	Rates

TABLE 6.62	Initial sector allocation 2017		
	Long	Short	Total
Agriculture	5	7	12
Rates	2	9	11
Non-Agriculture	7	3	10
Equities	11	3	14
Currencies	1	6	7
Total	26	28	54

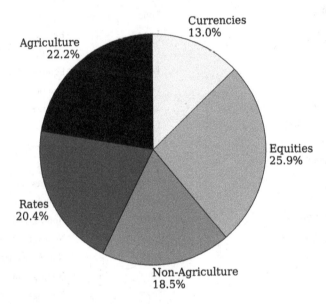

FIGURE 6.92 Sector allocation 2017.

Even a quick look at Figure 6.93 tells us that this was not a fun year. The MSCI World Index kept moving up in a nearly perfect trend for the entire year, ending at close to 25% up, while our strategy did nothing of the sort. We took an initial hit right off the bat, and then we got stuck in the -5% range for almost half of the year. Far behind benchmark, we tick up a bit by mid-year, only to lose it just as swiftly, and by the end of the year we have a tiny 3.7% trading gain, leaving us 20% behind the index. That's a pretty lousy year.

Now you'll have to explain why you failed to profit from an incredible bull market. You told your investors that you need trends to make money, and they all saw a massive bull market trend. Well, looking at the sector

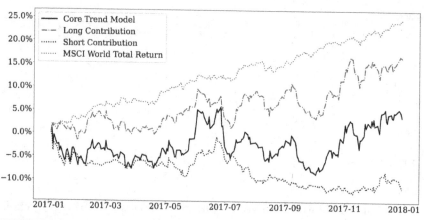

FIGURE 6.93 Strategy performance 2017.

performance in Figure 6.94, we see that we did make very strong returns in the equity sector. The problem was with all other sectors (Figures 6.95 and 6.96). Every other sector ended up making a loss this year. None of those losses were very big, but together they add up and their aggregated loss summed up to about the same as the gains on the stock markets.

The bull market of 2017 wasn't limited to the United States, and as you can see in Figure 6.97, Asia performed quite well too. This was just a full year of clear skies in this sector, with markets moving up almost uninterrupted for the whole year.

We started the year with nearly US$85,000,000, so that trading gain of US$3 million is really quite tiny. After nearly a percent of income from the

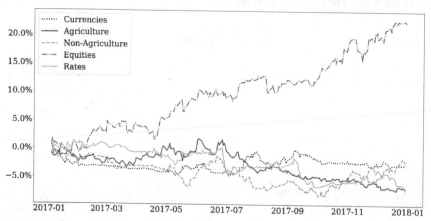

FIGURE 6.94 Sector performance 2017.

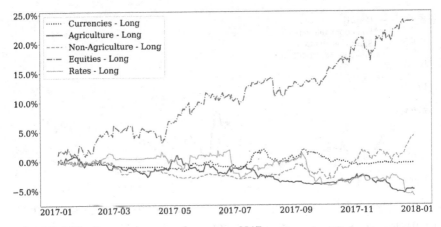

FIGURE 6.95 Long sector performance 2017.

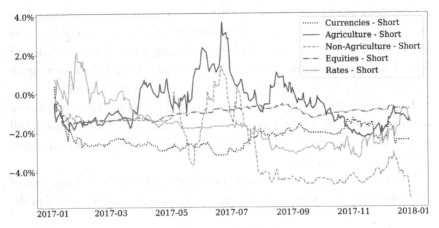

FIGURE 6.96 Short sector performance 2017.

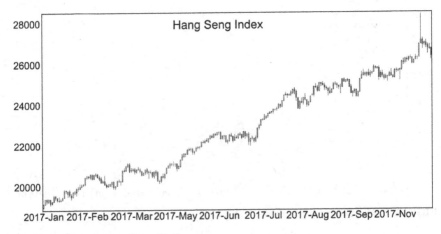

FIGURE 6.97 Hang Seng bull run.

TABLE 6.63 Sector results 2017

	Currencies	Agriculture	Non-Agriculture	Equities	Rates	All sectors
Long	−0.3	−5.0	4.3	23.6	−6.1	16.5
Short	−2.4	−1.5	−5.4	−0.8	−1.5	−11.7
Total	−2.6	−6.8	−2.1	22.4	−7.2	3.7

TABLE 6.64 Results 2017

	US$	Percentage
Starting NAV	84,305,179	843.05
Trading result	3,127,629	3.70
Interest income	745,210	0.90
Management fee	1,285,877	1.50
Performance fee	388,044	0.50
Net result	2,198,918	2.60
Ending NAV	86,504,097	865.00

interest side, and we're a little shy of 5% up before fees. After paying management and a little bit of performance fee, we return 2.6% net to investors (Tables 6.63 and 6.64). One measly tenth of the return they could have gotten from a passive index tracker. After a year like this, the pressure is on. Even if we now, in this chapter, have over a decade and a half of strong track record behind us, there is a risk of investors losing confidence and we really need another big win to prove ourselves once more.

■ 2018

This year we start off with a considerably smaller portfolio than last year, with a lot lower risk (Table 6.65). Only 35 positions all in all, with a clear tilt towards bullish stocks, and a mixed exposure in the rest (Table 6.66 and Figure 6.98). We're mostly short agriculture, but still long lumber and cotton. After the loss last year, there are two things we'd like to see happen this year. We'd like to see an absolute gain, and we'd like to see a relative gain. Failing both would look really bad.

At the start of the year, we get exactly what we want to see. A strong move up to +12% by February. Of course, if you've been paying attention during this chapter, you should know how the game works by now. From the +12%, we take a nosedive and crash down to -10%. As much as such moves

TABLE 6.65 Initial portfolio 2018

Market	Direction	Sector
Lumber	Long	Agriculture
Coffee C	Short	Agriculture
KC HRW Wheat	Short	Agriculture
Corn	Short	Agriculture
Cocoa	Short	Agriculture
Soybean Oil	Short	Agriculture
Robusta Coffee	Short	Agriculture
Cotton No. 2	Long	Agriculture
British Pound	Long	Currencies
FTSE 100	Long	Equities
CBOE Volatility Index	Short	Equities
S&P/TSX 60 Index	Long	Equities
E-mini Russell 2000	Long	Equities
E-mini Nasdaq-100	Long	Equities
E-mini S&P MidCap 400	Long	Equities
E-mini Dow	Long	Equities
Nikkei 225 Dollar	Long	Equities
E-mini S&P 500	Long	Equities
Henry Hub Natural Gas	Short	Non-Agriculture
NY Harbor ULSD	Long	Non-Agriculture
RBOB Gasoline	Long	Non-Agriculture
Copper	Long	Non-Agriculture
Gas Oil	Long	Non-Agriculture
Palladium	Long	Non-Agriculture
Silver	Short	Non-Agriculture
Brent	Long	Non-Agriculture
Crude Oil – Light Sweet	Long	Non-Agriculture
Platinum	Short	Non-Agriculture
Euribor	Long	Rates
5-Year U.S. T-Note	Short	Rates
10-Year U.S. T-Note	Short	Rates
2-Year U.S. T-Note	Short	Rates
Euro-BTP Long-Term	Long	Rates
Euro-Bund	Long	Rates
Eurodollar	Short	Rates

TABLE 6.66	Initial sector allocation 2018		
	Long	Short	Total
Agriculture	2	6	8
Non-Agriculture	7	3	10
Rates	3	4	7
Equities	8	1	9
Currencies	1	0	1
Total	21	14	35

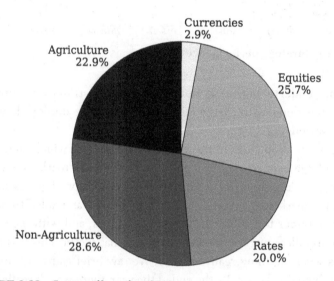

FIGURE 6.98 Sector allocation 2018.

are barely visible in a multi-year chart, they really hurt when they happen in front of you. For much of the year after that, we wobble along sideways in a -5% to -10% range, and we stay below the equity index. The really worrying development is that drop we see in Figure 6.99 in October, when we move all the way down to -20% while the stock market index only see a modest pullback.

After another really difficult year, at least we get a slight respite from the last month, when the stock markets fall hard while we gain. At the end of 2018, we manage to achieve one of the two goals we set out early on. We failed to produce absolute return, but a least we beat the benchmark index. Of course, setting out such goals is just an imaginary or

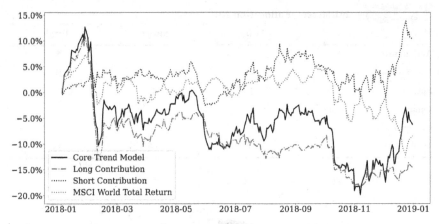

FIGURE 6.99 Strategy performance 2018.

motivational undertaking, as it doesn't affect the strategy in any way. That's just the thing with systematic strategies. Once deployed, we are effectively passengers.

That big scary drop early in the year, the sudden loss which ruined our year, was in large part created by a pullback in the stock markets. We were heavily long, took a short-term hit and triggered stops (Figures 6.100–6.102). As the markets recovered, we had stopped out and failed to participate. It was a rather tough year in the stock markets, and with the choppy and largely trendless market, we kept losing in that sector. This was one of those years where nothing really worked. We saw brief gains in some sectors, but nothing that lasted. By the end of the year, there wasn't really much of a difference in sector performance, and they all showed a slight loss to a slight gain, with a net negative return on the year.

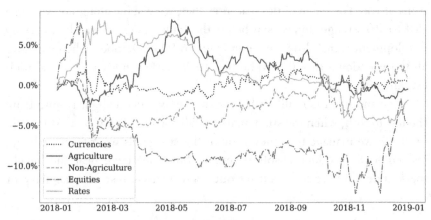

FIGURE 6.100 Sector performance 2018.

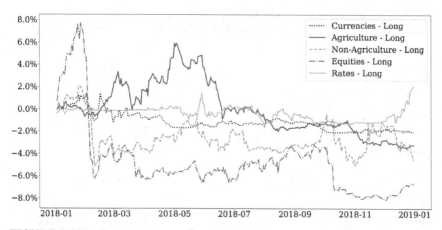

FIGURE 6.101   Long sector performance 2018.

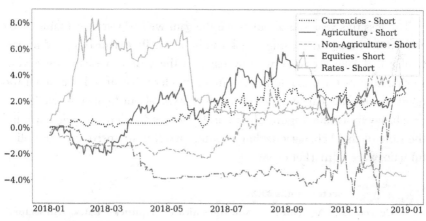

FIGURE 6.102   Short sector performance 2018.

The word crash is incredibly over-used as a descriptor of market pull-backs. What happened to the stock market in January of 2018 certainly felt like a crash at the time, and it was of course described as such in the media. A few years later, everyone struggles to remember what happened, or even that something did happen. Still, it was certainly a couple of very painful weeks for trend followers. Take a look at the price movement in Figure 6.103. We had an amazing bull trend in 2017, and then it really started accelerating as we entered 2018, building up some serious profits. And just then, when you least expected it, the markets just turned on a dime and you gave up several months' worth of performance in a matter of days. Easy come, easy go. These situations, painful as they are, represent the cost of doing business in this industry.

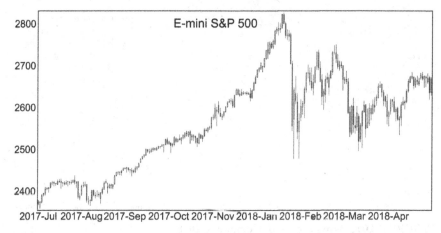

FIGURE 6.103 S&P 500's sudden plunge of 2018.

The loss this year was about twice the gain we had last year (Tables 6.67 and 6.68). Being on a losing streak can be mentally exhausting, and in particular that fake recovery we saw early in the year can easily break your spirits. Luckily for me, I don't remember much of that since I was on far too many drugs that year. No, not every stereotype about finance is true. I was on a heavy morphine regime after a pretty severe accident, and right around the time of that February decline I found myself in intensive care and blissfully unaware of market events.

TABLE 6.67 Sector results 2018

	Currencies	Agriculture	Non-Agriculture	Equities	Rates	All sectors
Long	−2.1	−3.2	−4.5	−6.7	2.1	−14.5
Short	2.6	3.1	5.6	2.7	−3.6	10.4
Total	0.4	-0.6	0.7	−4.9	−1.9	−6.2

TABLE 6.68 Results 2018

	US$	Percentage
Starting NAV	86,504,097	865.04
Trading result	−5,384,227	−6.20
Interest income	1,327,782	1.50
Management fee	1,193,032	1.40
Performance fee	—	0.00
Net result	−5,249,477	−6.10
Ending NAV	81,254,620	812.50

That was a bad year all around, even if we did beat the index. All in all, we lost US$5 million for investors, after having been paid a million and change in fees, and now we're in a drawdown again. No performance fees until we recover to fresh highs.

■ 2019

Being in a drawdown is always tough. It makes you feel as if you're working for free, since you don't get any performance fees until you get back up over that last high-water mark. We're also in a tough spot since we haven't really seen a proper victory since 2014. After the 50% return that year, we were heroes. Now, after four mediocre years, our annual Christmas card list is getting smaller and smaller.

The year is 2019 and after the mediocre stock markets of the previous year, we have built a bear market portfolio. We're short equity indexes across the board and that is rather unfortunately going to be the driving force in the first part of this year (Tables 6.69 and 6.70, and Figure 6.104).

TABLE 6.69 Initial portfolio 2019

Market	Direction	Sector
Lumber	Short	Agriculture
Lean Hogs	Long	Agriculture
Soybean Meal	Short	Agriculture
Live Cattle	Long	Agriculture
Soybean Oil	Short	Agriculture
Robusta Coffee	Short	Agriculture
Canola	Short	Agriculture
KC HRW Wheat	Short	Agriculture
Cotton No. 2	Short	Agriculture
Australian Dollar	Short	Currencies
Canadian Dollar	Short	Currencies
US Dollar Index	Long	Currencies
CBOE Volatility Index	Long	Equities
HS China E	Short	Equities
Nikkei 225 Dollar	Short	Equities
E-mini S&P MidCap 400	Short	Equities
E-mini Russell 2000	Short	Equities
CAC 40	Short	Equities
DAX	Short	Equities

(Continued)

TABLE 6.69 (Continued)

Market	Direction	Sector
E-mini Nasdaq-100	Short	Equities
EURO STOXX 50	Short	Equities
S&P/TSX 60 Index	Short	Equities
FTSE 100	Short	Equities
E-mini Dow	Short	Equities
E-mini S&P 500	Short	Equities
NY Harbor ULSD	Short	Non-Agriculture
RBOB Gasoline	Short	Non-Agriculture
Brent	Short	Non-Agriculture
Palladium	Long	Non-Agriculture
Copper	Short	Non-Agriculture
Gold	Long	Non-Agriculture
Gas Oil	Short	Non-Agriculture
Crude Oil - Light Sweet	Short	Non-Agriculture
2-Year U.S. T-Note	Long	Rates
Long Gilt	Long	Rates
Euro-Bund	Long	Rates
Euro-Schatz	Long	Rates
Short Sterling	Long	Rates
10-Year Govt. of Canada Bond	Long	Rates
Eurodollar	Short	Rates
U.S. T-Bond	Long	Rates
Euro-BTP Long-Term	Long	Rates
10-Year U.S. T-Note	Long	Rates
Euribor	Long	Rates
Euro-Bobl	Long	Rates
5-Year U.S. T-Note	Long	Rates

TABLE 6.70 Initial sector allocation 2019

	Long	Short	Total
Agriculture	2	7	9
Non-Agriculture	2	6	8
Rates	12	1	13
Currencies	1	2	3
Equities	1	12	13
Total	18	28	46

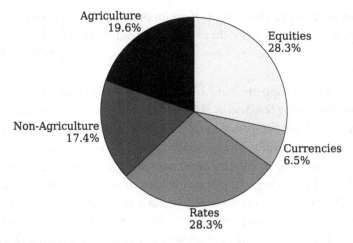

FIGURE 6.104 Sector allocation 2019.

With the stock markets taking off on the upside this year, our short exposure to that sector proved rather costly. As the markets gain 15% early on, we lose about the same amount. Not the kind of start we were hoping for. Our portfolio allocation adapts to the market conditions, as it always does, and we gradually recover from our lows (Figure 6.105). By October, we have caught up with the markets and we stand at about +10%, but that is before yet another ugly drop. Just when things finally looks so good, we fall right back down and end the year with a 5% loss.

Losing 5% in a year is not a disaster by itself. That happens. But this was the fifth poor year in a row. Not the fifth consecutive loss, but five years

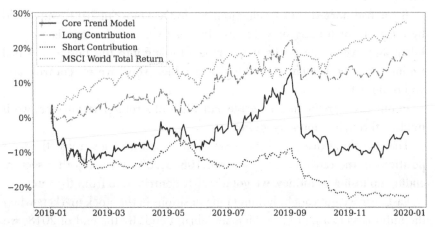

FIGURE 6.105 Strategy performance 2019.

without anything to show for it. If an investor had put US$100,000 in the strategy at the start of 2015, they would now only have US$93,000 after five years, and all along they've been paying you fees for the privilege of losing their money.

A year or two happens, but five? This is the worst crisis we've seen since starting this trading business in 2001 and it would be quite reasonable to ask if the markets have changed, if trend following no longer is a viable approach. Well, we have seen some fundamental market changes in the past years. The most obvious being that the interest rates situation changed. In the golden days of trend following, the primary source of returns were from the rates sector. This was because we started out in a very high interest rate regime and saw slowly decreasing interests. As interest rates decrease, bond prices rise, and simply being long year after year was the main source of income. This game is clearly up, given how low are the interest rates we are on.

The other major thing that changed is the risk-on, risk-off mentality of the markets. All too often, there is a single factor that everything depends on, some event which can turn almost all trends on their heads at once. This could be a US debt ceiling deadlock, a major election, FED decision, or similar. The markets have become too globalized, so interconnected, that markets which wouldn't show much correlation decades ago now suddenly move as one.

So, is the game up? Is it time to fold up shop, take the money we made so far and buy a small island somewhere? The thing to remember is that while this may be a tough crisis for the industry, trend following has been declared dead more often than Mark Twain. It's been a premature assumption every time, so far.

If you had started your trading journey in December of 2014, you would be forgiven for folding now. To have five bad years at the start is a career killer, and that is one of the major risks of going into this business. A bad timing for your launch, something over which you have no control, and you're done for.

In our case, having had a decade and a half of strong performance, we'll muddle through it and keep going.

The one thing that saved this year from a total meltdown was the long positions in the rates sector (Figures 6.106–6.108). With all other sectors ending up losing us money, we got a +20% contribution from the rates.

Last year we got caught holding long positions in the stock markets when the bull market came to a sudden and abrupt end. By the end of 2018, we have been short in the S&P and other stock markets for a couple of months, and even started making some money on it. But the short side is notoriously

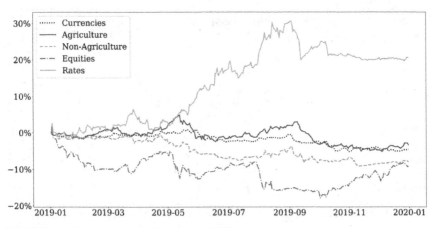

FIGURE 6.106 Sector performance 2019.

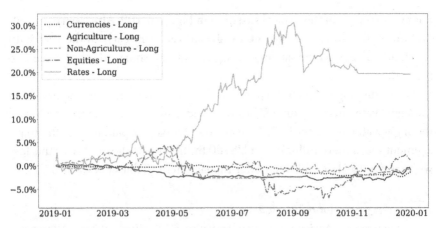

FIGURE 6.107 Long sector performance 2019.

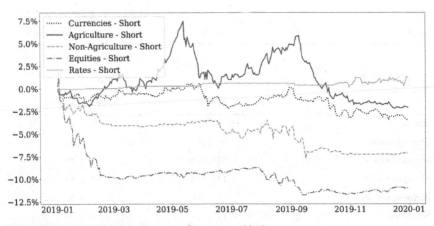

FIGURE 6.108 Short sector performance 2019.

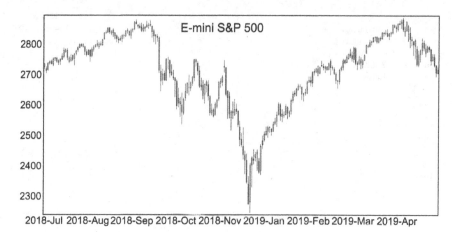

FIGURE 6.109 Trying the short side of the S&P 500.

tricky, as you see in this typical situation in Figure 6.109. After a sharp acceleration on the downside, we get a V-shaped recovery early in the year with substantial losses accompanying it. In general, the short side is very hard to make money from.

We're digging an even deeper hole for ourselves, moving further from the high-water mark. Our NAV moved under 800 after this loss of 5% and the high-water mark set in 2017 was 865. All we get paid here is the management fee, a mere million on a US$80 million portfolio, and after this loss we're down to U$77 million under management (Tables 6.71 and 6.72).

TABLE 6.71 Sector results 2019

	Currencies	Agriculture	Non-Agriculture	Equities	Rates	All sectors
Long	−1.3	−0.9	−1.2	1.3	19.6	17.5
Short	−3.6	−2.1	−7.2	−10.9	1.2	−22.5
Total	−4.6	−3.4	−8.1	−9.3	20.6	−4.9

TABLE 6.72 Results 2019

	US$	Percentage
Starting NAV	81,254,620	812.55
Trading result	−3,957,256	−4.90
Interest income	979,959	1.20
Management fee	1,141,344	1.40
Performance fee	—	0.00
Net result	−4,118,641	−5.10
Ending NAV	77,135,979	771.40

■ 2020

After five tough years, it would be nice too have an uneventful 2020. A nice, smooth year with no major drama or big news. And what could possibly go wrong in 2020? I mentioned earlier that we generally don't like single theme market regimes, where everything spins around one single event or situation. That's usually a bad thing for trend following, as it reduces the benefits of diversification. So I'm sure you're wondering how our trend model handled the shock of the worst pandemic in a hundred years, lockdowns, travel bans, and all the things that you have now spent so much time trying to forget.

Knowing what we know now about 2020, it may seem quite concerning that we're fully loaded on a bull market portfolio. We're long stocks across the board and short the VIX as well. That would certainly not be good if there's a sudden market shock. We're also long oil, mostly long agriculture and short rates (Tables 6.73 and 6.74, and Figure 6.110).

TABLE 6.73 Initial portfolio 2020

Market	Direction	Sector
Lumber	Long	Agriculture
Soybean Meal	Short	Agriculture
Soybean Oil	Long	Agriculture
Cotton No. 2	Long	Agriculture
Sugar No. 11	Long	Agriculture
White Sugar	Long	Agriculture
Lean Hogs	Short	Agriculture
KC HRW Wheat	Long	Agriculture
Live Cattle	Long	Agriculture
Feeder Cattle	Long	Agriculture
Coffee C	Long	Agriculture
Corn	Short	Agriculture
Japanese Yen	Short	Currencies
Australian Dollar	Long	Currencies
New Zealand Dollar	Long	Currencies
Canadian Dollar	Long	Currencies
US Dollar Index	Short	Currencies
British Pound	Long	Currencies
E-mini S&P 500	Long	Equities
Hang Seng Index	Long	Equities

(Continued)

TABLE 6.73 (Continued)

Market	Direction	Sector
HS China E	Long	Equities
S&P/TSX 60 Index	Long	Equities
FTSE 100	Long	Equities
Nikkei 225 Dollar	Long	Equities
EURO STOXX 50	Long	Equities
CAC 40	Long	Equities
CBOE Volatility Index	Short	Equities
E-mini Nasdaq-100	Long	Equities
E-mini Dow	Long	Equities
E-mini Russell 2000	Long	Equities
E-mini S&P MidCap 400	Long	Equities
Henry Hub Natural Gas	Short	Non-Agriculture
Gas Oil	Long	Non-Agriculture
Brent	Long	Non-Agriculture
Palladium	Long	Non-Agriculture
Copper	Long	Non-Agriculture
RBOB Gasoline	Long	Non-Agriculture
Euro-Bobl	Short	Rates
Euribor	Short	Rates
Short Sterling	Short	Rates
10-Year U.S. T-Note	Short	Rates
2-Year U.S. T-Note	Short	Rates
Long Gilt	Short	Rates
Euro-Bund	Short	Rates
Euro-Schatz	Short	Rates
5-Year U.S. T-Note	Short	Rates
10-Year Govt. of Canada Bond	Short	Rates

TABLE 6.74 Initial sector allocation 2020

	Long	Short	Total
Agriculture	9	3	12
Rates	0	10	10
Non-Agriculture	5	1	6
Equities	12	1	13
Currencies	4	2	6
Total	30	17	47

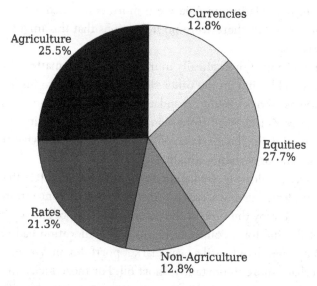

FIGURE 6.110 Sector allocation 2020.

This year started out in quite a worrying fashion, in particular in the light of our past five years and the pressure is on us at this point. We saw some larger swings and losses down to -17% at the start of March (Figure 6.111). This was, of course, a year like no other, and your memory of the events here are probably quite different depending on where in the world you were at the time. For me, being in Switzerland, I remember it very clearly. In January, there were minor news stories about yet another virus in some faraway part of the world. The story continued into February, but even at the start of March this wasn't anything of real importance to us

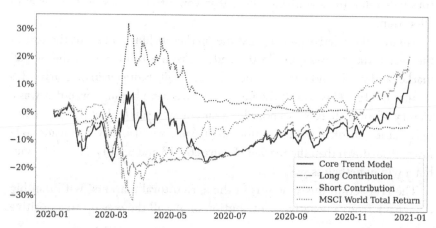

FIGURE 6.111 Strategy performance 2020.

here in Europe. My relatives in Asia were more concerned and we were concerned for them, but there were no indications that this might be anything more serious.

The situation changed dramatically in mid-March. In a matter of days, it went from some odd thing on the other side of the planet, to full-on panic mode. Lockdowns, shops closing, mandated working from home, schools closed. Downtown Zurich went from being a bustling tourist city to a ghost town in a matter of days. The markets, of course, didn't know what to make of this situation, and uncertainty usually leads to panic.

In terms of trend following, we handled this situation far better than most discretionary traders. Sure, we entered the year with a concentrated bull market portfolio, but by the time of the panic in March, we already had had a slow market decline for a couple of months. The allocation had changed and in mid-March we already had a bear market portfolio on. We were short stocks and, perhaps more importantly, short oil. For those lucky enough to have suppressed memories of 2020, this was the year when the oil futures price went negative. In theory, you got paid for taking possession of a barrel of oil.

During this most chaotic phase, March and April, we could clearly see the value of the short side of trend following. During this phase, we lost nearly as much as the overall market on the long side of our portfolio, but we gained substantially more on the short positions. All in all, we showed a welcome gain while the markets lost. If you aim to attract professional investors, this type of behaviour can be extremely valuable. The ability to act as a hedge during times of market distress. Even if you end up giving much of these gains back, as we do here in the following months, professional investors will value the stabilizing effect that your strategy has on their overall allocation.

We lose the relative gain against the market in June and spent the rest of the year trying to catch up. In the end, we're not too far from the overall market and we do end with a modest double digit trading gain of nearly 13% (Figure 6.112). This wasn't the big victory we were hoping for, but it was a victory of sorts. 2020 was a horrible year any way you look at it, and we not only came out of it with a double-digit gain, we also saw a considerably lower drawdown than the market (Figures 6.113 and 6.114). Not a big win, but a win nonetheless.

The real action this year was in the agricultural markets, with that big comeback from a negative contribution of 5% all the way up to a positive

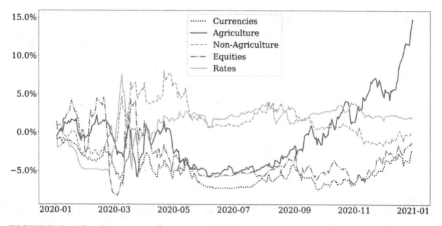

FIGURE 6.112 Sector performance 2020.

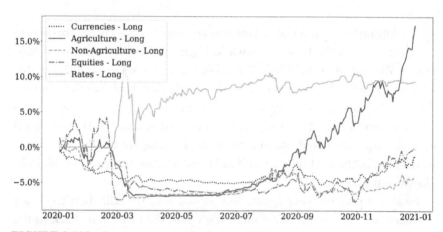

FIGURE 6.113 Long sector performance 2020.

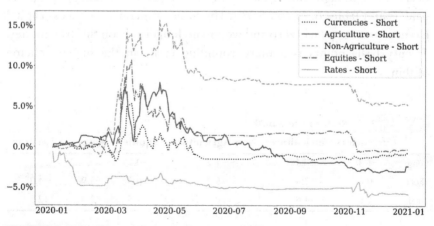

FIGURE 6.114 Short sector performance 2020.

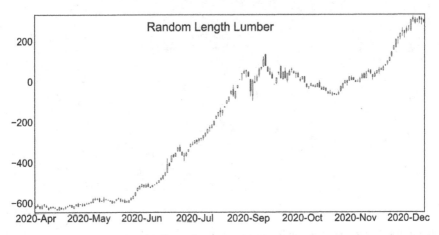

FIGURE 6.115 Lumber bull market.

15% addition to the portfolio. This was accomplished by many markets in combination, but the lumber shown in Figure 6.115 illustrates what happened. We had an incredible bull market run in the sector and the profits added up quickly. You may notice in this particular chart that the price on the y-scale goes into the negative. This is nothing to worry about, as it's just a cosmetic effect of long-term continuation charts. As mentioned earlier, I use calculated continuations in this chapter to illustrate price trends, but in the backtests as well as in real life, we trade on actual, individual contracts.

Finally, a positive year again! But as you see, we still didn't get any performance fees. Even this double-digit gain didn't push us back to the old high-water mark. We had a fund-high NAV of 865 in 2017. We're nearly there though, and just a tiny bit further, and we could get properly paid again (Tables 6.75 and 6.76). The interest income on excess capital has now gone to nearly zero and we can no longer rely on this free money. Twenty basis points is a mere rounding error in the bigger scheme of things.

TABLE 6.75 Sector results 2020

	Currencies	Agriculture	Non-Agriculture	Equities	Rates	All sectors
Long	−1.3	17.4	−4.2	−0.2	9.4	21.1
Short	−0.8	−2.4	5.2	−0.3	−5.9	−4.2
Total	−2.6	14.8	-0.2	−1.5	2.0	12.5

TABLE 6.76 Results 2020

	US$	Percentage
Starting NAV	77,135,979	771.36
Trading result	9,617,188	12.50
Interest income	184,422	0.20
Management fee	1,286,048	1.70
Performance fee	—	0.00
Net result	8,515,563	11.00
Ending NAV	85,651,541	856.50

■ 2021

So here we are, entering the final year of this 20-year journey. This sure was more fun the first ten years, wasn't it? It probably feels like it at this point, but things really didn't start to get tough until 2015. Still, that's six difficult years behind us, and you would be forgiven for starting to give up on the whole idea of trend following by now. Clearly it stopped working. Right?

Something quite unusual this year is that we have 12 positions in agriculture, all of them on the long side (Tables 6.77and 6.78, and Figure 6.116).

TABLE 6.77 Initial portfolio 2021

Market	Direction	Sector
Sugar No. 11	Long	Agriculture
Lumber	Long	Agriculture
Soybean	Long	Agriculture
Lean Hogs	Long	Agriculture
Soybean Oil	Long	Agriculture
Soybean Meal	Long	Agriculture
Canola	Long	Agriculture
KC HRW Wheat	Long	Agriculture
Corn	Long	Agriculture
Cocoa	Long	Agriculture
Cotton No. 2	Long	Agriculture
White Sugar	Long	Agriculture
Australian Dollar	Long	Currencies

(Continued)

TABLE 6.77 (Continued)

Market	Direction	Sector
British Pound	Long	Currencies
Swiss Franc	Long	Currencies
Euro FX	Long	Currencies
Canadian Dollar	Long	Currencies
US Dollar Index	Short	Currencies
Japanese Yen	Long	Currencies
New Zealand Dollar	Long	Currencies
FTSE 100	Long	Equities
DAX	Long	Equities
E-mini Nasdaq-100	Long	Equities
EURO STOXX 50	Long	Equities
HS China E	Long	Equities
E-mini Russell 2000	Long	Equities
CAC 40	Long	Equities
E-mini S&P MidCap 400	Long	Equities
CBOE Volatility Index	Short	Equities
S&P/TSX 60 Index	Long	Equities
E-mini S&P 500	Long	Equities
Nikkei 225 Dollar	Long	Equities
E-mini Dow	Long	Equities
Hang Seng Index	Long	Equities
Crude Oil – Light Sweet	Long	Non-Agriculture
Henry Hub Natural Gas	Short	Non-Agriculture
Gas Oil	Long	Non-Agriculture
RBOB Gasoline	Long	Non-Agriculture
Gold	Short	Non-Agriculture
NY Harbor ULSD	Long	Non-Agriculture
Palladium	Long	Non-Agriculture
Copper	Long	Non-Agriculture
Platinum	Long	Non-Agriculture
Euribor	Long	Rates
Eurodollar	Long	Rates
Euro-BTP Long-Term	Long	Rates
10-Year Govt. of Canada Bond	Short	Rates
2-Year U.S. T-Note	Long	Rates

TABLE 6.78 Initial sector allocation 2021

	Long	Short	Total
Agriculture	12	0	12
Rates	4	1	5
Non-Agriculture	7	2	9
Equities	13	1	14
Currencies	7	1	8
Total	43	5	48

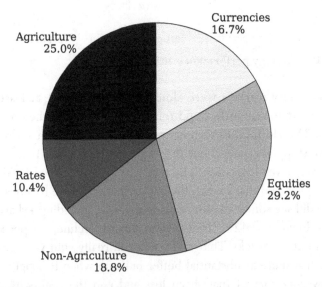

FIGURE 6.116 Sector allocation 2021.

On top of that, we have a fully loaded bull market portfolio with 14 positions directly betting on stocks moving up. We're mostly long metals and energies, and we have a very limited rates exposure at this point. There's a lot riding on this one after the mediocre performance we've had for a while now.

When the profits jump to +10% on the year in the first week, you probably won't feel much joy. We've seen that one before, haven't we? You would probably be expecting a quick move down to -10% or worse, just like we had a few times before. Well, just as you expected, there is a sudden change in performance coming in February, but this time it's in our favour. In fact, this is the year that will make you feel like you just woke up from a bad dream. The good times are back, and they're back in spades!

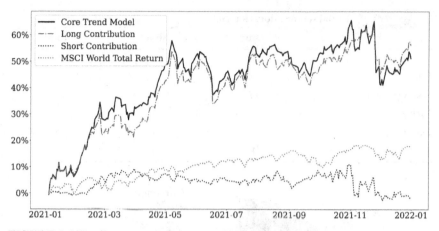

FIGURE 6.117 Strategy performance 2021.

The world equity markets were almost flat during 2021; at least that's how it looks next to our little trend-following strategy. At the end of the year, the MSCI World Total Return has netted about 15%, but we're so far ahead that we stopped caring about the index long ago. After that move up in February, we never look back. The next strong push ended in May and reached 55% plus, and that's when the equity markets were barely scratching 10%. We did see some volatility during the year, including a sharp drop from +65% down to +42%. That's quite a hard decline, 23 percentage points in a couple of weeks. Things like that can really ruin your year, but this time we had quite a substantial buffer built up when it happened. We end up recovering part of that sharp loss and end the year with a very respectable trading gain of 51% (Figure 6.117).

Finally, after six tough years, we prove that our approach still works and that our fees are justified. We were behind the traditional markets for a while but this puts us firmly in the lead again. The hero sector this year was agriculture. This sector was carrying the entire year. It wasn't the only sector that gained, but it gained far more than anything else. The overall year contribution for this sector was 35%, leaving just 16% for the rest to share and 13 of those came from equities, with the rest from non-agricultural (Figure 6.118). The currencies and rates showed a marginal negative contribution.

As for that rather large drop we saw late in the year, that was a combination of sectors. The stock markets fell a bit then, and our long equity index futures lost. At the same time, long positions in metals and energies suffered as well as some short rates (Figures 6.119 and 6.120).

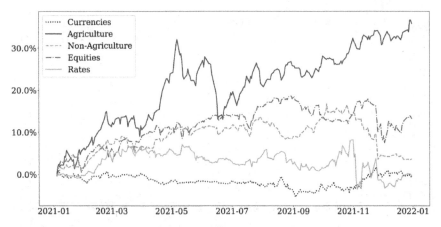

FIGURE 6.118 Sector performance 2021.

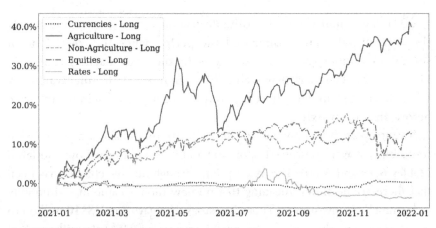

FIGURE 6.119 Long sector performance 2021.

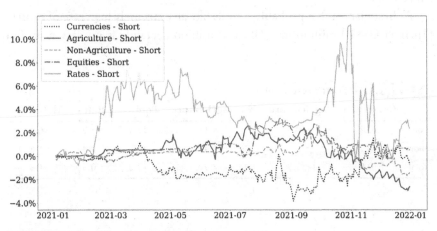

FIGURE 6.120 Short sector performance 2021.

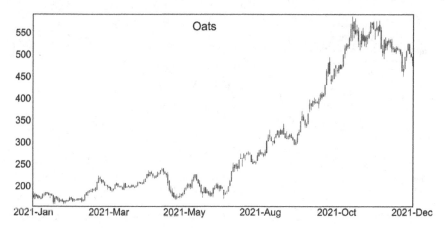

FIGURE 6.121   Oats in a bull market.

2021 saw a multitude of profitable trends across sectors but clearly the agricultural sector dominated the performance this year. One of several incredible trades we saw was in the oats market, shown in Figure 6.121. The market was already on an upwards-leaning trajectory when it started moving in a big way by mid-year, doubling in price before an orderly exit.

Twenty years have now passed since US$10 million and a noble mission to multiply it were bestowed upon you and it's time to see how you fared (Tables 6.79 and 6.80). The assumption throughout this chapter has been that there are no flows, meaning that no new money came in and nobody redeemed their investment. Those investors who gave you US$10 million to invest now find themselves the proud owners of US$120 million. And the change.

At first glance, that probably sounds like an extremely high rate of return. Turning US$10 million into US$120 million certainly is no easy task. But

TABLE 6.79   Sector results 2021

	Currencies	Agriculture	Non-Agriculture	Equities	Rates	All sectors
Long	0.3	40.0	7.1	12.5	−3.7	56.2
Short	−0.7	−2.6	−1.4	0.5	2.4	−1.8
Total	−0.9	35.9	3.7	13.2	−0.4	51.3

TABLE 6.80   Results 2021

	US$	Percentage
Starting NAV	85,651,541	856.52
Trading result	43,964,142	51.30
Interest income	216,443	0.30
Management fee	1,913,857	2.20
Performance fee	6,212,126	7.30
Net result	36,054,602	42.10
Ending NAV	121,706,143	1217.10

the actual return here, after all fees, is merely 13.3%. All it takes is a reasonable rate of return and time, and both you and your investors will make a lot of money.

We have seen plenty of problems in this chapter, plenty of things that could have done better, could have been improved. This was by no means meant to be a perfect trading strategy, but it still performed really well and would have been perfectly viable. The drawdowns were a little deeper and lasted a little longer than we would have liked, but they were survivable. Had we geared up the risk settings to 11 in an attempt to get rich quickly, any one of those drawdowns would have killed the entire venture.

The 13.3% return over a 20-year period is a very strong result. The strategy used for this chapter can certainly be improved upon, but it was designed to capture the bulk of trend-following returns while keeping very simple rules. To tell you the truth, it was also designed not to be too good. No, not to keep secrets from you, but rather to avoid giving you a false sense of confidence.

It would have been dead simple to make a backtest which performed far better, perhaps even gaining every year throughout these two decades. But what's the point of that? It's just a backtest. I'm trying to teach you something here in this book, and the lesson you should learn is certainly not to copy some backtested rules in a book and start trading.

But what about our own end in this? If investors' money grew from U$10 million to US$120 million, how much did we make? Well, there's a reason we work in finance. We made a grand total of US$17.5 million in management fees. Oh, and I almost forgot, we also made US$20 million in performance fees.

■ Year-by-Year Conclusions

After two decades of trading, it's time to evaluate how we performed and if all parties involved have reason to be happy or not. We have seen some amazing years and we have seen some nightmare years. We've even been through a worrying phase of five consecutive years of mediocre performance. We already know that both our investors and we, as the manager, made money, but that alone isn't enough to determine if this was all successful or not. Let's take a look at the big picture first, to see if the strategy made sense (Figure 6.122).

Take a close look at the four panes in Figure 6.122. The first two panes show the same data, but in the top one there is a linear scale whereas the

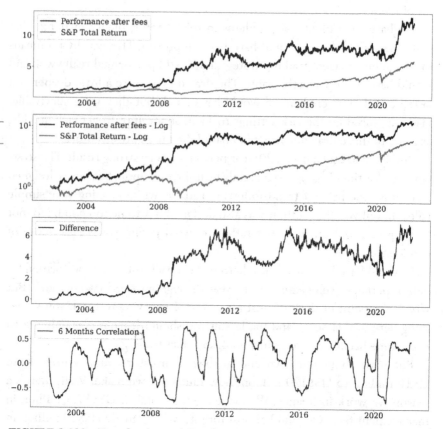

FIGURE 6.122 Trend strategy after fees, compared to S&P 500 Total Return.

lower uses a log scale. I have included both, just to demonstrate what a different impression the two scales can give. In both cases, the black line shows the performance of our little trading business, net of all fees. In these charts, and in particular in the log version, we see that the long-term performance of the strategy did beat the index, and that generated a large outperformance during the 2008 bear market. None of that should be news to us.

The third pane gives us a little more insight. This shows the simple difference between our trend-following trading results and the index. This graph may give us some mixed signals. It shows that much of the outperformance was created from 2008 to 2012, and that after this, we have kept an even keel with the index over time. That could be interpreted in different ways. You could say that it shows that trend following has ceased to outperform the markets, or you could say that trend following managed to keep pace with the markets during the most powerful bull market in our generation. Both are true.

Perhaps the most interesting story is told by the final and fourth chart pane in Figure 6.122. That shows you a six-month rolling correlation between our trend strategy and the stock market index. All too often, traders underestimate the importance of this factor. Your strategy, and thereby the product on which your trading business is entirely dependent, will be of much higher value to your customers if it is uncorrelated to the stock markets.

Forget about the amateur mind-set of just looking at returns. Unless you cater exclusively to small, amateur retail investors, this game is not about the highest possible absolute return. That is not how you raise capital and that is not how you build a trading business. Any professional understands that with high returns comes high risk and that simply going for the highest return is a sure-fire way of setting yourself up for major losses. Even more importantly, a professional understands the need for diversification and achieving a smoother long-term return on their overall portfolios. This is where correlation comes in.

Put yourself in the shoes of a regular asset manager, one who primarily buys stocks, a bit of bonds, and the occasional alternative product. This is probably one of your key target groups to pitch your fund to. For such a manager, most of their investments move up and down at the same time. When it comes to alternative products, they are looking for something which behaves differently, without being overly risky. Even if you produce the same returns as stocks over time, but make money during equity bear markets and lose during equity bull phases, that can be a very valuable product for them. It makes both their returns and the customers' returns smoother over time, reduces the portfolio risk, and keeps everybody happy.

Speaking of keeping everybody happy, it could also be of interest after two decades to look back and see who got what. Unless you just skipped the year-by-year review, you should be very aware of the potential profitability of this business. But you probably didn't pay enough attention to actually add up the numbers, so I will do it for you (Table 6.81).

Ten million were entrusted to us at the start of 2002 and at the end of these two decades, those investors have a cool US$121 million and change. We created US$111 million from thin air. And change. No, that's not really true, we created more than that. This amount, as much as it may seem, is not

| TABLE 6.81 | Monthly performance, net of fees |

	Jan	Feb	Mar	Apr	May	Jun	Jul	Aug	Sep	Oct	Nov	Dec	Year total
2002	−4.4	−1.0	2.5	−3.1	3.3	5.4	12.7	5.2	11.6	−8.3	−3.7	1.3	21.0
2003	10.0	6.3	−11.1	0.3	8.6	−2.7	-3.7	1.7	−3.0	13.1	0.6	−0.3	18.6
2004	2.2	14.3	2.3	−11.5	−7.0	−0.3	3.5	−6.1	3.2	6.5	5.1	0.4	10.7
2005	−2.8	0.1	−4.1	−5.5	0.9	1.5	3.2	0.9	7.5	−5.2	7.3	3.5	6.5
2006	11.0	−0.2	12.1	11.0	−5.5	−7.0	−5.8	1.3	3.8	−0.3	3.8	−1.0	22.9
2007	3.1	−6.6	−3.6	5.5	4.5	0.9	−8.7	−12.1	9.7	8.3	−1.0	6.2	3.7
2008	14.7	24.3	−10.0	−2.8	6.1	1.1	−10.9	0.3	19.4	32.8	8.7	4.2	114.9
2009	−0.2	2.9	−1.2	−2.7	8.7	-4.1	4.0	4.4	5.3	−3.8	12.2	−4.6	20.9
2010	−3.5	1.3	5.9	1.5	−10.2	0.9	−5.2	5.5	8.1	13.9	−8.3	16.1	24.7
2011	7.1	4.5	−4.3	6.2	−9.6	−10.0	9.8	1.4	8.0	−16.9	10.3	−0.7	1.2
2012	−1.5	3.8	−1.9	−1.1	−0.6	−12.0	6.6	−8.4	−3.5	−5.5	−0.2	2.3	−21.1
2013	1.9	−4.6	3.8	0.4	−0.4	−1.4	−1.1	−5.2	1.5	5.3	0.8	0.4	0.9
2014	−1.5	3.3	−2.7	5.4	−0.3	3.6	1.7	6.3	13.9	−4.8	9.6	6.0	46.9
2015	8.2	−0.9	0.9	−1.9	−0.4	−6.5	−4.1	−2.7	8.5	−12.2	7.2	−1.2	−6.9
2016	2.1	7.6	−9.1	0.6	−2.2	8.8	0.6	−5.4	3.4	−4.9	7.3	2.1	9.6
2017	−7.1	3.4	−1.2	1.7	3.9	−3.3	0.8	−0.3	−6.1	8.8	2.8	0.4	2.6
2018	7.2	−11.5	−0.7	3.8	−6.4	0.1	−0.6	6.6	−2.2	−10.0	1.2	8.7	−6.1
2019	−10.3	−0.5	3.3	5.2	−5.6	4.7	3.9	10.4	−14.8	−3.6	1.3	3.7	−5.1
2020	−14.1	−1.5	15.5	−2.7	−8.8	−2.2	5.5	4.4	−3.3	0.8	5.2	16.1	11.0
2021	5.3	17.7	3.0	10.3	0.7	−2.6	4.5	−1.2	1.0	5.6	−11.7	6.0	42.1

our full trading gain. It's just what the investors get to keep. And of course, while the idea of making US$10 million become over US$120 million may seem outlandish on the surface, it represents a realistic 13.3% annualized return.

All in all, our trading gains these twenty years amounted to over US$140 million. On top of that, we earned US$8 million in interest on excess capital. That's nearly US$150 million. Can you guess what happened to the balance?

Over these years, we pocketed a cool US$17.5 million in management fees and nearly US$20 million in performance fee. Now tell me that you would rather have just traded your own money and avoided all the stress.

CHAPTER 7

Counter-Trend Trading

It seems so far as if the age-old concept of trend following still works. Sure, it's not as easy sailing as it once was, but it still provides attractive long-term results, beating the markets both before and after risk adjustment. Declaring trend following dead every couple of years has become a national pastime and it's getting quite hard to take such assertions seriously any more. But that doesn't mean that trend following is the only game in town or that you should focus solely on this or any other specific strategy style.

This book is primarily about trend following but I would also like to add some value to you readers by showing different approaches. The most obvious alternative to futures trend following would be to flip the cards and go full counter-trend. A dip buying strategy is by definition against the trend and does pretty much the opposite of what we have been seeing in this book so far. It probably sounds counter-intuitive that a book about trend following should discuss counter-trend models, at least if the purpose is other than to trash them.

My personal view is that it's very dangerous to identify yourself with any specific trading strategy or even market philosophy. Trend following is a tool, just like quantitative trading is a tool, and so is the futures market. Focusing on something may be a good idea in that you can get better at something that you spend a lot of time and energy doing, but you shouldn't reject other methods just because you found one that works. Trading is neither sports, religion, nor politics, and you should keep an open mind and be ready to study and use anything which might be helpful.

■ Building a Counter-Trend Model

The counter-trend model I will demonstrate aims to buy dips in a bull market. I'm sure you're wondering why we don't apply a symmetrical approach and short rallies in bear markets as well, and I'll let you in on the secret. Counter-trend models tend to work quite poorly on the short side, even more so than for trend following. You're probably better off just skipping the short side altogether.

There's one more piece of information for you to unpack in that first sentence of the previous paragraph. I said that we're buying dips in a bear market, and that's a significant piece of information. There are two ways of thinking about counter-trend trading, and this tells you which one I'm aiming for.

You could try to go against the main, long-term, dominating trend of the market. That would be the inverse of what we're doing in the trend-following space. That is a very tricky way to go, and carries quite a bit of risk, should the trend keep running. The other type of counter-trend trading approach would be to trade in the direction of this dominant trend, but to enter on pullbacks, betting on a return to that trend. What you usually do is to try to enter about at the point where long-term trend followers stop out of their positions, and then you ride it back up for a short-term gain, or stop out pretty quickly if things don't materialise. That's what we'll do here.

As before, I try to keep the rules clean and simple. As I like to stress, what I'm showing you in this book, in all of my books, are demonstration models to prove a point. You should never trade any rules that anyone gives you, and certainly not any rules anyone sells you. The point here is for you to learn how to construct models, and giving you exact rules to copy and trade would very much defeat that purpose. Study these models, learn from them, and build your own production grade models.

We are only looking to buy dips in bull markets. In my view, the dynamics of bear market rallies tend to be so different from bull market dips that we cannot use the same logic, or at least not the same settings. In order to keep things reasonably simple, we are going to focus on bull market dips.

That means that we need to know if there is a bull market on. We need to define what a bull market is. I will define a bull market here as when the 40-day exponential moving average is above the 80-day exponential moving average. Exponential moving averages are quite popular among technical analysts as they are said to react faster. What they do is to up-weight recent observations compared to older ones.

There is one very important thing to understand when working with exponential moving averages, however. This is a classic source of confusion with many technical analysis indicators, i.e., the age-old question about why your exponential moving average is not the same as mine. While it may sound as if a 40-day exponential moving average only uses and only needs 40 daily closes, that's not the case. The exponential weighting starts with the previous value, and that means that it never really drops data points. It merely down-weights them into oblivion over time.

What is important to understand here is that you will get a slightly different value for a 40-day exponential moving average if you apply it on a half-year time series history for a market, than if you apply it on ten years' worth of history for the same market. I guess that what I'm trying to say here is, please refrain from sending me emails about why your EMA is a little different from mine.

Once we know that we are in a bull market, we will look for pullbacks. An easy way to quantify pullbacks is to measure the distance from a recent high, but this needs to be put into some sort of context. Clearly it wouldn't make sense to trigger a trade on a pullback of ten dollars, for instance, as a ten-dollar pullback in gold is quite different from the same in gasoline. Neither would percentage pullbacks make any sense, given the vastly varying volatility across the futures markets.

No, what we need to do is to standardise the pullback to the volatility of each market. A simplified way of measuring volatility is the average true range (ATR), as we used earlier for position sizing, so we'll keep using that. What you will find in the actual financial industry is that standard deviation, in its various forms, is used to measure volatility, but for our purposes here, the ATR is good enough.

So in this model we will use a 40-day standard deviation of price changes both for position-sizing purposes and for pullback. A pullback will be measured as the difference between the current price and the highest close in the past 20 days, divided by the standard deviation. That will tell us how many standard deviations we are away from the highest price in about a month.

This results in an analytic that can be compared across markets. You could use the same process for stocks, bonds, commodities, and other markets, as it takes the volatility into account. In this model, we are going to buy to open if we are in a bull market, as defined by the moving averages described above, and we see a pullback of three times the ATR.

Figure 7.1 illustrates the kind of logic we're going for here. In the top part you see the S&P 500 index, along with two exponential moving averages. With this being a bull market period of 2021, the faster moving average remains above the slower, as would be expected. This means that we are free to take long positions, if the pullback reaches our trigger value.

At the bottom of the same graph, you see this pullback analytic. This is simply the difference between the close price and the higher close in the past 20 days, divided by the 20-day average true range. If this dips below 3, we go long.

As for the exit, we are going to use a really simple logic, just to demonstrate the entry idea. I want to show that what is important with this kind of model is the entry. That does not mean that everything else is unimportant, but a mean reversion style model like this is very dependent on a solid entry logic. That's not the case for many other types of strategies.

To see if there is any predictive value in the entry method described, we are going to use two simple exit criteria. First, if the trend as defined by the two moving averages turns bearish, we exit on the following day. Second, if that does not happen, we hold the position for 20 trading days, approximately one month. Then we exit.

You are probably wondering why there is no stop loss point and no target exit price here. Those things may very well make sense, and I encourage you to try it out. The aim here is to teach you concepts and provide ideas for further research. Replicate what is shown here, try it out, modify it, and make it your own.

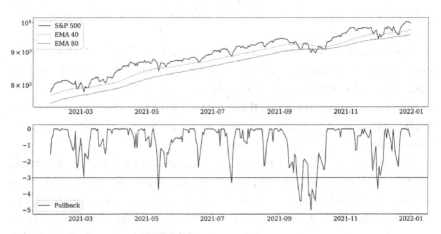

FIGURE 7.1 Counter-trend logic.

The rules we arrive at then are:

- Long positions are allowed if the 40-day exponential moving average is above the 80-day exponential moving average.

- If the price in a bull market falls back three times its average true range from the highest closing price in the past 20 days, we buy to open.

- If the trend turns bearish, we exit.

- Position size is volatility parity, based on average true range.

■ Counter-Trend Performance

The first thing that you'll notice when looking at the long-term performance of this simple counter-trend model in Figure 7.2, is that it has a rather smooth long-term performance. Comparing it to the trend-following model looks a bit like the rabbit and the hare, with trend following occasionally showing substantial outperformance, only to lose it again. Over a 20-year time horizon, the two showed quite similar return numbers in the end.

If you look a bit closer, you'll see how the counter-trend model is much more prone to sudden, sharp moves in the short term. That is clearly a cause for concern, and the result of the fact that we are trading less liquid contracts which may occasionally exhibit unusual behaviour. In the current iteration of this counter-trend model, we have also chosen to greatly

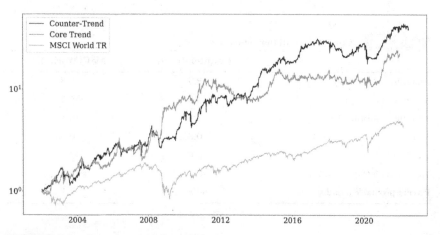

FIGURE 7.2 Counter-trend performance.

simplify the rules, with a somewhat silly exit method and without proper risk management. The reason for skipping such things here is to show off the general concept, how counter-trend logic works in isolation. I want to convince you that this is a viable approach to the futures markets, and if you agree on that, I encourage you to continue this model and improve it on your own.

Comparing the performance to the global stock markets, we get the figures in Table 7.1. Bear in mind that while we have loaded trading costs on the strategy, we have not applied any management or performance fees. Still, the long-term performance is comparable to that of trend following. An annualised return of nearly 20% with a maximum historical drawdown of less than 45% is respectable, and if you actually realise a Sharpe ratio of 0.89 in real life with a reasonably large asset base, you'll be very successful in this field. Arguably, the strategy is highly volatile but the returns do compensate you for the risk. It would be a simple matter to dial the position sizes back, of course, for a lower return, lower volatility, and lower drawdown.

In finance and trading, the game isn't about the highest possible return. It matters how you got there, and what risk you had to take. In terms of mathematical finance, we look to volatility to measure the risk, and we see it as the payment used to buy the performance. What you want to do is to pay as little as you can, and get as much as possible. In this case, you want to have as high return as you can, at the cost of the least volatility. The primary way to achieve something like that is diversification. And to get the most value out of diversification, you need low correlation numbers.

TABLE 7.1 Counter-trend performance

	Counter-trend	MSCI World TR
Annualised return (%)	19.7	8.3
Max drawdown (%)	−43.0	−56.2
Annualised volatility (%)	25.5	16.1
Sharpe ratio	0.83	0.58
Best month (%)	24.0	12.2
Worst month (%)	−20.1	−19.8
Percent profitable months	60.8	62.1

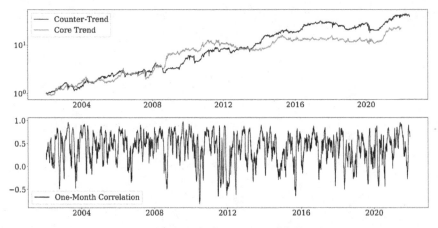

FIGURE 7.3 Counter-trend correlation to trend following.

What you see in Figure 7.3 is that the correlation at times peaks up to extremes around 0.75–0.8, but those are just temporary spikes. Most of the time, the correlation hangs out in the 0.25–0.50 area, which is right where we want it. At times, it even goes all the way deep into negative, which is of course brilliant. Those of you who have been around mathematical finance a while are already thinking about whether it makes sense to combine the models, trading both at the same time. And, yes, it absolutely does. This is the direction you would want to take, to look for ways to diversify not just in terms of markets, but in terms of style.

FIGURE 7.3

CHAPTER 8

Systematic Trading Without Time Series

M uch of this second edition is quite similar to the original 2013 release. The data and performance are updated, the trading rules streamlined and commentary is added. Those are all things that are expected from a second edition of this kind. But I also want to be sure to add something new and unique, something which may surprise the reader and add unexpected value. So in this chapter, I will demonstrate a method which complements trend following well, a method which uses very different types of inputs and hopefully will help open readers' eyes to brand new ways of approaching the markets.

That's right. Here, at this late stage of the book, I'm going to throw out perhaps the most valuable gem in this book, now that we've shaken out those who did not have the attention span to get through the year-by-year Chapter 6.

Practically all systematic trading models, regardless of style or asset class, use price time series in one way or another. After all, it's hard to imagine what we could do without time series. Trend analysis, for instance, relies completely on such series. Whether you're trying to follow trends or buy a dip, the knowledge of how the price moved in the recent past is a vital piece of information. You can't know that the market dipped without knowing what it did last week and last month, and you can't follow trends without the same information.

In this chapter, I will demonstrate how a complete trading model can be built without any historical price information at all. As always with any trading rules I show, this one too is designed as a demonstration model, to teach a concept. It is not meant for you to simply start trading from. I will demonstrate that the concept used is valid and can add value on its own, in this isolated type of approach. In reality, should you wish to use such a concept, you may want to combine it with more traditional approaches, rather than going for this very pure approach used for teaching.

■ Term Structure

We already touched briefly on the concept of term structure early in this book, but we didn't really look closely at just how important this factor is. Let's start with an overview of this phenomenon first, to make sure you're up to speed. Then I'll go into how we can use the rather weird-sounding terms contango and backwardation to construct trading models, and hopefully make a bit of money.

Futures contracts have a limited life span. There is a date when each contract ceases to exist. This means that there is not just one futures gold contract, but a rather large amount of them. At any given time, there will be one specific contract that has the highest liquidity. Most people would trade the contract that's closest to expiry, as long as it has not passed the first notice date.

The first notice date, usually a month before expiry, refers to the date when a contract becomes deliverable, and someone still holding it can be called upon to make or take delivery. As traders, we don't really want to be part of that, but it's not really a risk in reality. Your broker won't let you keep positions open after that date anyhow. First notice date is a concept primarily in commodity futures, and that's the only sector which we are going to trade in this chapter. It's in the commodity sector that term structure trading is of most interest.

Figure 8.1 shows a snapshot in time of how the term structure of soybean looked, at that particular point. As with any financial data, this is ever changing, of course. Figure 8.1 shows the expiry dates on the x-axis, and corresponding price and open interest for each contract.

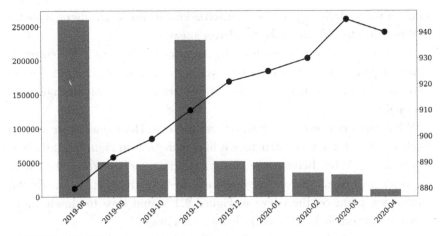

FIGURE 8.1 Term structure in contango.

In this example, you can see that each consecutive point on the curve is a little higher up than the previous one, i.e., contracts are more expensive the longer time there is until they expire. That situation is called contango. The reverse, if each point was to get cheaper, would be called backwardation, which is what you see in Figure 8.2.

The closest contracts tend to be traded fairly close to the underlying asset. The less time left to expiry, the closer the price tends to be. The reason for that is simple. At expiry time, the value of the contract is the same as the

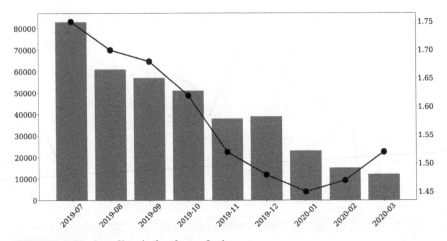

FIGURE 8.2 Gasoline in backwardation.

value of the underlying, as it will be settled for it. But when there is plenty of time left, other factors take the driver's seat.

There are multiple reasons for why the price further out in the future is different, but as quantitative traders we rarely need to dig deep into these reasons. Factors in play include interest rates, cost of storage, and seasonality.

What matters is how to interpret this pattern. Here is a simple way to think about it. If the term structure is in contango, as in Figure 8.1, there is a bearish bias. Why? Because the closer a contract gets to expiry, the closer the price will be to the underlying. So if the underlying stays exactly the same, each point on the curve in Figure 8.1 would have to slowly move down until it finally hits the underlying asset's price.

The reverse is therefore true for backwardation, which then has a built-in bullish bias. The underlying would need to move down simply for the points on the backwardation structure to stay the same. If the underlying does not move, the contracts need to come up to meet it.

The chart shown in Figure 8.3 shows a theoretical situation, where a futures contract starts out in a state of contango. As you see, the price would then start above that of the underlying market, trading at a premium. As you see here, if nothing else changes, then for each day the contango contract has to move a tiny bit down, getting a tiny bit closer to the underlying. We already know that the two will by necessity be the same at the date of the expiry, so it will slowly approach that point.

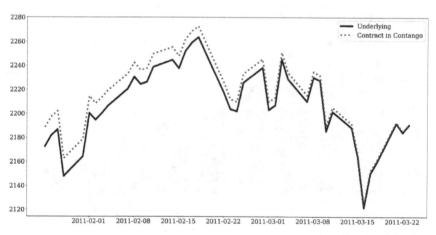

FIGURE 8.3 Contract in contango.

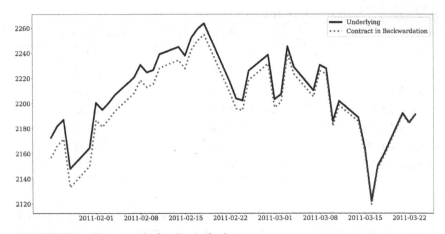

FIGURE 8.4 Contract in backwardation.

You see the inverse situation in Figure 8.4, where the futures contract starts out below the underlying, trading at a discount. For each day, we slowly, slowly approach the underlying until finally aligning with it at the end of the contract's life. It's important to understand that the contango and backwardation effects do not guarantee that the price will move up or down, merely from which direction it will approach the underlying. In that way, this effect acts as a tailwind or headwind, adding a bullish or bearish factor to the equation. We are still very much dependent on the direction of the underlying asset, but this term structure effect gives us a boost in either direction.

Now if you understand the general idea, you are probably already thinking about how to quantify this effect.

■ Measuring Term Structure

While there are different ways to quantify the term structure, I will demonstrate a methodology which I believe makes intuitive sense. This involves calculating an implied annual yield, or cost of carry, if you will. It needs to be annualised, so that the resulting number can be compared across different delivery dates. As always in finance, time matters. If a contract three months out is traded at a 2% discount, that is more significant than if a contract 12 months out is traded at the same 2% discount, similar to how it's preferable to make a hundred dollars today than in a year from now.

TABLE 8.1 Term structure data

Expiry	Price	Open interest
14 March 2019	907.50	295,414
14 May 2019	921.50	206,154
12 July 2019	935.00	162,734
14 August 2019	940.25	14,972
13 September 2019	943.50	7,429
14 November 2019	952.00	75,413
14 January 2020	961.50	7,097

The first point in the curve, the closest contract, expires on the 14th of March 2019 (Table 8.1). That contract, the SH9, is currently traded at 907.50 cents per bushel. No, you don't really need to know much about bushels to trade soybeans. The next contract out is the SK9, expiring on the 14th of May the same year, and that's traded at 921.50 cents per bushel.

The SK9 expires 61 days after SH9. If, theoretically, the underlying, cash soybean does not move at all, the SK9 would need to move from 921.50 down to 907.50 in the next 61 days. That makes for a loss of 1.52%. A loss of 1.52% in 61 days, would be the equivalent of an annualised loss of 8.75%.

$$\left(\left(\left(-0.0152+1\right)^{(365/61)}\right)-1\right)=-8.75\%$$

This gives us a number that we can both relate to and compare across markets and expiration dates. We have a quantifiable, comparable yearly yield number. If we now apply the same logic to that entire table, we will have converted the price curve to an annualised yield curve and now we have something that can be used to create some pretty interesting trading models.

Table 8.2 tells you where on the curve you would theoretically get the best return. But you also need to take liquidity into account. Often you will find that there is a substantial theoretical gain to be made by trading far out on the curve, but that there simply is no liquidity available.

But in this case, we see that there seem to be a nearly 9% negative yield in the May contract, which is the second closest delivery and it seems to

TABLE 8.2 **Annualised carry**

Expiry	Price	Open interest	Days	Percent difference	Annualised carry (%)
14 March 2019	907.50	295,414	0	0.00	0.00
14 May 2019	921.50	206,154	61	−1.52	−8.75
12 July 2019	935.00	162,734	120	−2.94	−8.68
14 August 2019	940.25	14,972	153	−3.48	−8.11
13 September 2019	943.50	7,429	183	−3.82	−7.47
14 November 2019	952.00	75,413	245	−4.67	−6.88
14 January 2020	961.50	7,097	306	−5.62	−6.66

have sufficient liquidity to consider. This logic forms the basis of what our next trading model will do.

It's worth noting that we have only used a snapshot of current data to arrive at this curve. No time series have been used of any kind, merely the current price of a range of contracts.

■ Using Term Structure for Trading

As a demonstration of just how powerful term structure can be as an analytic, I will construct a very simple model to isolate the phenomenon. This is perhaps the most overlooked and underused analytic in the futures space, and if you really want to improve your futures trading, this is one area which you really should study. What I will show you in this chapter is akin to a teaser, scraping the surface of what can be done. As always, remember that any trading rules that I show you are purposely simplified to make a specific point. What I try to show is that even simple rules can get the job done. After that, it's up to you to try variations and fine-tune the details.

So having said that, here are the simple rules that we'll use for this particular demonstration:

■ Trading only once per week.

■ Broad investment universe, across all asset classes.

■ Once a week, for each asset class, we calculate the annualised carry, or implied yield if you want, for each point in the curve.

- For each market, gold, S&P, oil, etc., we check the steepest point in the curve.

- For contango markets, we require a minimum annualised slope of 15% to enter a short.

- In the case of backwardation, we're happy with 7.5% slope, tilting the exposure slightly towards the long side.

- If so, we take a position and hold until next week. Long for backwardation, short for contango.

- Positions are, in the interest of simplicity, equal-sized with a target total gross portfolio exposure of 200%.

- And that's it!

No time series data used, no technical analysis, indicators, not even any stop loss points or so-called money management schemes applied. All we did was to check the futures chain, do a simple implied yield calculation and trade off that. There has been no optimisations or other tricks involved here, and I can assure you that it's quite easy to improve upon these rules and build something better. Still, let's see how this odd-looking model pans out in a backtest.

If you have never been exposed to the concept of term structure before, this all may still seem a little confusing. I can assure you that it's really quite simple, despite the odd-sounding terminology. All you do is to check the current prices of each point in the futures chain once a month, calculate the implied yield, and you're ready to trade.

The question now is, of course, if this simple model, without any time series data at all, can hold up to a classic trend-following model.

In Figure 8.5 we see that even this simplified approach to pure term structure trading actually performs quite well. We had a brief period of underperformance in the first couple of years, but, after that, the outperformance was quite consistent. We also see how trend following as a strategy levelled off and slowed in performance, as we should know quite well after the year-by-year Chapter 6, but the term structure approach showed no such deterioration. For both of these curves in Figure 8.5, slippage and commissions have been accounted for, but management and performance fees have not.

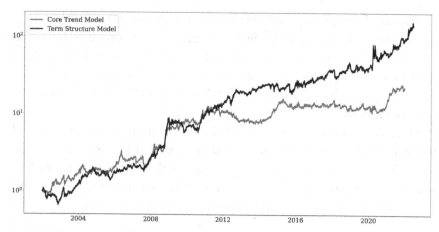

FIGURE 8.5 Term structure model performance.

■ Limitations of Term Structure Models

And why, you ask, doesn't everyone trade this way? Or at the very least, why not all the big players with an excess of propeller heads to research strategies? The latter part is easier to answer. We've mentioned earlier that most trading activity takes place in a single contract at any given time. One contract, for instance, the October 2022 contract, might be the main contract. At some point, often at quite predictable patterns, trading activity migrates over the course of just a day or two, from one contract to the next, and then there will be a new king of the hill.

Almost all futures traders stay with the main contract and roll to the net when everyone else does so. That's where you'll find the most liquidity, and it will be cheaper and easier to trade. It's true for small and big traders alike, and that's the normal way of dealing with the issue of limited futures life span. But as a smaller trader, and in this context small means that you're trading less than US$50 million, you could get away with doing some trading in less liquid months. You just need to be really careful with your executions. The spreads can be wide and market orders are not advisable.

If you manage billions of dollars and trade at high leverage, as most futures houses do, it gets very difficult to trade these less liquid months. That's why there is a small guy advantage in the term structures business. The degree of liquidity problem you may face varies from market to market, and of course from delivery to delivery. You need to be very careful when designing these kinds of models, and even more careful in executing them.

The other reason why more traders are not including term structure is more curious. In the retail trading community, term structure trading is very rare and it's even quite unusual in the smaller, under US$50 million, professional sector. This is something that has always surprised me, as this type of approach has so much to offer. It simply isn't very well known or very well followed.

There is, of course, a reason why I decided to write a book about trend following back in 2012. It was a well-known, well-followed area, often somewhat misunderstood and an area ripe with misinformation, system sellers and self-proclaimed gurus, but well-known nevertheless. And, of course, the title *Following the Term Structure* just wasn't as catchy.

CHAPTER 9

Tweaks and Improvements

In this chapter I provide some ideas on the type of improvements that may prove beneficial to our core strategy. There are several possible objectives when it comes to tweaking a strategy such as this one, and while not necessarily the most important, increased profitability is only one. If increasing the annual compounded return is the only objective, all you need to do is increase the leverage to just slightly shy of risking a complete blow-up. This is, of course, just stretching the theoretical arguments and not how reality looks. It is important to be able to achieve a high enough annualised return for the strategy to be of interest to investors and worth the time and effort involved in achieving it, but in reality it is much more important, and difficult, to reduce volatility and correlations to similar products.

If you can reduce your drawdowns, lower the volatility levels, and achieve a slightly different return profile from the average CTA product, you will find your product much easier to sell. Most of these subjects would require a book of their own to analyse properly and my intention in this chapter is only to point you in the right direction for further research on these topics. After all, in order to really trust and trade strategies with a potential 1,000 to 1 leverage, you need to do some serious research either way.

■ Trading Synthetic Contracts

Do you sometimes get the feeling that trading all asset classes on all the world's exchanges is not enough diversification? This can at times be very true and if you are looking for ways to achieve uncorrelated returns and separate yourself from the pack of trend followers, you may need to look beyond just trading single markets. One way to do this is to construct synthetic contracts, or spreads, if you prefer, and treat them just like they were a normal futures market. The idea is that you take two or more contracts that are in some way related, make a new time series showing the difference between the prices of the two markets, and then apply standard trend-following strategies on this. When you trade it, you will always have a long leg and a short leg of the trade, theoretically cancelling out the commonalities of the markets involved and trading only the differences.

A simple example is the classic gold against silver trade. At times, silver may show stronger relative performance than gold during prolonged periods, whereas the opposite may be true at other times. By treating the difference in the two prices as a time series all by itself, measuring trends and breakouts as we do for all other markets, you can trade this practically the same way by going long on one of them and short on the other. There are a couple of differences, however, that are important to remember. First, if you start off with two equally balanced legs of the trade and successfully hold onto it for some time, you may find yourself with a very mismatched position. As the long leg increases in price, that position grows larger. If the short position decreases, it grows smaller. You need to keep an eye on this and make sure your position remains roughly balanced. A second concern is that the volatility of spreads such as this is usually much lower than that of the individual contracts. As gold and silver commonly move up and down on the same days but in different degrees, you need to take on much larger notional positions in each asset to get sufficient profit potential. This means a potentially greater risk, but it can also mean much higher margin requirements, depending on how your broker views this kind of trade and how it calculates the combined margins of these trades. Some brokers simply add the margins up, which would make these spreads practically impossible to fund.

Besides gold to silver, there are many popular spreads to use for this purpose, not least in the energy space. The crack spread as an example refers to the theoretical profit margin of an oil refinery, that is, the difference between the crude oil price and the petroleum products that are extracted from it. A common way to trade this is to have the crude on one leg and gasoline and heating oil on the other, usually in a ratio of 3:2:1. You can essentially make up any sort of spread combination you like, but do ensure that the contracts have a real-world connection and reason why they move in similar ways. If you pick contracts that just happened to have similar return profiles for a while but could potentially decouple, you may end up taking a larger risk than you bargained for.

■ Correlation Matrices, Position Sizing, and Risk

If you are serious about the field of managed futures and trend following, this is an area in which you may need to do some hard work. After you have replicated and fully understood all other aspects of diversified trend following, this is likely to be the area where you need to spend the most time to perfect your strategy design.

If anyone asked me what the single biggest flaw is in the core strategy we have used up to this point, my answer would be that the strategy treats every position completely independently and does not take into account how related they are to each other. The position sizing and risk management are therefore done on a position level and not on a portfolio level. There are two main reasons why I have let this flaw remain in the core strategy. First, it works quite well without it, showing strong results at acceptable volatility and drawdowns. Second, the topic is complex enough to warrant another few hundred pages to treat properly.

Consider a situation where there has been one overwhelming theme dominating the real-world developments for some time. Perhaps there is a serious bear market in equities, primarily driven by negative European Union developments, as in 2011/2012. This may have caused most bond futures to trend up for a prolonged period of time while the dollar gained strength and commodities moved down. So we have a fully invested portfolio with long bonds, short equities, short currencies against the dollar, and short commodities. The question then is: do we have many different trades or one single bet on the same theme? It may be fine that we just have a concentrated bet, because that is how the strategy is designed and what happens in some markets, but the risk level will be very high and the more these positions go in our favour, the larger the difference will be in the risk level intended by our position-sizing formula and the actual risk level. With such a portfolio, we need to be very aware that if the underlying economic and political situations suddenly change, all our positions are likely to move violently against us at the same time. Whether it is still a profitable trade or not depends on how much profit we managed to build up before the inevitable reversal.

Two things about a change in our existing positions when they are held for a longer period of time, which will affect their potential impact on the portfolio. Long positions going in our favour will by definition grow larger while short positions moving down will shrink in size. Furthermore, the volatility level that each market had at the time of position entry, on which the sizing was based, will change over time. This is not taken into account at all at the moment and neither is the fact that many of our positions may in some market conditions show practically identical daily moves.

Using the ATR method for judging volatility and as a proxy for risk is a decent estimator but a highly simplified concept compared to what most futures managers would do in reality. Most of us would use Value at Risk (VaR) or similar concepts instead and some stick to the good old margin-to-equity ratio.

You can use VaR for risk reporting, risk management and risk control and once you have large enough assets under management, it makes sense to implement such a system. VaR methodology takes into account how each position is related to each other, that is, their covariance against each other. This has the added benefit of being able to run pre-trade simulations such as calculating the incremental VaR on your portfolio, should you take on a new position. The possibilities this opens in terms of risk control on a portfolio level are quite vast and potentially very valuable if you are looking for risk reduction and return smoothing.

If you don't have the possibility of implementing a full VaR system, you should at least be aware of the relationship between the markets you trade and look for methods to use this information in your risk management. The first thing you should do is to build a correlation matrix of the instruments you are looking to trade, or a covariance matrix if you so prefer. Make the table dynamic so that you are able to analyse the relationship between the markets over many different time periods. What you are likely to find is that at times the overall covariance between most markets in diverse asset classes goes up dramatically. These periods are often very profitable but also highly risky.

When you build a correlation matrix, there are a few things to keep in mind. First and foremost, you want to use the log returns as your basis of calculation and never the actual prices to get data. This is not at all difficult but very necessary if you don't want to end up with nonsense data. The basic formula to get the log returns for one period is simply $\ln(P_t/P_{t-1})$. However, when you are dealing with daily correlation data for global futures you have another problem to take into account and that is the different closing times of the different markets. Using one-day returns may be counter-productive if you are trading futures across the globe. If the S&P makes a big move in the afternoon in New York, the Nikkei is likely to make a big move the next day and you end up with a date mismatch. The most common solution to this problem is to use a return over several days instead of just one. For instance, if you use a rolling 10-day return, ln (P_t/P_{t-10}), as your basis of calculations you have smoothed this issue out and made it but a rounding error.

There are many ways to implement a risk-management strategy for a futures strategy by taking these relationships into account and this is an area where you may want to spend some time thinking things through before going live.

■ Optimisation and Its Discontents

Modern software can easily run through a few tens of thousands of iterations of our core strategy and tell us exactly which parameters would have been the best in the past few decades. It may be tempting to let your workstation go nuts and run through every possible permutation of the strategy to make sure you get the very best possible parameters. Unfortunately, this is another one of those potentially very expensive illusions.

Don't lose track of what we are really doing here. We are trading a concept, a general idea. What we need to know is whether that concept would have worked reasonably well in the past and then we need to make up our minds whether we believe that this same concept is likely to work well in the future. We need to stay objective in the evaluation process and look into all the details on what went well and what did not in the past simulated results. The optimisation process does just the opposite. It hides the potential problems and lulls you into a false sense of security.

Perhaps your optimisation process tells you that you should run the core strategy with a 57-day breakout period, a trend filter using 53 and 92 days on the long side and 41 and 113 on the short side. I did not bother to run this optimisation, and so those numbers are completely made up. Whatever they end up being, consider the reasons for showing the best results. If you look into the details, you are likely to find that this set of numbers worked best because they managed to avoid a few really bad losses by a hairline. They had their stops just that one day before a big loss or they did not enter just before that major correction that hit the other iterations.

If you want to push optimisation even further, why not let it use different parameters for different years? You may come to the conclusion that if you put stops very tight every second year, that will give better results. I think you see the point here. Optimisation will produce so many nonsense results that it is not worth bothering with.

Look at the broad concepts instead. Make a few different versions of the strategy, representing different conceptual ideas, and test them against each other. Find out which concepts work and you get some real value out of your testing, instead of being told if you should have a moving average period of 93 days instead of 100.

■ Style Diversification

For all the possible tweaks, improvements, and enhancements you might be thinking of, there is one which will, with a high degree of likelihood, add the most value. This book has had a strong focus on diversification, but we have only really looked at one way to diversify. The foundation of systematic futures trading is a solid investment universe, with markets from all major asset classes included. The fact that we can trade everything from soybeans to bonds to oil to currencies, in the same manner, is what our strategies are built upon.

If you apply trend following to one, two, three, or even five markets, there is a great element of luck involved. Your diversification simply won't be sufficient for long-term stable returns, so you will be at the mercy of luck. If you happened to pick markets which will trend well for the next few years, you might be fine. But the odds are against it.

This much should already be very clear to you, if you made it all the way to this point in the book. It shouldn't come as any surprise. But what most people are missing is a different kind of diversification, usually referred to as style diversification.

While I focused on one strategy in this book, I also just showed you two quite different ways of approaching systematic futures trading. In those

chapters, we saw that counter-trend trading and curve trading can both produce attractive returns. What if we traded all three of these strategies
together? Would that perhaps improve our overall returns? Only one way
to find out.

For this demonstration, I will use the three models we've seen so far, with
trading costs included as well as slippage, but no other costs. Have a look
first at the three backtests in Figure 9.1.

Looking at a long-term graph like can be dangerously misleading. We
might get a general idea of the behaviour of a strategy, but it would be
impossible to determine which of these strategies is preferable to another.
The human eye, or brain for that matter, simply doesn't work that way. It
would appear from a visual inspection that the curve trading strategy is
vastly superior to the counter-trend model, but if you look closer at
Table 9.1, you should come to quite a different conclusion.

Table 9.1 shows that all three model have reasonable returns, with similar
volatility and drawdowns and attractive returns. Be careful in drawing too
many conclusions from the fact that the curve and counter-models show
higher returns. We already know that trend following has had a few difficult
years recently and that very much affects the long-term values. Trend following is also a much more liquid strategy, able to take far greater capital
than the other two. While you can safely deploy tens of billions on trend
following, you would struggle with even a few hundred million for
curve trading.

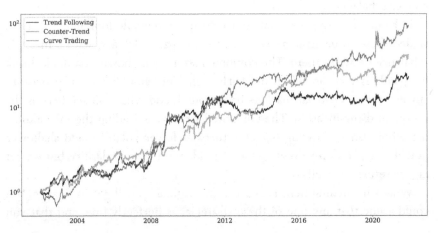

FIGURE 9.1   **Three futures trading approaches.**

TABLE 9.1   Comparing the approaches

	Annualised return (%)	Maximum drawdown (%)	Annualised volatility (%)	Sharpe ratio	Best month (%)	Worst month (%)	Percent profitable months
Trend following	16.9	−42.4	26.9	0.72	47.2	−18.9	53.8
Counter-trend	19.7	−43.0	25.5	0.83	24.0	−20.1	60.8
Curve trading	25.4	−39.2	30.4	0.90	66.7	−19.0	63.8

If we would now like to combine these strategies into a single portfolio, we would need to decide on what weight each of them should have. One way to approach this would be to decide that trend following is your main strategy, and should therefore have a larger weight. Another would be to down-weight the curve strategy as it trades less liquid contracts and is thereby less scalable. You could also decide to scale the weights dynamically based on realised volatility, holding more of the less volatile strategies. While all of these are valid choices, as long as you have good reasons for it, I'm sticking with the simplicity which underpins this book, and going with equal weights. Except, instead of having 1/3 weight in each, I'm going with 34% trend following, and 33% of the others, because a third would be irrational. I have done a monthly rebalancing of these weights, which makes sense for experimenting but in reality you would likely want to set threshold limits to trigger rebalancing.

In Figure 9.2, you see what your return curve would look like if you had traded these three strategy versions for the past 20 years, with a monthly rebalance between them. The combined strategy is shown as a thick, black line, and, as you can see, it did fairly well. This shouldn't be a surprise to anyone with a financial markets background, and what you see here is the power of diversification. The combined strategy is leading the race almost the whole time, showing higher returns at lower volatility and shallower drawdowns. Not only do we get a safer ride with lower volatility, but we get higher returns as well.

What's happening here is as close to magic as you'll get in finance. You could argue that any one of these strategies is perfectly fine, and that you

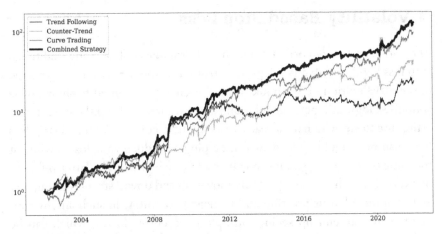

FIGURE 9.2 Combined strategy performance.

should focus on a single style and keep your portfolio pure. But that would mean that you miss out on this free effect of style diversification.

The numbers in Table 9.2 look almost too good to be true, and in this field you should always be sceptical of anything that looks too good to be true. In this case, it's absolutely true as a theoretical, mathematical example. To actually implement this and realise such numbers is, of course, a whole different matter. The point here is not that you will get a Sharpe ratio of 1.3 if you follow these exact rules. If that's your takeaway from this book so far, I'm afraid you have missed the plot.

What I'm saying here is that there is, without a doubt, a huge value to be had in diversification. Across markets and across styles. Together, they can achieve incredibly impressive results. Ignore style diversification at your own peril.

TABLE 9.2 The value of style diversification

	Annualised return (%)	Maximum drawdown (%)	Annualised volatility (%)	Sharpe ratio	Best month (%)	Worst month (%)	Percent profitable months
Trend Following	16.9	−42.4	26.9	0.72	47.2	−18.9	53.8
Counter Trend	14.7	−27.8	16.9	0.89	13.9	−13.9	60.8
Curve Trading	25.4	−39.2	30.4	0.90	66.7	−19.0	63.8
Combined	27.3	−23.8	20.2	1.29	40.0	−14.2	67.1

■ Volatility-Based Stop Loss

The core trend model presented in this edition does not have any traditional stop loss logic, and that is a departure from how the model was constructed in the 2013 edition of this book. With this change, I wanted to show how a simplified logic still gets the job done and I wanted to keep the book interesting for those who have already read the first edition. Adding a stop loss logic can be a double-edged sword, helping to reduce your losses while at the same time making you more vulnerable to whipsaws. The latter refers to markets where the price repeatedly moves up and down, strongly enough to kick you out of your position and to trigger re-entry. In such an environment, you may end up seeing multiple consecutive losses, which can be quite demoralising.

Adding stop loss logic is not primarily a matter of making performance better or worse, it is more a matter of changing the profile of the performance. That makes it in large part a matter of preference, and you would be well advised to experiment with variations to see which kind of return profile you are personally comfortable with and, if you manage external money, which kind your clients are likely most comfortable with.

For some types of trading approaches, a fixed stop loss point is used and the position would be closed if the price touches that level. But for trend-following models, where the aim is to stay with the trend for as long as possible, it makes more sense to maintain a trailing stop loss. This means that as the price moves in our favour, the stop loss point will keep moving with it. The stop will never move farther away from the price, and that means that for a long position, the stop will move up as the price moves up. What you would do is to decide on a distance, and then the stop point will be continuously adjusted up each time that we make a new high.

But that still leaves the most important question of how we define such a stop distance. Setting the stop distance to five dollars, for instance, wouldn't make much sense, given the very large differences in price levels involved. A five dollar pullback means something quite different if an asset is trading at US$20 or at US$300. You may think that a percent-based stop distance would make more sense, but that still doesn't work. For a market such as an equity index, a 2% move may be normal while a 0.2% is very rare for a money market futures market. At the same time, a 5% move is just a regular Thursday for palladium, and these days in the oil markets as well. No, we need to look beyond dollars or percentages.

The solution to this should be obvious, if you have paid attention to the section early in this book where we discuss position sizing. The key is to use volatility adjusted stop distances, and since we have already calculated the average true range for the position sizing, we can use the same for the distance. Remember how we used the ATR as a simple proxy for volatility. There is, of course, nothing wrong with using standard deviation of returns, but let's use what we already have.

The ATR tells us what kind of price range to expect from a market in an average day, so conceptually we could use that to define how many normal days' worth of performance we are willing to give back. The first edition of this book used a stop distance of 3 ATR units, and we would then always give back three daily price ranges before stopping out.

Figure 9.3 demonstrates the principle, showing a bull market trend in the natural gas market. We see here how the price breaks out into a new bull trend in April, where our trend-following approach would then go long. This position would be kept as the price advances, and the stop keeps being moved higher and higher. As the price turns back down in early July, the stop is quickly hit and we exit the position.

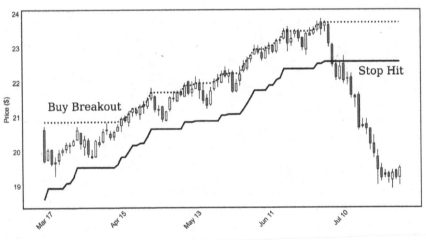

FIGURE 9.3 Trailing volatility stop loss.

CHAPTER 10

Practicalities of Futures Trading

The work does not stop after you have designed a robust-trading strategy, rather the contrary; this is when things really begin. Now you need to deal with all the little practical details of the implementation of your strategy and if you have not traded global futures before, you may be in for a few surprises if you are not prepared for them.

■ Required Asset Base

Whether you opt to trade diversified futures for your own account, for managed client accounts or as a hedge fund, you need make sure you have a capital base sufficiently large enough to make full use of the diversification effects without taking on unhealthy levels of risk. If there is a catch to diversified futures trend trading, this would be it. For stock traders the capital base is not a big concern, because their position sizes are divisible into very small amounts and you can easily have 40 open positions in a US$1,000 account and get the same diversification as a fund of a US$100 million. Futures are not divisible in the same way, however, and if your capital base is not large enough, you cannot take on many positions without racking up the risks higher than the desired level. In this strategy, positions are sized so that they will target a desired daily average impact on the overall portfolio and if you have an insufficient asset base that formula will indicate that you should buy only a fraction of a contract, which means that you should not buy at all.

To illustrate the problem, say you have an account of US$150,000 and you get a buy signal in live cattle. This contract has a size of 40,000 lbs and the ATR at the time of the trade signal was US$0.017. Using the risk factor 0.2%, you would then end up with the following formula for your position size:

$$\text{Trade Size} = \left(150,000^{*}0.002\right) / \left(0.017^{*}40,000\right)$$

The formula would arrive at a trade size of less than half a contract and then you obviously have a problem. To trade diversified futures with too small an asset base would force you to increase the risk factor and if your asset base is significantly smaller than what is required, you will leave the field of professional trading and enter the field of gambling. Trend trading with an asset base of less than US$1 million is, in my opinion, a bit on the reckless side and even with that amount it can be a bit of a stretch and you may have to make some compromises. I am, of course, aware of stories of people who started trading these strategies on margin accounts of US$10,000 and made millions, and if you feel extremely lucky, you could try it. If 1,000 readers of this book do so, my bet is that about 998 of them wipe out their money in a matter of weeks or months, while two of them make huge returns in a short time before they either end up wiping out as well or are smart enough to quit or reduce risk once they have won their first jackpot. But this book is not about gambling strategies and I strongly recommend against anyone entering this field with less than US$1 million to back them up.

Trading mini contracts can help a little if you are low on base assets but the availability is not great and the liquidity in some can be low. In the equity world there is an abundance of mini contracts but for some sectors they are hard to come by. In particular, in the very important rates sector there is a clear lack of proper mini coverage. The agricultural sector has some minis but they are limited and often illiquid with spreads that are too expensive.

Even if you have US$1 million, you sometimes get trading signals of 1.5 contracts or 0.7 contracts, and so on, and you need to decide in advance what to do with such signals. The prudent course of action is of course to round down, but you also want to avoid ending up with too few positions. With a smaller asset base in the range US$1–5 million, you may also need to be more restrictive with your investment universe. As we have seen, increasing the investment universe while keeping all else equal directly increases the risk of the overall strategy, we hope, along with the expected return. You could therefore decrease the number of instruments in the universe to decrease risk, but if you trade too small in a number of markets, your diversification effects will get too small. There is no easy way to trade diversified futures with smaller assets, but if you do attempt it, be sure to do your maths well so that you are aware of the risks involved.

■ Going Live

So the day has come for you to go live. All the testing has been done, you are comfortable with the strategy choices you have made, your accounts are opened, the structures are in place and clients' assets are on the accounts. Excellent, but now the hard part starts. A common question that is often not thought of until quite close to the go-live date is what exactly is to be done on day one. Should you immediately enter all positions that your backtest simulation currently has open or should you wait and just enter into new signals as they come along and slowly build up a portfolio?

For other types of strategies that answer might not be as clear but in this context there is only one correct choice. You absolutely need to enter into all positions on the first day or you will get a return curve that may look very different from what you expect. You need to calculate the position size for each open position in the simulation based on the day when the trade signal came in, not on the day when you go live, and then enter into the positions when your trading goes live. So if you go live on 2 January and your simulated strategy would have entered into a long soybean trade on 10 December the previous year, you need to calculate the theoretical size that you would have held if you had been trading on 10 December, using the volatility numbers from back then. The reason is, of course, that you want to make sure that your real results match your simulation.

If you don't enter into all positions right away, you will not get the same return curve as your simulations predict and you would simply be taking a gamble that the discretionary override, which is what the approach of only taking new signals would really constitute, will tip in your favour.

You may see situations that look scary on the first day and it may be difficult to enter into them: perhaps a long position that already has a much higher profit than the statistical average and just had two weeks of shooting up like a rocket. The problem is that if you don't buy it now, when will you do so? Perhaps it falls back down a little, perhaps not. Perhaps it continues for a year before being stopped out. If you don't enter all positions right away it will take quite a while before you achieve any meaningful diversification and even longer before your live track record is in sync with simulations. If you happen to go live just before a very profitable phase of the strategy, it may take longer to recover the underperformance. Perhaps you start just before a bad period too but that is impossible to predict, and therefore the wise decision is to just stick with the programme.

■ Execution

A practicality you need to think about before commencing trading operations is just how you are going handle the executions when new trade signals are generated. Our strategy in this book assumes that you place market orders before each exchange is open and get the stated open price with a realistic slippage, but this is of course a simplification of reality. The exchange openings can be at very different times of the day and perhaps in the middle of the night for you. Some markets have several trading sessions that you need to take into account and others are practically traded 24 hours a day, making the definition of "open" a little fuzzy. There is also the question of liquidity, of course, where in particular some commodity markets can be quite illiquid part of the day, making market orders at those times subject to higher spread costs.

From my own experience, as well as that of colleagues at other futures management companies, I can say for sure that there is a wide range of opinions and different approaches on this subject. Some of the traders have everything automated, with their analytical software sending orders directly to the exchange using pre-programmed algorithms for when and how to execute each market. Other funds have large staffs of execution traders who sometimes are given as much as a week to enter or exit after a signal has been given by the analytical software. For a large fund that could potentially make a significant market footprint when they enter and exit, it makes sense to give execution traders the discretion of spreading the trade over a few days but there are also larger funds that use automatic programs to achieve the same thing. For a smaller fund or trader, it is of course possible to set defined times of the day when trades are made for different markets and then use a bit of common sense whether to enter a market order or limit order.

If you do decide to trade in manually to try to get a better price, make sure you measure the result compared to theoretical market orders over time. A good execution trader can beat the average market order but most people cannot do that over time and the core business here is the longer-term trade and not the relatively small difference made by minor variations in the execution price. If it takes a lot of time or costs a lot of money and makes little difference, or even has negative impact, there is little point in keeping up the manual work. Your decision on this aspect is a matter of preference and highly subject to your own skills as an execution trader.

Depending on your geographical location as well as on your sleep cycle, if you trade global futures, you are not likely to be awake at all times when the strategy wants to trade. Assuming you trade only in the opening as the core strategy in this book does, you have quite a bit of time difference between the opening of Japan, Hong Kong, Singapore, Europe, and North America.

If you execute each transaction manually, you are likely not to be around for the opening of each market and thereby your entry price may differ significantly from what your simulation predicts. One way to counter this is to put in market-at-open orders before going to sleep, but if something big happens overnight, you may have a problem.

Another simple way to counter this discrepancy between simulated and actual executions is to make your simulations aware of the problem. If you live in Europe and know that you will not be awake for the opening of Japan, Singapore, and Hong Kong, you could simply build into the simulation software that trades are taken at the close for these markets instead of at the open, or even delay execution one day. Try it out in your simulation and see whether it makes a difference to the results or not.

■ Cash Management

One thing you never really see in your simulations is the practicality of cash management. This is just one of those things that are simplified and ignored in most simulation software and although it is not terribly complicated, it is still something you want to be familiar with before starting to trade futures.

When you open your trading account, whether it is for your own money, a hedge fund or for a client account, you have to decide on the base currency of that account. This is the main currency in which all performance will be calculated. Your account can also have one or more sub-accounts in different currencies, which is what you as a futures trader need. What you want to do is to make sure you have a sub-account for each currency of the futures in your universe. The instruments covered by this book, which are likely to cover what you need, are traded in USD, CHF, EUR, GBP, HKD, JPY, and CAD, so these are the accounts you need to set up from day one. When you take on a new position, you need to have enough collateral in your account and you should make sure that you always have much more than you need in terms of collateral. Some brokers may require you to post collateral in the same currency while others are happy with the equivalent in another currency, which would likely be your account base currency.

Futures contracts are marked to market on a daily basis and the daily gain or loss is settled through the clearing house at end of business. So if you have your accounts all set up, put US$1 million in your base USD account and happen to lose £2,000 on long gilts today, you will find yourself in the red on the Sterling account. Note that this is regardless of whether or not your long gilt position is still open. The net gains or losses are always settled daily and the balance shows up on your profit and loss cash accounts. Now you have a choice of doing a spot currency transaction to cover the negative balance on your Sterling or to ignore it and pay the interest rate on the overdraft.

To avoid this problem, you could transfer an initial amount to each account to cover potential losses. This would mean that you open a currency exposure for those currencies you may not want. This currency exposure is not likely to be very large in terms of percent of the whole account, so again this leaves you with the choice of leaving it as it is and calling it a rounding error or hedging it away. Unless your account is very small, currency futures make for excellent hedging vehicles. They are cheaper and easier to trade than currency forwards and the spreads are much tighter. The only real negative aspect of using currency futures for hedging is that you cannot trade exact amounts, only multiples of the contract value, which is usually around US$100,000–150,000 equivalent for the big contracts. Minis are normally available and liquid enough in this sector, though.

The picture I am trying to paint here is that cash management and its implications are not an exact science and that there are no easy answers on the best course of action. Some might transfer a few hundred thousand to each account and ignore the relatively minor currency exposures; others have great deals on the rates and leave the negative balance as it is, and some may transfer enough money and maintain currency hedges on it. It will not make much difference to the bottom line at the end of the year either way, but it is still a practical detail that needs to be addressed. Table 10.1 shows an example of some sub-accounts.

A certain amount of cash is always needed in your accounts to pay for the settlements of futures and to use as collateral. You may be able to use bonds or similar instruments as collateral as well, depending on your broker and your negotiation position, but having some liquidity on the books cannot be completely avoided. Make sure you have enough to settle your losses and that you are able to pay up for any potential investor redemption. If you have to sell off bonds that you intended to keep to maturity because of unexpected investor fund outflows, then something has gone wrong in your cash planning.

Having said that, it is of course in your interest to keep the cash to a minimum while at the same time at safe enough levels to be able to settle the said expenses and outflows. There are two reasons why you want to minimise the cash on the books and though one of them is well known, the other is increasing in importance these days. The more widely understood reason is the additional interest income you can get from placing excess liquidity with the government, and even though the yields these days are far from what they used to be, there is still validity to that argument. Even if you manage to get only 0.25% on the portfolio in a year, it is still free money and while the risk-free moniker can be discussed, it is as close as you get.

The other reason is that any cash held by your bank or broker will evaporate into thin air if they go bankrupt. I don't much care if a broker claims that accounts are segregated and that there is no risk, because we have all seen that this is not always the case in real life. All it takes is a former senator with apparent gambling problems as CEO and a billion bucks of customers' money can vanish in no time. No matter how much

TABLE 10.1 Sub-accounts overview example

Account	Currency	Cash available	Unrealised P&L	Account value
5611.77512-124/U	USD	34,124,566.86	−131,548.22	33,993,018.64
5611.77512-124/E	EUR	124,886.12	146,324.87	271,210.99
5611.77512-124/C	CHF	−12,781.20	34,819.15	22,037.95
5611.77512-124/G	GBP	14,379.08	−2,674.00	11,705.08
5611.77512-124/H	HKD	14,721,927.45	2,456,874.23	17,178,801.68
5611.77512-124/J	JPY	−132,453.00	278,226.00	145,773.00
5611.77512-124/C	CAD	74,558.98	−4,235.73	70,323.25

reassurance you get, the truth is that any cash you have in your accounts is likely to either disappear or be locked up in limbo for years if your broker suddenly goes belly up, whereas security holdings such as government debt should be returned to you intact.

■ Higher Volatility in Drawdown Mode

A factor that is easy to forget is that your volatility will be significantly higher whenever you are in a drawdown. When you are having a good year and making good money and new highs, your overall performance moves slower than when you just had a bad period. This may sound a bit odd, but take a moment to think about it. The reason for the slower moves in good times has nothing to do with market climate or the strategy as such and this phenomenon is true for practically all hedge funds, managed accounts, and similar structures as long as they charge a performance fee.

When your current result is better than at the last time the performance fee was settled, part of your profits will be offset to account for the accrued performance fee. The money is not physically removed from your account but the accrued liability will be accounted for in the performance calculations. If you charge 15% performance fee on a managed account or fund and you gain 10% from the recent highs, your track record will reflect a gain of only 8.5%. On the other hand, if you are in a profit since the last performance fee settlement and you suffer a loss, the same percentage of the loss will be absorbed by the decrease in the performance fee liability.

Performance fee therefore works as a stabiliser, dampening both the positive and negative moves in the fund or account as long as you hold a profit since the last high-water mark. On the flipside of that, your volatility is higher as a result when you are in a drawdown since there is no performance fee stabiliser any more. This can work in your favour, helping you regain the old high-water mark quicker, but it can, of course, also accelerate steep losses if you are not careful.

■ Portfolio Monitoring

Having your fund net asset value (NAV) and the intraday profits and losses ticking in real time in front of you is a mixed blessing. It is certainly convenient and reassuring to be able to follow your positions intraday. It lets you stay current with the developments in the markets and how your fund responds to it and it gives you a good feel for your portfolio composition and return profile. This type of monitoring is usually available from most futures brokers and if it does not suit your needs, you could use your Reuters, Bloomberg, or whatever market data system you have and build your own Excel monitoring screen that calculates the P&L for you.

The question is, of course, whether intraday, tick-by-tick monitoring contributes anything positive. Having the real-time values ticking in front of you does not help your trading and if you have a strategy that just trades on end-of-day values anyhow, it serves only to increase your stress level and distract your attention from more important tasks. There is very little rational reason why you would want to stare at a ticking portfolio screen during the day if you run a strategy such as the one in this book.

Of course, despite having said this, I have to confess that I spend much more time than I should watching that screen and I know just how addictive it can be.

■ Strategy Follow-Up

Once you are up and running, trading live money and, I hope, showing good results, the actual work is far from over. One of the most important tasks going forward is to benchmark your actual results with the expected results from your simulations as well as from other futures managers. If you spent all this time developing a solid trading strategy and it turns out that your returns are not closely tracking the expected simulated returns, you need to figure out what is wrong. There will, of course, always be small discrepancies between simulations and reality but they should be within a reasonable range and random, and not systematic. If you are a little worse one month and a little better another, that is not a big deal, but if you are always a little bit worse, then there is a risk that you missed something in your modelling of the strategy and you may find that the negative bias will continue over time. I advise that you err on the side of caution and make sure from the start that the assumptions in your simulations are conservative. Add higher slippage and commissions than you believe you will see in reality.

Set up a spreadsheet where you do daily calculations of your trading result, net of all fees, including accrual management and performance fees as well as all other external costs, and compare this each day with the predicted simulation results. Track closely any trend in the divergence and attempt to locate where it comes from. If you realise that there is a systematic difference between your results and the simulations, you have a real problem and you had better figure out where it comes from before things get worse.

It helps getting to the details if you calculate daily profits and losses per instrument, both for your actual trading and for your simulations. Most simulation software does not have such an option built in, but if you get one that has an open enough architecture, you can just add this yourself. It is not too difficult and you don't need to be a master programmer to build a plug-in to your analytical software and augment the functionality a little.

Having the best simulated results possible is a poor comfort if you find your real trading failing to replicate it.

CHAPTER 11

Modelling Futures Strategies

In this book, you've read about a futures trading strategy which seems to produce strong returns over time, and has the potential to form the basis of an entire trading business. The rules have been clearly described and they're easy to follow. Before you go out and start your trading adventures, deploying these rules with real money, there is a very important question you need to ask yourself.

Do you really trust some weird European just because he wrote a few books? No matter how handsome and funny this guy might be, simply taking a bunch of trading rules from a book and trusting someone else's backtest is not a good idea. This is a point which I have tried to make over and over in my books, and it worries me that I might not have gotten that point across. I write books to teach ideas and concepts, to broaden your horizons, and show you what's possible. I do not, ever, intend for anyone to just take the demonstration trading rules from my books and go out and trade them as they are. That just isn't a good idea. Never trade anyone's rules, no matter who they are. Even if they are really clever, handsome, and funny Europeans who just can't refrain from sarcasm.

■ Why You Need to Do Your Own Research

When it comes to trading rules, it's all very personal. You should never ever trade rules which you haven't developed and tested yourself. There is no such thing as The Best Trading System and you should treat any such claims with the greatest of scepticism. It's perfectly fine to read research, to get inspiration and ideas, and certainly to buy my books, preferably multiple copies so you can give them to all your friends. But in the end, you need to verify every claim, replicate the research, test the ideas, and make up your own mind. Even if the historical claims turn out to be true, that is not necessarily an indication of how things will work out in the future. In the end, you might pick up some ideas and be able to incorporate them into your own approach. But what you need to do is to verify claims made, to treat everything with a healthy dose of scepticism, and always do your own research.

In reality, most trading models are developed for a specific purpose, in particular, if you're running a business. When you design your strategy, you're not just randomly looking for something that makes money. It would be like starting a company in any other industry with the business plan summarised as "Making Money". Even your friendly neighbourhood crack dealer has a better business plan than that. Odds are that when you start your trading business, you're planning to take advantage of some gap in the market, or to replicate some niche strategy which is attracting a lot of money at the time.

If your trading strategy isn't designed for a specific purpose, you probably just have a bunch of random indicators thrown together, mixed and matched until a good-enough backtest emerged. Those types of trading models rarely have any predictive value, or business value for that matter, and they usually fail pretty quickly.

Whatever you do, never ever trade someone else's rules without doing your own, deep research. In my books, I try to provide all the details, everything you need in order to do this research. I suggest you start by replicating the rules, test it out for yourself, and then continue to improve, adapt, and make it your own.

■ A Word about Programming

A quantitative trader really does need at least a basic understanding of programming or he or she will be quite helpless in this business. It doesn't matter if you never did any programming before or if you feel that this is not your main area of expertise. Since you are reading this book I'm going to go ahead and assume that you have a certain degree of determination to either get into this business or become better at it. Understanding programming is a vital part of that process and something you need to face. Even if you have access to a team of propeller heads who can build to your specifications, you are still seriously disadvantaged by not understanding the details and not being able to tweak and innovate on your own. Having a secretary does not negate the need for the ability to type. Point and click system building and simplified scripting languages are for consumers and we are shooting for the big leagues here, so buckle up, buy a programming book, and learn how to write some code.

■ Settling on a Research Environment

Next thing you need to do is to settle on a primary environment for developing your strategies. This is an area where we've seen an incredible amount of progress since the first edition of this book came out. Back in 2010, when I first started writing this book, the choice of backtesting software was quite limited. There were, of course, as today, hundreds of different software packages, but they were all very similar and all had the same limitations. Most of those packages are still available, and still surprisingly popular among hobby traders, but I would advise you to stay clear of them.

Be careful in screening the available software solutions and make sure to pick a platform which is really up for the task. If you come from the hobby side of trading, you're likely working with retail-oriented technical analysis software, such as MetaStock, TradeStation, TradeSignal, MetaTrader, or WealthLab. There are so many of these, and they all have one thing in common. They are simplistic, outdated, and will greatly limit your creativity. The worst are those that use proprietary scripting languages. Those are aimed at people who don't take trading seriously enough to bother learning proper tech. Luckily, there is no more need for any of these old software packages or their proprietary scripting languages. Big boy tools have become readily available for everyone.

A few of these retail packages use C# or similar open languages to construct trading strategies, and while those are a little less restrictive than the rest, they still tend to be quite limited in the end. The fact of the matter is that any backtest environment made by someone else will be limiting, one way or another. Unless you want to construct your own backtester, all you can do is to pick a software package which best fits your needs and opens the most possibilities to get creative.

The first think that you need to accept if you want to be a trader is that learning programming is becoming unavoidable. Simply put, if you don't understand programming, you will be quite helpless in this game. If you think that programming is for programmers, that such menial tasks are beneath you, then the best of luck to you. If you believe that you can simply hire a programmer and tell him or her what to do, then you really have missed what this is all about. Either take this seriously, or stay away from it. Learning coding is unavoidable.

The good news is that you don't need to be an expert programmer. You need to know enough, and know how to figure stuff out when required. Knowing enough means that you need understand how backtesting works, the limitations of your software and methodology, and naturally a solid understanding of statistical analysis. If you understand these things and if you can code the strategy yourself, you will have a deep understanding of what your strategies do, of the underlying assumptions, the limitations, and the inevitable problems involved. This is the only way you can trust the rules, and if you can't trust the rules, you certainly won't be able to follow them when things get tough.

So you do need to figure out what kind of environment you need for your research and backtesting. A good environment for developing trading strategies should have an extreme level of flexibility, allowing you to do just about anything. Even things that the developers of that environment never imagined. It also needs to be able to handle large amounts of data and process such data quickly. We're crunching huge amounts of numbers here and most of us aren't ready to wait for hours for a backtest to be completed.

These requirements lead us down one single path. We need a sophisticated, powerful quant developing environment, one which is easy to learn, quick to develop in, and can handle fast analysis of large time series. While there are a few valid choices, there are plenty of more that just lead to a waste of time. Be sure to pick a proper, industry-standard platform, something which has considerable development support and isn't likely to simply go away any time soon. If you have no set choice, I would very much encourage you to go down the Python route.

■ Python and Zipline

From a finance and trading point of view, Python as a programming language is objectively special. It's not just yet another language with some different syntax and minor differences. It's a potential game-changer and something you really should pay attention to.

Python is very easy to learn. Whether you are new to programming or a seasoned C++ coder, you can get into Python very quickly. The syntax is deliberately very easy to read. If you know nothing about Python and are shown a bit of code, right away you will see what it does. That's not true for most programming languages.

Python is, to a large extent, purpose-built for finance. There are tools available which are designed by hedge fund quants and made available to everyone for free. Tasks which would take a lot of programming in a C style language can often be done in a single line of code. Having programmed in many different languages for the past 30 years, I have never seen a language where you can get things done as quickly and easily as in Python.

In the past few years, Python has emerged as the quant's language of choice. This has resulted in a substantial community and a large amount of open source tools. For people working in finance, the quant community are surprisingly open to sharing stuff.

There are some clear issues with Python, of course. Given that most people using Python at the moment are hard-core quants, documentation tends to assume that you already know everything and there is a clear aversion to anything user-friendly. For someone entering this space, the first barrier to overcome is what at times look like a certain techno arrogance.

Daunting as it may seem when you first get started, learning Python really isn't all that hard and the payoff is high. But, of course, Python alone doesn't just do your backtesting for you. That gives you two options. You can construct your own backtester in Python, if you're proficient enough in programming, or you can pick a suitable backtesting package for Python and adapt it to your needs. The latter is far easier, and I would very much suggest that you use a little Python library called Zipline.

There is a long and colourful story behind Zipline, though most of it is no longer important. The company which built it made it available, free, and open source, before going under some years later. While some assumed that the demise of Quantopian, the company which build Zipline, would be the end of that backtesting library, it was rather the opposite. As Quantopian died, the open source community took over Zipline and its development and maintenance got a significant boost.

One of several reasons why Zipline is great tool for futures traders is that it can realistically trade individual contracts. Most backtesters simply use calculated continuations for testing, which has all kinds of realism issues.

Having this native ability to work with tens of thousands of individual contracts not only brings a higher level of fidelity, but also opens up all kinds of interesting opportunities for creative strategy design.

Since the demise of Quantopian, there have been multiple forks of Zipline by different developers or teams. As of writing this, the most interesting is *Zipline-reloaded*. Free and open source, and ready for you to play with.

■ Sourcing Your Data

A backtester without data is as useless as simile in a trading book and settling on a backtesting software is only half the solution. There's a multitude of providers of financial data, ranging from free to extremely expensive and they vary greatly in coverage, quality, and various technical aspects. If you already work in the financial industry, you probably already have your preferred data sources all lined up, but you may perhaps need something a little different for backtesting futures strategies, in particular, if you decide to take the more realistic route and use Zipline to backtest on individual futures contracts.

It may be tempting to go with some free data source. There's no shortage of websites where you can download plenty of history, free of charge. While there's perfectly fine open source software, I would not particularly trust the quality of free data. If you do use such free sources, make sure that you build in checks in your code for unexpected data spikes, and you might want to use multiple free sources to cross-check against.

Free data is generally more readily available and of higher quality for stocks, in particular, American stocks, but, for futures, it gets a little trickier.

As we mentioned before, there are two related concepts in terms of time series for futures. We have the individual contract series and we have the calculated continuations. What exactly you need from a data provider depends on how you intend to use it and what your software is capable of. Old school software solutions are only really capable of using the continuations. They use a single pre-calculated continuation series for each futures market and thereby greatly cut down on the amount of data processing needed. However, it's not a very realistic way of testing. A better solution would be to use every single individual contract for backtesting. That can easily amount to tens of thousands of individual time-series. If you have a solid backtesting environment set up, such as a Python-based system with Zipline or similar engine, you can then dynamically calculate the continuations when needed.

But you're probably looking for an actual data source recommendation, and I will give you one. There is a low cost, high quality source which provides data on hundreds of thousands of individual contracts and offers a custom-made Zipline interface as well. This set-up is likely to save you quite a bit of time in getting started with backtesting futures models.

For this book, I have used the data provider Norgate Data exclusively for this reason, and all the backtests and analytics in this book were done using Norgate in combination with Python and Zipline. In fact, my 2019 book *Trading Evolved* (Clenow 2019), is also entirely based on this set-up and it explains in detail how to set up such an environment, and how to use it to construct backtests. If you want to dig deeper into the subject and learn how to code backtesting strategies, that should be the next book on your list.

■ Data Storage

You have two main ways you can go in terms of data storage. Either you can rely completely on your chosen data provider and let your strategy modelling software and tools work directly against this source or you can create your own local database. If your software talks directly to your vendor's database, you will be a little more vulnerable and if their source happens to be down while you need to work, that can cause a bit of a problem. Some vendors shut down for maintenance on weekends, for instance, and perhaps you need access to the data then. Other vendors will automatically send you text files with data on a daily basis, which will counter the risk of server downtime on their side but it still makes you very dependent on their technical formats and standards. This is very much a matter of preference, but I like to create generic database solutions in-house, so that the critical part of the business will always be shielded from the particulars of any individual data provider. This makes it easier to switch provider if needed or mix data from several providers and in general gives you much more freedom and control over your own data. Setting up a MySql database or similar and having your strategy modelling software speak directly to that are both inexpensive and easily done.

■ The Dangers of Backtesting

This book has shown you quite a few backtest results and has drawn plenty of conclusions from them, so it may seem odd that I now warn you about backtesting. As a tool, backtesting can be very helpful but as the expression goes, a little bit of knowledge can be a dangerous thing. This book is not about backtesting, mainly because that's a subject which would require not only a book on its own, but multiple books to properly explain it. But I will try to give you the gist of the problem, to make you aware of the main pitfall.

There is an old industry adage: "I have never seen a backtest that I didn't like", meaning that you can, on purpose or by accident, make a backtest look exactly the way you want it to. After all, you are analysing static, historical data and you can keep tweaking until the results show the kind of numbers you were looking for. The way most people approach backtesting is the so-called *Groundhog Day* method, or infinite trial and error. For the slightly younger readers, perhaps *The Edge of Tomorrow* may be easier to relate to. Perhaps you start out with a theory about how you can apply some indicator to a market, and then you go test it. After it didn't work out very well, you study the details and find that your stop loss point was a little too tight, so you move it a little further away. Your results improve, but not enough, so you go study the details some more, and decide to add a trend filter. And this iterative process can go on and on, until you learn to become a better human being like Bill Murray or kill some giant blue alien like Tom Cruise. But in this case, you continue until you have a perfect-looking backtest, with amazing results. This is likely to lull you into a false sense of security, and make you think that you have somehow discovered the Holy Grail of trading.

It's really quite easy to make a perfect backtest, one which appears to prove the possibility of a Sharpe ratio of 15, of hundreds of percent per year return with almost no drawdowns. But such backtests are merely curve fitting and lack any sort of predictive power, and with a devastatingly high probability, they will crash and burn in real life.

Since this really isn't a book about backtesting, I would very much encourage you to pick up a copy of the excellent book *Systematic Trading*, by Robert Carver (2015), which is the best book I am aware of on this particular topic.

CHAPTER 12

Does Trend Following Work on Stocks?

■ Define Trend Following

The primary reason for the high emotions about trend following on stocks is likely a discrepancy in definitions. Trend following as a strategy originates from the futures world and that's the kind of trend-following methodology I'm talking about. In the futures space, we have a fairly limited set of markets to trade, but they are highly varied and can offer a high degree of diversification. That assumption forms the very basis of trend following.

If you apply a standard trend-following futures model to a single sector, any sector, it's likely to show poor performance. You might perhaps pick agricultural commodities, as that's the most diverse sector and most likely to work. And, sure, you might get lucky and enter at a time when this particular sector has a good run for a year or two, but then the party is likely over. What we see in the long-term analysis is that we simply cannot predict which sector will perform and which will not in any given year.

If you pick a financial market, like rates or equities, your probability of success will be much lower still. The reason for that is not the lack of trends in the equity markets. They have trending periods and non-trending periods like any other market. It's just that it's an extremely homogeneous market. All the markets in your investment universe would move up or down or sideways at the same time and you would simply not have any diversification. You either have a big beta bet on, or you don't.

When stocks rule the roost, you'll be flying high. After all, you would be just long stocks in a strong bull market. But that's hardly trend following; that's just a variation of a buy and hold and hope for the best. When the markets get choppy, pulling back a bit only to continue back up, you'll quickly be left behind. You'll start stopping out at the worst point and fail to keep up with the index.

In sideways markets, you'll take hit after hit and bleed money. Month after month, perhaps even year after year, you will keep losing. That's what happens in sideways markets when you apply trend-following models, and that's the reason why proper trend following trades multiple asset classes. While one asset class experiences sideways market conditions, others are likely to trend. That's why futures trend following has worked so well for so many years.

But worse still will be the bear markets. Equity bear markets are notoriously tricky. They tend to be sharp, sudden, and prone to violent countermoves. You'll make money fast and then lose it and more before you know what hit you. What we have seen empirically is that during bear markets, it's not the short equity positions that provide the most valuable protection. It's rather the trend-following positions in rates, commodities, and currencies.

After we get over the whole concept of having little to no diversification, we have the next obstacle to deal with. Instead of a limited universe of fifty to a hundred futures markets, we now have tens of thousands of stocks to pick from. Running a trend model that just selects trending stocks from that many markets would pose some interesting problems. How large a portfolio are you willing to accept? A hundred positions? A thousand?

You need a way of limiting the pool of stocks you pick from or you will get overwhelmed. You will also need a way to rank your stocks, based on some criterion. If you don't, you will end up having nearly the entire investment universe flag buy signals in a bull market.

With futures, you can take on almost any exposure level, given the built-in leverage mechanism. Face value exposure can be nearly irrelevant in terms of risk. After all, a million-dollar position in platinum carries a very different risk profile than a million-dollar exposure to the three months Eurodollar market. With futures, leverage is easy and cheap. Not so with stocks, where it gets really expensive to borrow for exposure over 100% of your portfolio.

So let's assume that you make some necessary modifications to your trend model. You add methodology for investment universe inclusion, which of course needs to deal with historical realism in terms of what might have been available and reasonable at any given time in the past, for your back-tests to make sense. Then you probably remove the short side, not to get killed every time the markets turn sour. Next, you'll need a ranking methodology to pick the best trends, based on your criteria. Perhaps some sort of trend strength indicator that you come up with. And let's not forget a portfolio allocation algorithm, to decide how you size your positions. As you're likely limited by a maximum of 100% long exposure, you need to figure out how to best deploy that, and how much to allocate to each position. Perhaps even limitations per sector or geographical area might be needed.

And now, after you have done all of this, you might actually have a pretty good trading model. But it's not a trend-following model. It's probably a momentum model.

There is nothing wrong with a momentum model, and, in fact, I've written a whole separate book on the topic (Clenow 2015). But the construction of individual stock-picking strategies requires so much care, unique to this particular sector, that it would simply be a misnomer to bundle it up with something like trend following. What you will get in the end is a model which piles up beta when beta is good. It will be highly dependent on the health of the equity markets. You will see all your big profits during bull markets, and you will hopefully have some sort of defence mechanism in place to limit your losses during bear markets. In the end, it's more of an aggressive relative approach, rather than an absolute return approach. And, no, I would not recommend hedging out the market with futures, but feel free to try a backtest.

So, in the end, the answer is this. No, trend following does not work on stocks, but there are some related types of strategies, such as momentum, which work just fine. But it's not trend following.

■ What about ETFs?

Another common question I've heard many times over the years is about exchange traded funds, or ETFs. If you accepted my view that trend following, as it is generally understood in the business, does not lend itself well to stocks, then you might reasonably be curious about ETFs.

On the surface, it looks like ETFs might be a suitable type of instrument for trend following. We have ETFs tracking equity indexes, commodity markets, interest rate markets, and currency markets. This potential for diversification means that it's at least worth exploring. I'll save you the suspense and tell you up front that, sadly, ETFs are no substitute for futures and not a very practical market for trend following.

First, look at the available investment universe. On the equity side, we're well covered. We have low-cost instruments with low tracking error for pretty much any index we'd want to trade. Safe to say, we're covered in this sector. Next, rates. We do have some interesting ETFs in the rates sector, even if they are not as clean and pure as the equity futures. But I'll give you that one, fine. For currencies, we have a few. Not all that many, but I'll be generous and say that we're OK here too.

Then things get a little tricky. There are a few ETFs which track individual commodities, such as oil and gold, but they are few and far between. In the agricultural sector it's even trickier, and among the reasonably liquid ETFs you'll mostly find ones that bundle up a whole bunch of commodities in one fund. That, of course, completely defeats the purpose of diversification, at least, the kind of diversification which we need.

The thing that really kills trend following on ETFs, however, is not the investment universe availability, even that is a severely limiting factor. The true problem is that these are cash instruments, paid up front. Leverage is expensive and limited, so what do you do when you get a trade signal telling you to take on a 250% position in a rates market, when you already have a few hundred percent exposure on? You just can't build the kind of exposure which would be needed, and you would be bound by cash utilization.

This doesn't mean that the ETF market is horrible or that you should never invest in or trade ETFs. There are some truly horrible ETFs, of course, with the worst offenders being those that are essentially structured derivatives, repackages, and sold to people who don't know what structured derivatives are. But there are also great ETFs, and the most plain and best-known ones, such as the SPY are among them. The idea of exchange traded funds is brilliant and it serves its purpose, even if some issuers use it to sell toxic derivatives. For asset allocation models, for instance, ETFs are your go-to instruments. But for regular trend following, they are not a great choice.

CHAPTER 13

Trading for a Living

M ost people reading a book like this either dream of trading for a living, or they are already doing just that. This chapter is meant both for those of you who do not yet trade for a living, and for those of you are, but are doing it wrong. Yes, in my view, there is a wrong way to trade for a living. Somewhat ironically, it is exactly this wrong way that most people outside the industry see as the ultimate goal. To trade your own money for a living. Having goals and big dreams is a good thing, but you should be careful in picking those goals. I hope that by the time you've finished reading this chapter, you will agree with me that dreaming about trading your own money for a living is the wrong dream.

■ How Much Does a Good Trader Make?

If you think that you want to trade for a living, the first thing you need to ask yourself is how much you expect to make. I don't mean your salary, bonus or dollar trading gains but rather in terms of percent. Sometimes when I speak at conferences around the world, I ask the audience for a number. I ask them how many percent per year, on average, a good trader makes. It's a very interesting exercise, and very telling. People who come from the financial industry or have been trading professionally for some time tend to have very different expectations from hobby traders.

The somewhat frightening situation tends to be that the numbers from the hobby traders tend to be five to ten times as high as the numbers from the professionals. The professionals, when asked for percentage returns of good traders, usually say something like 15–20%. Depending on the definition of good, they may even say 25%. But the hobby traders rarely come up with triple digit numbers. I hear 100% a year, even several hundred per cent. Just how high the numbers are can depend on the type of conference, and at times I have heard the most absurd insistence on how a good trader can make at least 2.5% per day.

A mere 2.5% per day might not sound so great, until you actually stop and do the maths. Let's assume for a brief moment that this was achievable. That it's something that actually happens in the real world, at a frequency higher than extinction-causing meteor strikes. If you put US$10,000 to work on such a strategy, how much would you have after one year?

Five million dollars. That's how much. Yes, 2.5% per day compounds to over 50,000% on an annual basis. But why would you stop after one year? In two years, you would have US$2.5 billion. Your first trillion comes in year three and in another year or two we start reaching the kind of numbers that few people outside of the mathematics department at MIT know the names for. Inconceivable.

But it's not nice to ridicule the mathematically impaired, even when they are delusional. This was, of course, an extreme case, but it's more common that people answer around 100% per year. Well, even then, the numbers quickly spin out of the realm of reality. The same US$10,000 traded with an annual gain of 100% per year would move quite quickly indeed. In one year, we'd have 20k, the year after, 40k. We'd make our first million in seven years and a decade in, our 10k is up to 10 million.

I'm sure you've heard stories of people who have done just that. We all have. Curiously, most of them decided to become trading mentors or performance coaches or TikTok stars after building their fortune in the trading field. You can safely assume that the percentage of these stories which are actually true is so low that it can be approximated to zero.

And if you're still sure that you know of this one person who has actually done this, in a real, verified way, then let me tell you about this Jamaican fellow I know of who ran 100 metres in 9.58 seconds. He really did that, but that doesn't mean that I or anyone else have a chance of doing the same.

Another way to look at the few true stories of outsized success is the famous coin-flipping thought experiment. Imagine a nation-wide coin-flipping competition. Everyone gets paired up, one on one, for a game. If you lose, you're out. If you win, you go on to the next round. Round after round, and we would get fewer and fewer people left. But, by mathematical certainty, someone will keep winning. Again and again, they call the coin correctly. When there are just a handful left in the country, they would be seen as superstars. They would be on TV, being interviewed about their incredible coin-flipping skills, and they would write books about their technique.

No, returning to the realm of mortals, to the real world, we can easily observe what the very best have achieved in the long run. Some of the very best have become billionaires by realising a long-term annualised return of around 20%. That is a world-class number, and if you were thinking of 40% or more, you need to ask yourself if you have credible reasons to think that you can double the performance of the best in the world.

Of course, in any given year, anything can happen. By luck or skill, you might double your money one year, but you will also have negative years. Anyone might double their money one year, but it won't happen every year.

This book shows you trading strategies which in theory can give you very high returns over time. But there are quite a lot of "what-ifs". What if the markets change and trend following doesn't perform for the next ten years? What if you happen to start trading just before the biggest drawdown in history? What if you can't keep trading for 20 years, to really achieve that high return? What if you miss a trade, what if you get a poor execution, what if?, what if? Reality is simply not as cooperative as a lab-grown backtest.

You would do well in accepting that 20% per annum over a longer time is a respectable target to shoot for, but that you will probably never reach it. But if the bad news is that you're unlikely to reach 20% compounded over time, the good news is that you don't have to. That you can become independently wealthy by compounding at 15%, perhaps even less.

And note that I did say that you can, meaning that it's within the realm of possibility. I didn't say it's likely and I didn't say it's easy. It's not that kind of a trading book.

■ Getting a Job in Trading

Once you have done all your research, designed and refined your strategies, tested them and feel confident in their results, it's time to figure out what you want to do with it. One obvious way is of course to try to get a job in the industry. The financial industry can be a lucrative place to spend your time. There aren't all that many industries where you can make meaningful money being an employee. In most professions, there is a natural ceiling to your compensation but rightly or wrongly, in some parts of finance there really isn't. After all, how many jobs are there out there where a 20-something kid can pull seven figures and add another figure to that a few years later? Sure, it's not all that easy to land a seven-figure job, but most people are quite happy with six.

You shouldn't underestimate the value of having a salary. If you manage to get into the quant finance space, you would get paid well and get an education at the same time. You learn from people around you, from the industry and the experiences will further your personal growth, all while pulling a decent pay cheque.

One thing to keep in mind of course is that jobs in the financial industry very rarely are what those outside think it to be, and they are most certainly different from popular culture depictions. Most people with the word trader in their job title do nothing remotely similar to what hobby traders would assume, and their daily tasks involve little related to topics in a book like this. In a smaller bank, for instance, it might involve taking phone orders from an asset manager, who is buying securities on behalf of his customer. You then call up the trading desk at an investment bank, who places the actual order in the market. Neither of these industry professionals have any actual interest in any trading strategy or even outcome of this trade. They work on commissions or fixed fees.

A common perception is that a bank or financial firm will just allocate a pool of money to someone to sit around and trade as he or she sees fit. That you might be given a so-called prop book, a proprietary account, to trade with your own clever strategies. That's so rare that we could round down the number of such job roles to zero. They do exist, of course, just like there are people working full-time on building exact architectural replicas of construction projects in Lego. Working in the financial industry can be very rewarding, but to a large extent, it's just a job.

If you do aim for the type of job where you get to trade your own strategies, you might want to look at the so-called buy side. The financial industry is roughly divided into the buy side and the sell side. One way to look at this divide is that the sell side are selling financial services while the buy side buys them. Think of the sell side as investment banks, selling execution, brokerage and analysis, while the buy side is asset management, which needs such services. If you understand that part, you could guess the power dynamics between the two sides.

As the age-old gag in the business goes, the true differences between buy side and sell side is that if you're on the buy side, you can yell obscenities before you hang up the phone. The buy side includes the hedge fund industry, and that's where you may find a bit more freedom to trade.

A very common question I've been asked over the years about trying to get such jobs is whether they might try to steal your strategies. Imagine having spent years perfecting your trading model and then demonstrating it at a job interview at a hedge fund, only for them to steal your ideas and never give you the job in the first place.

That's not likely to happen. It just doesn't work like that. Not that it would be against some sort of moral code of the hedge fund industry, because that industry isn't all that much into morals in the first place. It just wouldn't make any sense. Any fund or trading company which might be interested in stealing your ideas are amateurs, and you wouldn't want to work for them anyway.

What you have built, no matter how great, isn't likely to be something amazingly revolutionary which will change the direction of the industry. Even if you have come up with something really impressive, it won't be something that someone else can simply pick up and copy. If it was, someone else would already be doing it. No, if you really have come up with some impressive research, it would make a whole lot more sense to simply hire you, to continue to do such research. Trying to steal your work and reverse engineer it would be more costly than to just buy you.

They will try to rip you off, of course, but that's part of the business. They'll try to underpay and overwork you, but not steal your stuff. The concept of the super-secret trading code worth massive amounts of money is largely a myth. It just doesn't work like that. Your code, no matter how great it is, would need to be adapted and fitted into the company's framework, business strategy, customer demands, etc.

And how do you go about getting a job in the financial industry? The same way you get to Carnegie Hall, I suppose. The competition is tough, as it tends to be with anything worthwhile. Perhaps you went to Princeton and your daddy plays golf with Jamie Dimon, but if not, you have some work ahead of you. Find a way to make yourself stand out, to get noticed, or your job application will drown in a sea of thousands of others.

■ Trading Your Own Money

Trading for yourself is without a doubt the most common dream among hobby traders, but I will try to convince you here that this is the wrong dream. It doesn't make sense.

The first thing that you need to understand is that almost all day traders end up losing all or most of their money. The stories you hear of the social media stars, the influencers, and the gurus, it's not real life. The markets do not work that way. The stories are either made up, greatly exaggerated, or you might just hear about the gains and not the losses. Even if they were true, if such black market magic existed in the real world, using these supernatural abilities to trade for yourself still wouldn't make any sense.

What it comes down to is a simple risk assessment, best illustrated by example. Assume for a moment that you have worked hard and saved up US$100,000, and that you're now ready to start off your trading journey. You've done your research and you have a solid trading strategy to deploy your hard-earned money on, ready to trade for a living.

How much money do you need to live on? If you're based in Zurich, London, or New York, you probably need six figures to break even, but those are expensive locations. How much you need to take out of the account each year for living expenses may vary, but it's something that you do need to account for. With entry-level jobs in finance often paying in the low six figures, you would likely want to achieve this and hopefully more.

The second question would be what kind of risk you need to accept from trading, in order to have a shot at achieving such returns. Perhaps you decide that you need US$50,000 return per year to live on, from your US$100,000 trading account. That's 50%, and more than double of what Warren Buffett has accomplished. Does that sound realistic?

Even if you somehow are sure that you can average 50% return in the long run, which isn't very likely, your ride wouldn't be all that smooth. One year you're +80%, the next you're at −60%. It might even out to a positive number, but try telling your landlord that when your rent is due.

Another issue here is that you are giving up the compounding effect. Imagine the first year starting out exactly according to plan, and you actually reach your target 50%. Since you have living costs, you now withdraw US$50,000 from the account and the next year you start out with the same US$100,000. You will never grow the account this way. Worse still, if the second year ends up at −30%, you now have only US$70,000 on the account, you had zero income, can't pay your bills, and you need 70% trading gains to get your target US$50,000.

When you trade your own money for a living, you will be forced to take on too high risk. You will be taking all the risk and you will be giving up most of the upside by taking out a salary. No, take my word for it, trading your own money for a living does not make sense. I would even argue that making the decision to trade your own money for a living is in itself, a bad trade, and it makes you a bad trader by definition.

■ Trading OPM

If you want to be a professional trader and if you have accepted that trading your own money for a living isn't the answer, than you need to look at trading other people's money (OPM) for a living. You can throw in your own as well, nothing wrong with that. Trade your own money while you're at it, but your main income will come from trading other people's money (OPM).

Don't fall into some sort of thought trap of believing that it's somehow brave to trade your own money and cowardly to trade others. This is finance. We're not out to prove something to ourselves or to others, we're in and out for a buck and we don't take prisoners. This is all a numbers game, and specifically about number of dollars.

Go back to the example of the previous section. You've done your research, you're happy with your trading strategy and you've got US$100,000 to trade. But this time, you clever up and rather than just deploying your own money, you decide to go on a fund-raising spree until you manage to raise US$10 million of other people's money. That means convincing others to trust you and your trading approach, and allow you to trade their money along with your own, for a fee.

And there is, of course, the key to this little equation, the word "fee". You now get a basic income just from fees, which means that you can trade more responsibly, instead of aiming for unrealistic returns. Setting trading targets too high means taking too much risk, and taking too much risk means that you'll blow up sooner or later. No need for such irresponsible risks any more, not with the fees.

Let's say you get a fee structure of 1+10 from your investors. That means that you get a 1% management fee, for showing up and turning on the lights, and you get to keep 10% of the profits you generate for your clients. It's a fair deal.

With US$10 million under management fee, you now get US$100,000 in salary, taking the stress off paying rent and feeding the dog. If you end up making 20% gain, that's US$2 million for your customers of which you'll get US$200,000. All of that with lower trading risk than you would be forced to take if you traded just your own cash. Throw your own money in the pile, and you can make trading gains, or losses, on your own money at the same time.

The management fee is always there, even if you have a bad year. That is not unethical, it actually works in everybody's interest. If a manager has only a performance fee, they will be incentivised to take on high risk in hopes of high pay, and they will have an incentive to simply shut down the shop after a loss, rather than to try to recoup it.

The really nice thing about asset management is how it scales. It's not all that much more work to manage twenty million, compared to ten. But your pay is double. The industry scales well and if you're clever, you can raise substantial amounts without having to add too much cost.

If you look at this from a trading perspective, the risk and reward comparison should be clear to you. By trading for yourself, you take a very high risk for quite a limited upside. In contrast, if you choose to trade other people's money, you take a fairly low risk for a nearly unlimited upside potential. A good trader would make that call in a split second.

■ Reasons Not to Trade OPM

Looking at just the mathematics, it's hard to find reasons not to go the professional way, and trade other people's money. The numbers are clearly there and it makes for a superior deal, but trading other people's money may not be for everyone. There are a few reasons why it might not suit you.

Some say that they just want to trade, not run a business. That's fine, but it's just an explanation as to why you decided to make a bad trade, in going the solo route. Another common reason is that you don't feel comfortable with risking other people's money. Well, if you're not confident in your trading, you certainly shouldn't risk your own money on it either. A third reason in the same category would be that you don't want to deal with client relationships and sales. Again, that's just a reason for making a bad economic call.

On the more valid side, you might object that you simply don't know any investors and would have no idea how to raise US$10 million. Well, that's not easy, but it can be done. It means learning new skills, getting to know the right people, and working hard. Difficult, but not impossible.

Regulations are important and that's also a valid obstacle. Some jurisdictions are tougher and more expensive than others and you really do need to read up about your local rules and regulatory bodies before trading other people's money. Find out which regulatory body is responsible in your area, call them, and find out what it takes. What you don't want to do is to ignore regulations. That could get you shut down real fast.

Finally, a very valid reason for why some traders don't raise external money. Some types of strategies rely on small pricing inefficiencies or they trade illiquid markets. Such strategies can at times have limited capacity, and it might not be possible to trade them on a large scale. Luckily, trend following is able to scale to very large trade sizes so that won't be a problem for you with those types of strategies.

CHAPTER 14

Final Words of Caution

This book deals in highly leveraged derivatives strategies and, as such, it is wise to dedicate the final chapter to the risks and problems that may arise.

■ Diminishing Returns of Futures Funds

The trend-following business used to be much easier and it is getting tougher and tougher to achieve the big number returns. In the 1980s and 1990s, most managers in this business had stellar compound returns with hardly any lasting drawdowns, but those days seem to have been replaced with higher volatility and more uncertain results. The core trend-following strategies are still profitable, given enough time, but the return profiles have changed somewhat in the past decades.

It's hard to find indexes which accurately reflect the trend-following industry, but one of the most widely followed is the Société Générale Trend Following Index. Figure 14.1 shows this index at the top, and five-year rolling returns at the bottom. This is to show you the long-term profile and how it changes over time.

What you see there is that the five-year rolling returns used to be quite high and then kept falling, consistently, year after year. Just a year or two ago, you could have simply extrapolated this falling trend, pun very much intended, and claimed that trend following would become a negative sum game. But then we had that bottoming out of the returns back in 2020 and

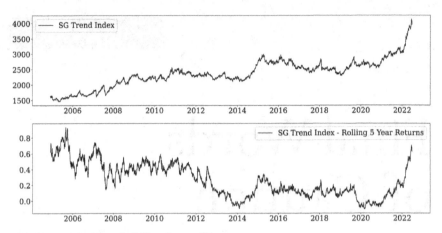

FIGURE 14.1 Trend-following rolling returns.

a sharp rise. Just when everyone least expected it, trend following came back in a big way.

Addressing the decline in returns first, one obvious factor is the interest rate situation. The absolute optimal condition for trend following is when we have high interest rates, while they are slowly and steadily decreasing. In such a situation, we print money on both ends. We get free money on excess capital, due to the high interest rates, and at the same time we stay long bonds to profit from the trend in decreasing rates. That game can, of course, only last so long, as we have seen in recent years. If rates keep decreasing, they will sooner or later reach such low numbers that two things happen. First, our free income is gone, and, second, they really can't go down much more.

As of writing of this book, we are starting to see interest rates move up again, even if we are very far from the good old days of the 1980s and 1990s, but it is not up to me or any other systematic trader to speculate on where this may be heading in the future. Should rates continue to hike, we would, however, be well positioned to take advantage of it.

Regardless, what we are seeing in 2021 into 2022 shows us that while trend following had a slow phase, it's far from dead. In 2022, the stock market was taking a beating while trend following saw record returns, once again providing its worth in terms of diversification and crisis alpha.

■ Setting the Initial Risk Level

One of the most important decisions you need to make before starting actual trading is what risk level to aim for. Setting your position sizes is the key control factor for setting the risk and if you set it too low, you will not be able to get enough returns to attract capital, but if you set it too high, you risk having the kinds of drawdowns that scare investors off.

When you are making this call, keep in mind that the maximum drawdown will probably be higher than what your simulations predict and perhaps it will happen soon after your launch. The fact of the matter is that this happens more often than one might think. The real reason why a new fund starts with this type of strategy and finds sufficient initial investors for it may be that trend-following strategies just had a very good run and got plenty of attention. This is exactly what happened to so many new funds after 2008. This strategy absolutely dominated the headlines and massively outperformed practically all other strategies, except of course those who were massively betting against the Credit Default Swaps markets. It is much easier to find traction for a venture like this after a very good return period and investors tend to come into these funds after these good years. The problem is that they will come in with an expectation that the good times will continue in the near future, and, as we have seen in this book, this is not often the case. After a very strong performance period, we are likely to see some troubled times, large drawdowns, and volatile years of sideways or losing results.

Funds that launched just after 2008, or after other good periods as well for that matter, found themselves in a very dangerous position. If you invested in a typical trend-following futures fund at the start of 2009, after having read all about the strategy that beat the markets in the otherwise disaster year that had just passed, you would be in for a very tough ride. Most trend followers had large losses in 2009, many over 20% drawdowns during that year. Plenty of the new capital that came into trend-following funds in early 2009 had already left by the end of that year as investors got scared over the difference in what they thought they would get and what reality looked like. For those who stayed in, 2010 was for the most part a bad year as well. In the last half of 2010, the profitable trends came back and started making the money back for the patient investors.

So if you had launched a new fund in early 2009, you would find yourself over a year and a half later with a likely drawdown of 20–25%, perhaps more. A fund that had been in business a couple of decades longer with a good track record could survive this, but a new fund likely would not.

What I want to say about this is, be very careful when you start out. If you set a high risk level, you may perhaps look like a hero if you get lucky and get some good trends soon after the launch, but if you are unlucky and get a bad year or two, you are out of business. Survival must always be the first priority and this means starting out at a comfortable scale, making sure you are able to handle a bad period, even if it happens to come along at the very start.

I hope my attempts at giving a fair and balanced picture of the reality that faces a trend-following futures manager has not discouraged you from getting into the business. For all the possible pitfalls, this is still a very good business to be in and even with the diminishing returns of the past years, there are no real signs that cross-asset trend following should not be profitable in the future.

■ Going Live

Fast-forward some years, and after reading this book and a few more, you have spent years doing all your research. You constructed your own quant modelling environment, studied statistics and programming, and designed your very own trading algorithms. Then you went out there in the real world and fought the harsh street-by-street battle of seed capital raising and you got enough together to actually start. Now what?

The all-too-common confusion is what to do on the very first day. You could start off with a big pile of cash, and only take new positions when your model gives you a trading signal. This means that it may take some time for you to reach a full portfolio, but you would only get fresh signals rather than risking an entry in the middle of a trend. Makes perfect sense, doesn't it?

The only problem is that this doesn't make any sense, if you stop and think for a moment. If you only take the new signals, your actual portfolio will deviate substantially from your backtest and research. By making that choice, you also made the assumption that new signals are more valid and more likely to be profitable than signals that open other positions. What we have seen so far in this book is that diversification is key and that you simply can't predict which markets or sectors will perform best in the future.

It is the interaction between positions which makes diversified futures strategies so interesting. The vast potential for such diversification is unique to the futures space and this is what we need for our strategies to be successful in the long run. By taking only fresh signals, it will take you quite some time before your portfolio becomes fully diversified and until then your risk will be highly concentrated on more or less random positions and sectors, depending on the order and timing of new signals.

That means that the only way it makes sense to go to live is to take all positions on the first day. You would have a walk-forward tracking portfolio based on your backtest and research. The past year or months before going live, you have probably been paper trading this exact strategy, building your confidence in the methodology and learning the daily routine it requires. When the big day comes, and you finally have all those sweet millions in the investor trading account, you need to replicate this paper portfolio as closely as you can, and then simply keep following the plan.

Just keep swimming.

■ Author's Website

www.clenow.com

■ Research Papers, Articles, and Websites

303

Absolute Returns, www.absolutereturns.com (accessed 24 August 2012).

Automated Trading System, www.automated-trading-system.com (accessed 24 August 2012).

Barclay Hedge, www.barclayhedge.com (accessed 24 August 2012).

Basu, Devraj, "Capturing Commodity Backwardation", *Futures* magazine, May 2011.

Basu, Devraj and Stremme, Alexander, "The Economic Value of Linkage between Spot and Futures Market", WBS Finance Group Research PaperNo.92, papers.ssrn.com/sol3/papers.cfm?abstract_id=1099839, February 2009.

Burghardt, Galen and Walls, Brian, "Two Benchmarks for Momentum Trading", in Galen Burghardt and Brian Walls, *Managed Futures for Institutional Investors: Analysis and Portfolio Construction*, John Wiley & Sons, Inc., Hoboken, NJ, 2011, pp. 99–127.

Cooper, Tony, "Alpha Generation and Risk Smoothing using Managed Volatility", *SSRN Electronic Journal*, August 2010.

Faith, Curtis, "The Original Turtle Trading Rules", 2003, http://www.benvanvliet.net/Downloads/turtlerules.pdf (accessed 24 August 2012).

IASG Managed Futures Database, www.iasg.com (accessed 24 August 2012).

Kaminski, Kathryn and Lo, Andrew W., "When Do Stop-Loss Rules Stop Losses?", paper presented at EFA 2007 Ljubljana Meeting, January 2007.

Koulajian, Nigol and Czkwianianc, Paul, "Black Box Trend Following: Lifting the Veil", Quest Partners LLC, 2010.

Koulajian, Nigol and Czkwianianc, Paul, "Know Your Skew", Quest Partners LLC, 2011.

National Futures Association, www.nfa.futures.org (accessed 24 August 2012).

Standard and Poor's, "Standard and Poor's Indices Versus Active (SPIVA)", www .standardandpoors.com/indices/spiva/en/us (accessed 24 August 2012).

Wilkes, Thomas and Fletcher, Laurence, "Special Report: The Algorithmic Arms Race", Reuters, 2012.

▪ Books

Carver, Robert, *Systematic Trading*, Harriman House, Petersfield, Hampshire, 2015.

Carver, Robert, *Smart Portfolios*, Harriman House, Petersfield, Hampshire, 2017.

Carver, Robert, *Leveraged Trading*, Harriman House, Petersfield, Hampshire, 2019.

Chande, Tushar, *Beyond Technical Analysis*, John Wiley & Sons Inc., Hoboken, NJ, 2001.

Clenow, Andreas, *Stocks on the Move*, Equilateral Publishing, Zurich, 2015.

Clenow, Andreas, *Trading Evolved*, Equilateral Publishing, Zurich, 2019.

Clenow, Andreas, *A Most Private Bank*, Equilateral Publishing, Zurich, 2021.

Fabozzi, Frank, *The Handbook of Fixed Income Securities*, McGraw-Hill, New York, 2005.

Faith, Curtis, *Way of the Turtle: The Secret Methods that Turned Ordinary People into Legendary Traders*, McGraw-Hill, New York, 1997.

Gyllenram, Carl, *Trading with Crowd Psychology*, John Wiley & Sons Inc., Hoboken, NJ, 2000.

Ineichen, Alexander, *Absolute Returns*, John Wiley & Sons Inc., Hoboken, NJ, 2003.

Ineichen, Alexander, *Asymmetric Returns*, John Wiley & Sons Inc., Hoboken, NJ, 2007.

Leeson, Nick, *Rogue Trader*, Time Warner, London, 1997.

Lefèvre, Edwin, *Reminiscences of a Stock Operator*, John Wiley & Sons Inc., Hoboken, NJ, 1923.

Livermore, Jesse, *Reminiscences of a Stock Operator*, John Wiley & Sons Inc., Hoboken, NJ, 2010.

McCrary, Stuart, *How to Create and Manage a Hedge Fund*, John Wiley & Sons Inc., Hoboken, NJ, 2002.

Raschke, Linda and Connors, Laurence, *Street Smarts: High Probability Short-Term Strategies*, M. Gordon Publishing Group, Los Angeles, CA, 1996.

Rogers, Jim, *Hot Commodities: How Anyone Can Invest Profitably in the World's Best Market*, John Wiley & Sons, Ltd, Chichester, 2004.

Schwager, Jack, *Market Wizards: Interviews with Top Traders*, Harper, New York, 1992.

Schwager, Jack, *Schwager on Futures: Technical Analysis*, John Wiley & Sons Inc., Hoboken, NJ, 1995.

Schwager, Jack, *Schwager on Futures: Fundamental Analysis*, John Wiley & Sons Inc., Hoboken, NJ, 1998.

Ugrina, Tony and Gyllenram, Carl, *En Aktiespekulants Psykologi*, Liber AB, Stockholm, 2004.

Wong, Max, *Bubble Value at Risk: Extremistan and Procyclicality*, Immanuel Consulting PTE, Singapore, 2011.

Andreas Clenow is a Swedish Swiss author, financier, and entrepreneur based in Zurich, where he is the Chief Investment Officer of a family office. He has been a tech entrepreneur, a financial consultant, a hedge fund manager, a financial engineer, a quantitative trader, a financial advisor, a board member, and a middle management corporate bureaucrat during his illustrious career.

INDEX

Page numbers followed by *f* and *t* refer to figures and tables, respectively.

European Union, 255
Excel, 68–69, 273
Exchange rates, 22–23, 38
Exchange traded funds (ETFs), 148, 285–286
Execution, 54, 74, 251, 268–269
Exponential moving average (EMA), xvi, 52, 60–63, 72, 236–239

F

Fabozzi, Frank, 40
Fiduciary responsibility, 13, 153
Filter rules, 56–57
Following the Trend (first edition), xix
Free government money, 78–83
FTSE 100 index, 6, 39
Fukushima tsunami, 170–171
Futures, 8–12
  as a business, 11–15
  and correlation matrix, 69
  cross-asset trend following with, 1–19
  currencies, 37, 38t
  diminishing Returns of, 297–298
  diversified, 4, 49, 300
  and equities, 39–40
  gold, 37
  modelling, 275–282
  strategies, 18, 69–70, 104–105, 194, 257, 275–282
Futures, management of, 1–2, 8–9, 82–83, 117, 164
  and benchmarks, 273
  benefits of, 96
  comparison to world equity markets, 8
  diversified, 4, 21, 32
  and equity portfolios, 103, 120, 255
  and execution, 268
  trend-following, 46, 300
  and volatility, 256
Futures contracts, 22, 35–37, 60, 270.
    See also Contracts
  backtesting, 31, 280
  bond, 42
  and continuations, 30
  deliverable, 32
  in backwardation, 246
  in contango, 246
  lifespan of, 244
  losses during, 10

price correlation of, 68–69
Futures exchanges, 21
Futures sectors. *See also* Commodities
  agricultural, 31–33, 33f
  currencies, 37–38
  equities, 39–40
  non-agricultural, 34–37, 34f
  rates, 40–43

G

GBP (Great Britain Pound), 270
GDAX index, 39
German Schatz, 154
GFC (2008 Global Financial Crisis), 91–92, 92f
Global Financial Crisis (GFC) (2008), 91–92, 92f
Great Britain Pound (GBP), 270
Great Depression, 149
Groundhog Day (film), 76, 282

H

Hang Seng China Enterprises, 40
Hang Seng index, 39
Hedge funds, xiii–xix, 12, 55, 179, 185
  and buy side, 291
  CTA-managed, 1–2, 6–7, 83
  futures, 53, 109, 120
  managed accounts vs, 14–15, 265, 272
  and managed futures markets, 8
  management of, xvii, 6–7, 19, 66
  and moving average, 59
  mutual funds vs, 6
  quants, 279
  and timing, 88
  volatility of, 16–17, 272
Hedging, 8, 11, 22–23, 220, 269–270, 285
  cost of, 26–28
  cost-of-carry model of, 35
Henry Hub natural gas (HH), 34
Hong Kong, 269
Hong Kong dollar (HKD), 270

I

IBM, 21–22, 37, 99
Initial risk level, 298–300

N

O

P

Q

R

S